one
bad
mother

one
bad
mother

In Praise of Psycho Housewives, Stage Parents, Momfluencers, and Other Women We Love to Hate

Ej Dickson

Simon Element

New York   Amsterdam/Antwerp   London
Toronto   Sydney/Melbourne   New Delhi

SIMON
ELEMENT

An Imprint of Simon & Schuster, LLC
1230 Avenue of the Americas
New York, NY 10020

First Simon Element hardcover edition February 2026

SIMON ELEMENT is a registered trademark of Simon & Schuster, LLC

Simon & Schuster strongly believes in freedom of expression and stands against censorship in all its forms. For more information, visit BooksBelong.com.

For information about special discounts for bulk purchases, please contact Simon & Schuster Special Sales at 1-866-506-1949 or business@simonandschuster.com.

The Simon & Schuster Speakers Bureau can bring authors to your live event. For more information or to book an event, contact the Simon & Schuster Speakers Bureau at 1-866-248-3049 or visit our website at www.simonspeakers.com.

Interior design by Laura Levatino
Illustration on p vi by Shutterstock

Manufactured in the United States of America

10 9 8 7 6 5 4 3 2 1

Library of Congress Control Number has been applied for.

ISBN 978-1-6680-5111-5
ISBN 978-1-6680-5112-2 (ebook)

Let's stay in touch! Scan here to get book recommendations, exclusive offers, and more delivered to your inbox.

For my mother, who taught me how to be brave.

For my father, who taught me how to be honest.

For Alex, S., and M., who taught me how to be grateful.

Contents

one
bad
mother

Introduction

This Was a Bad Idea

or, Why I Should Lie to People More

Writing this book may have been a bad idea.

This thought first crossed my mind the summer of 2023, when I was at my husband's boss's birthday party in Vermont. Our two kids—Harry, then six, and Marco, age ten months[*]—were with us, and the entire evening was a performance of dutiful wifedom, chuckling at jokes and expressing intense interest in other people's kitchen renovations. I tried to maintain a balance between getting as buzzed as possible and making sure that my children did not run into the road and get dragged underneath a Green Party voter's Subaru.

At one point, I was talking to a middle-aged couple when they asked, with the routine manner of a dentist asking a patient to open wide, what I did for a living. They were from Arizona, a state that, prior to this meeting, I did not fully believe existed outside the context of the caffeinated beverage brand and the 1987 romantic comedy *Can't Buy Me Love*.

"I'm a writer," I said. "In fact, I just sold my first book."

---

[*] These are pseudonyms, in case my children ever want to run for public office someday. Which they won't, for reasons that will become apparent over the next 275 pages.

"Wonderful!" they said. "And what is it about?"

"Bad moms," I responded breezily.

Within a single second, I watched their eyes flicker to me, holding a glass of rosé, to Marco in his BabyBjörn, going to town on a piece of Camembert, then back to me again. Their expressions took on a different cast. They looked as if I had just announced, with great pomp and circumstance, that I had to retire to the facilities to empty out my DIVA Cup.

"Well," the woman finally said after a lengthy silence, "I can think of one bad mother in particular."

"Oh, really?" I asked. "Who?"

"My mother-in-law," she said.

She laughed. Her husband laughed. Marco laughed, spitting out bits of Camembert in the process. And I laughed, wondering what had just happened.

This occurred a few times that evening: There was the same scan from me to baby to wineglass, followed by the inevitable mother-in-law joke. At first, I thought I was just imagining things, but as I downed rosé after rosé, my baby strapped to my chest, I realized these people didn't see my book as a book at all. They saw it as an admission of guilt.

As naive as it may sound, I was surprised by this reaction. The guests at this party were all blue-state voters, art collectors, *New Yorker* cartoon–understanders. Many of them were mothers themselves. I had assumed that they, like me, would be skeptical of the concept of the "bad mother," viewing it as an outdated and somewhat misogynistic cultural trope, like paying a bridal dowry or using a tanning bed. I was mistaken.

Over the past few months, I've gotten similar reactions when I've told people I was working on this book. And I think I understand why: Women in particular have been so deeply inculcated with the stigma surrounding bad mothers—and perhaps feared they might be perceived as one—that my interest in the subject was enough to arouse suspicion. They must have been wondering: Who was this rosé-guzzling, infant-wearing reprobate? Why was she so interested in bad moms, anyway? And why was her baby permitted to eat so much cheese?

* * *

What I should have told those Arizona-based interlocutors is yes: By lots of people's standards, I am a bad mom. I text my friends Patti LuPone TikToks while Marco is on the floor playing with his toys.* I don't enjoy pretend play or cooking or cleaning or birthday parties. There are times when I don't particularly like being a mom. There are times, though they are far fewer, when I don't particularly like my kids. I drink (sometimes). I curse (often). And one night, when Harry was a toddler, I got so bored reading *If You Give a Mouse a Cookie* over and over again that I opted for Vincent Bugliosi's *Helter Skelter* instead.†

I know that I am not alone in this regard, and there are plenty of mothers who feel the same way that I do. But it's extremely easy to feel otherwise. I once saw a thread on X (formerly known as Twitter) where women were sharing the most "controversial" things they do as parents, and the responses ranged from things

---

* Though in my defense, there's an argument to be made that watching Patti belt a G5 during the 1980s Tonys performance of *Evita*'s "A New Argentina" serves an educational purpose.

† I don't think it did any long-term harm, though. I just asked him if he knew what Spahn Ranch was, and he said no.

like "We don't put any limits on TV when we are at home" to "I let my kids pick out their clothes" to using a backpack with a leash for an autistic child at risk of running away. Without exception, these were all either things I had done or could completely understand why another parent would do, particularly if safety issues were involved. I concluded that these women were either lying for fear of being judged or had so deeply internalized this fear that they had been led to believe their parenting choices were "controversial," instead of totally normal and understandable (or, in some cases, the safest and most reasonable option).

I am also aware that the fact that I am openly admitting some of these things—in both the indelible and increasingly irrelevant form of print, no less—reflects a position of privilege. For middle-class white women like me, there are few long-term material consequences for calling yourself a "bad mom," other than possibly being yelled at by other middle-class white women on the internet.* For low-income women and women of color, however, that is not the case. It's terrifyingly easy to find news stories of such women being arrested for neglect for leaving their kids in the car while they do a quick gas station run, or of moms who are reported to child protective services (CPS) for paying too much attention to their phones while their kids are at the playground. Many of these women are not "bad" mothers at

---

* These types of women are often referred to as "Karens," but that seems highly unfair to the Karen (pronounced kuh-REN), a Southeast Asian tribe that is one of the largest ethnic minorities in Myanmar and presumably does not share a predilection for leaving one-star ratings for cruise line buffets on Tripadvisor.

all—they are simply women who, for various reasons, fall outside the (impossible) standards for "good" motherhood as established by our culture. As a result, they are far more likely to face social or practical consequences for publicly admitting to reading their infant a true crime classic than I ever would.

So what are the qualifications for being a "good" mom? The way I see it, they're fairly self-evident. A good mom shows up to class field trips, remembers to bake peanut-free cookies for the PTA bake sale, and never, ever raises her voice at Target. She leaves crudités out for her guests when they come over and limits herself to only one glass of sauvignon blanc (it's always sauvignon blanc, the Blake Lively of white wines). Her kids hit their developmental milestones on time and eat gluten-free pea-and-mango-infused organic gummy snacks and never, ever do things like hit or push or yell "Slayyyyyy, bitch!" to a friend as a message of encouragement at the playground.* She has an expertly curated Instagram presence, an endless collection of nap dresses, and she never, *ever* has to hand off the stroller to her husband when she gets diarrhea in the middle of a family nature walk at a botanical garden.†

The qualifications for being a Bad Mom, however, are harder to pin down. If you need evidence of this, look no further than the range of results for the phrase "bad mom" on Google News. When I first started working on this book, I created a Google Alert for the phrase, and in one day alone, I saw it had been used to describe the following:

---

* Yes, this happened once; and yes, it was embarrassing, but obviously I'm kind of proud of it.

† See above.

1. *Game of Thrones'* Sophie Turner, who had recently been photographed drinking at a bar with her coworkers on the brink of a contentious divorce from her then-husband, Joe Jonas.[1]

2. Ruby Franke, the mommy vlogger who pleaded guilty to aggravated child abuse charges after her twelve-year-old son showed up at a neighbor's doorstep appearing malnourished, with tape on his arms and legs.[2]

3. A mother in the *New York Post* who practiced "gentle parenting" and did not sufficiently chide her three-year-old son for wetting his pants.[3]

4. An octogenarian Irish woman whose only crime, as far as I could tell, was dying with her middle-aged son in a house fire.*[4]

When I was looking at these search results, I was reminded of something Steven Mintz, a professor of history at the University of Texas at Austin who studies the nuclear family model, told me about the expansiveness of the "bad mom" label when I interviewed him for this book. "What's great about the concept of the bad mom is it's unlimited," he said. "A bad mom can be overly intrusive or neglectful. A bad mom can be permissive, or a bad mom can be authoritarian."

---

* To be fair, I think this was more the result of bad search engine optimization than of an anti-mom bias in the *Irish Examiner.*

With the bad-mom label, says Mintz, "*any* behavior is suscep-tible to criticism."[5] The woman who ties up her kid and deprives him of food; the celebrity who goes out for a night of drinking with her colleagues; the geriatric Irishwoman who has stopped converting oxygen into carbon dioxide: all of them are grouped together in the same grimy bucket, mired in an amalgamation of misogyny and shame. The term "bad mom" is used so often, and with so little differentiation, that it should be almost totally devoid of meaning. But it still has the power to shame us, to subjugate us, to force us to sit down and shut up and stay in line. Not even Sansa Stark is impervious to its sting.

This didn't necessarily have to be the case. During the early 2000s, there was a mounting backlash against the idea of the perfect mother, with books like Ayelet Waldman's *Bad Mother* and Judith Warner's *Perfect Madness: Motherhood in the Age of Anxiety* skew-ering helicopter parenting and modern-day mommy myths. The in-ternet also played a huge role in destigmatizing speaking out against the pressures of motherhood, thanks to mom bloggers like Heather Armstrong, a.k.a. Dooce, writing frankly about her experiences with postpartum depression or sex after having kids.

With the advent of Instagram and other image-based social media platforms in 2010, as well as brands increasingly entering the mom blogger space, showing "the dirty side of the room" of the mothering experience—as Armstrong once put it in an interview with me—fell somewhat out of favor. Still, there was a sense that women were col-lectively pushing back against the narrative that they had to be pretty and perfect and self-sacrificing all the time, that they were angry and exhausted and just wanted the rest of the world to give them a fuck-ing break. TV shows like CBS's *Mom*, Bravo's *Odd Mom Out*, as well as the hit 2016 film *Bad Moms*, reveled in showing nice suburban mothers smoking, drinking, and having sex with PTA dads. Moms on social media proudly posted memes like "The most expensive part of having kids is all the wine you have to drink" and "Motherhood— powered by love, fueled by coffee, sustained by wine"[6]—content that would have had them drawn and quartered by the mommy police just a few years prior.

But even as many progressive mothers and momfluencers proudly self-identified as "bad moms" and argued for the relaxation of the rigorous standards surrounding motherhood, the discourse around being a "good" or "bad" mother was still incredibly confusing.

When I had my oldest, Harry, in 2017, and my youngest, Marco, in 2022, I learned this firsthand. Sure, there was a movie with Mila Kunis doing Jell-O shots[7] and fucking the guy from *Crazy/Beautiful*; sure, people were telling me it was fine if I formula-fed and it was OK to give my kids an iPad every once in a while and I should just do whatever I could to take care of myself, 'cause you got this, *ma-ma*. But on the other hand, I was also constantly fielding questions about why I didn't breastfeed and seeing studies that screen time raised the risk of children exhibiting symptoms of autism[8] and having art school students stare daggers at me when I tried bringing my stroller into a coffee shop.

Even if a handful of social media influencers told me it was fine to be a "bad mom," I learned fairly quickly that nothing could reduce the intense feelings of judgment, shame, and scrutiny I felt— particularly in the age of social media, when total strangers have unlimited power to police others' parenting. At best, becoming a mother makes you feel like you are constantly taking up other people's valuable space; at worst, it makes you feel like you are a criminal (and if you are poor or nonwhite or neurodivergent or gender nonconforming, you may be treated like one).

As I write this today in early 2025, the cultural climate for mothers in the United States has only gotten worse. The GOP's battle against reproductive rights coincides with the popularity of "trad wives" like Nara Smith and Hannah Neeleman, a.k.a. Ballerina Farm, who seemingly preach total self-abnegation for wives and mothers while making gummy worms from scratch and chugging raw milk. On social media, there are countless threads and subreddits criticizing women for being too poor, too rich, too self-sacrificing, or not self-sacrificing enough, to the point where it is not uncommon for commenters to report total strangers to CPS. It's never been easier to be considered a bad mother, and in some ways, the stakes accompanying the very act of mothering in the United States have never been higher.

Because of this perpetual state of surveillance, and because I am a mother myself, I've become obsessed with the concept of the "bad" mother in popular culture: where it came from, how it has evolved, and what purpose it serves in controlling women. I started researching the quote-unquote bad mothers throughout history and pop culture, women whose actions are reviled by mainstream society and whose aesthetics are incorporated into gay men's Halloween costumes: the Joan Crawfords, the Momma Roses, the Mrs. Robinsons, the dance moms. I found that if we take a closer look, we might find that we could actually learn something from them—though they are not necessarily the lessons those in power may want us to glean.

* * *

I have to start by listing a few things that this book is not: For starters, it's not comprehensive. I am a white, middle-class woman, so my examination of many of the issues in the book will by default be through this lens. And though I felt it was important to speak to people from a wide range of backgrounds, there are almost certainly going to be voices and experiences that are going to be left out. For instance, while I'm sure there are many examples of bad mothers in, say, ancient Mesopotamian mythology, I've chosen to largely limit the scope of this book to American history and popular culture, which means there will be a lot more references to Kris Jenner than to, say, Gilgamesh's mother.*

Further, though I do, like 70 percent of mothers in the United States, work full-time (as a senior writer for *New York* magazine), it is a comparatively low-stress job (though I can't say I enjoy constantly being yelled at by anti-Semites, misogynists, and Swifties on X) and one that affords me the resources to pay for high-quality childcare, a luxury that many working mothers in the United States cannot afford. As a result, my perspective on these issues is informed by privilege, and I'd be doing the reader a disservice if I did not acknowledge that.

This book is also not a defense of bad mothers, nor is it an argument that all the women we perceive of as bad moms are, in an M. Night Shyamalan–esque twist, actually good parents after all. It does not, for instance, focus at length on women who are actually convicted in a court of law for being bad mothers—or, more to the point, women who physically harm their children. I hesitate to refer to these women as "actual" bad moms or "objectively" bad moms because such a binary is counter to the goal of this project. We are all unfortunately well aware that cruelty and violence exist in the world,

---

* No disrespect intended to Gilgamesh's mother, Ninsun, the goddess of wild cows, who, according to her Wikipedia page, seems like a very nice lady.

and mothers are no less likely to display these traits than anyone else. I'll be discussing a few of these women, but I am less interested in defending them, or drawing the distinctions between who actually is and isn't a "real" bad mom, than in examining the sociocultural factors that contribute to this perception in the first place.

Throughout the writing of this book, however, I kept being reminded of something Mintz told me. In his view, many child abuse cases adjudicated in court are not instances of physical abuse, but could more accurately be characterized as "cases of parenting under poverty," as he puts it. Some hypothetical examples he cited were, say, a mother being charged with neglect for unknowingly leaving a child under the care of a relative who sexually abused them, but they could also include a low-income mother leaving her child at a park in order to go to work because she doesn't have childcare,[9] or a single woman being charged with abuse and neglect for serving fast food to her obese child.*

When Mintz says that most cases of child abuse are really cases of parenting under poverty, he is not saying that there are not truly evil or deranged women out there who intentionally harm their children, nor is he letting mothers accused of harmful or neglectful behavior off the hook. But he *is* saying that many cases of mothers mistreating children stem not from a lack of love or care but from mothers in desperate and incredibly difficult circumstances.

---

* These are both real cases. In 2014, Debra Harrell was charged with criminal neglect for dropping her nine-year-old daughter off at a park a few blocks away from her workplace at McDonald's. And in 2009, Jerri Gray was similarly charged with neglect when social services expressed concern about her fourteen-year-old son, Alexander, weighing more than five hundred pounds. Harrell's case was dismissed in 2016. As of 2011, Gray still did not have custody of her son.

Consider the tragic case of Raquel Nelson, the Black single mom convicted of misdemeanor vehicular homicide when her four-year-old son was hit by a drunk driver while they were jaywalking across a busy highway, because she couldn't afford a car and the bus dropped her off far from a crosswalk.[10] Or Niveen Ismail, a Kuwaiti-born single mother who lost custody of her toddler after leaving him in his crib to go to work. (A jury found her innocent, but her parental rights were permanently revoked.) Or Beata Kowalski, the woman who took her own life after she was falsely accused of Munchausen syndrome by proxy and barred from seeing her ailing daughter, Maya, as documented in the Netflix series *Take Care of Maya*.[11] There are so many of these stories, all of which stem, at least to some degree, from a social infrastructure that fails to support women trying to care for their children in deeply trying and complex situations.

I am keenly aware there is a large, highly profitable market for vilifying such women (I, too, have subscribed to true crime podcasts where two drunk ladies giggle about dismemberment between hawking smart toothbrushes). But if there is one thing I hope to accomplish with this book, it is to invite people, particularly other mothers, to resist the urge to join the chorus calling for such women's heads. Indeed, I would go so far as to say that it's our responsibility to decry the horrific nature of such tragedies while pushing for systemic social change to prevent them from occurring again. When we deem someone a "bad" mother, we are often referring to some of the choices she has made as a parent, and it's important to note these choices are not made in a vacuum—they are a product of a complex web of individual circumstances and social, economic, and political forces working in tandem to deprive women and children of much-needed assistance.

I wanted to write this book in part to deconstruct the myth of the bad mom—where it comes from, what purpose it serves, and the insidious ways it continues to pop up in our culture. In doing so, I wanted to reevaluate some of the women who have been reviled throughout history—and, in the process, take some much-needed pressure off ourselves.

But there was also another reason, one that came up when I was doing an interview with a source for this book. Linda Seidel, a professor emerita of English at Truman State University, wrote *Mediated Maternity: Contemporary American Portrayals of Bad Mothers in Literature and Popular Culture*—one of a very small handful of books on the subject of bad mothers in contemporary popular culture—so, naturally, I was curious about what drew her to the subject. Her response to my question staggered me.

"I was interested in writing about bad moms because I *was* a bad mom," she said.

When she told me this, I initially didn't know how to respond. My first instinct was to make her feel better about herself and reassure her that wasn't true, or ask her all sorts of qualifying questions. *Well, sure, you may have done* this, *but don't* all *moms do that at one point or another?* I asked her. Or: *At least you didn't do* that. *Only a truly* bad mom *does* that. I was trying to assuage what I assumed to be her deeply ingrained sense of guilt, and in doing so, I suppose I was trying to assuage my own.

Still, Seidel was unwavering. She insisted that over the course of her son's upbringing, she had been a bad mom: ill-prepared and emotionally distant. She wrote the book because she "didn't want to just depict these other people who were supposed to be bad mothers without owning up to my own behavior," she told me. But while she says she takes responsibility for her poor parenting decisions, "It's easy to be a bad mother in this culture. Because it's made so difficult to be a good one," she said.[12]

I have no way of knowing whether Seidel was right, but I do know exactly what she means. I feel like a bad mom basically every day of my life, and not in a cutesy, #winemom, "reasons why Mommy drinks" type of way. I feel like a bad mom when I let Marco cry for a few seconds in his crib so I can wash some dishes. I feel like a bad mom when I'm writing this book and Harry begs me for the twentieth time to put down the computer and stop working. And I feel like a bad mom when Harry has a meltdown because we go a different way to school in the morning, and Marco is crying, and the dog is pulling at his leash, and I have a meeting in five minutes, and I lose my cool and yell at him. And I can honestly say that while I don't regret having children, I have had plenty of moments when I have regretted becoming a parent, when I thought that I wasn't cut out for any of this and someone else could do a much better job than I could. I don't know whether this is true. But I do fight like hell every day to prove this feeling of unworthiness wrong.

So I am taking this opportunity to admit, to any readers of this book or Arizona-based party guests: I'm not a very good mom. I'm impatient, and selfish, and frequently I get frustrated that parts of my life don't look the way that I'd like them to, and I really, *really* love being on my phone, and I acknowledge that these traits may do harm to my kids in the long run, in ways that may take years to fully become clear. But as bad of a mom as I may be, I try every day, in ways both big and small, to be a better one. And I've learned to let go of the idea that I am entirely to blame for my badness. Because if there's one thing I've learned in writing this book, it's this: As quick as we are to accuse women of being bad moms, no one wants to talk about how the world makes it very, very hard to be a good one.

* * *

Around the time I was finishing this book, Donald Trump was re-elected president. At first, it wasn't immediately clear how, if at all, it would affect the day-to-day of how I parent, as my kids are still too young to really be cognizant of politics. (I would like to say that Harry, who was seven at the time, said something adorable and heartbreaking and insightful the morning I told him Trump won, but really he just asked to play *NBA 2K24* on his Switch.)

Raising a thoughtful, compassionate, and, above all else, happy child is near impossible under the very best of circumstances. Obviously, we are not living under the very best of circumstances. Under the current president, we have already seen the mass deportation of migrant children, the removal of protections for gender nonconforming kids, the near ban on life-saving reproductive health care in many US states. He has made it abundantly clear he plans to make life more difficult for women and children, and it's only going to get worse, not better.

And as we enter this new age of uncertainty, reminding oneself that you are an imperfect person striving constantly to become a better one, that you have the hardest job in the world and you are showing up day after day to do it the best you can, seems all the more imperative.

This book is not for the women who, against all odds, somehow become "good" moms. If you have balayage hair and great Botox and a closet full of nonelastic pants, if your kids hit all their milestones on time and eat their greens and say cute things about Ruth Bader Ginsburg that you post on social media, and you had absolutely no trouble breastfeeding, please feel free to put this away and buy *Girl, Wash Your Face* instead. This book is for the moms who kinda *get* why Joan Crawford freaked out about the wire hangers. It's for the moms who get drunk after their kids go to bed and text their friends gossiping about whether Ms. Rachel has a secret nipple piercing. It's for the moms who know the cards are stacked against us to be good but keep trying to be better anyway. You got this, *ma-ma*.

1

The Marvelous
Mrs. Mommy Paradox

Why Being a Working Mother
Is Like Doing Ayahuasca

The last years of the 2010s—that period between Trump's first election and the Covid-19 pandemic—were a more innocent time. It was a time when we all thought that Ellen DeGeneres was nice, that vaping was actually good for you, and that Jack Antonoff's involvement with Taylor Swift's career was on the whole beneficial.*

One reflection of that optimism was the popularity of *The Marvelous Mrs. Maisel*, the Amazon Prime series starring Rachel Brosnahan as an upper-middle-class housewife who becomes a stand-up comedian. Created by *Gilmore Girls* showrunner Amy Sherman-Palladino, *Maisel* was perfectly suited for the pussyhat era: a portrait of a scrappy self-made woman who becomes a successful

---

* Culturally, we haven't quite reached a consensus on this one, but I can say that in my household it is considered something of a statement of fact that the *Lover* era was a high-water mark.

comic, triumphing over obstacles such as her gender, her genteel upbringing, and the fact that not a single one of her jokes is funny.*

When the first season aired in 2017, it was praised for many things: its warmth, its attention to detail, its portrayal of 1950s gender dynamics, and its casting of Brosnahan, who imbued the frustrated housewife trope with charm and vigor (and slayed in an array of jewel-toned A-line dresses while doing so). And I suppose I appreciated all those things about *Maisel* as well, as it did prompt me to make some rather ill-advised ModCloth purchases.

There was one thing about *The Marvelous Mrs. Maisel*, however, that left me and my husband a bit confused, to the point that we'd pause an episode a few times every season to discuss. It was about Midge Maisel's children. Specifically: Where are they?

We are told at the very beginning of the first season that Midge has two children under four: Ethan and Esther. In the first season, however, we hardly see Ethan within Midge's classic six, and in the rare cases that we do, he is usually exhibiting antisocial behavior for comic effect. And Esther is essentially a wraith, rarely seen and only occasionally alluded to, despite being a member of a demographic that is not exactly known for being chill and under the radar (i.e., a baby). Midge is almost never seen discussing childcare with her parents or her ex. In the context of the show, her being a mother is essentially an afterthought. *Maisel* erases poor Ethan and Esther, treating them largely as a logistical obstacle to be dealt with.

At the time that *Maisel* started airing, I had just had my first child. Even when I was writing, or on a call, or catching up with friends, Harry was rarely absent; he was always there, napping or asking for

---

* I mean, look, obviously humor is subjective, but I think we can all agree: George Carlin she ain't.

milk or Goldfish or "Baby Shark" on Alexa. Yet here was Midge, raising two little kids essentially on her own, with seemingly ample time
to jet off to Paris or flash her boobs to Village beatniks.

I was so struck by the absence of the kids on the show that I
wrote about it for *Vox* a few years ago.[1] Some believed my critique
was sexist, and that I was inordinately focusing on Midge's role
as a mother rather than the purpose of the show, which was her
personal trajectory toward self-fulfillment.*[2] The more surprising
argument, however, was that Ethan and Esther's absence was in-
tentional on Sherman-Palladino's part. Of course Midge was never
around for her kids. She was a bad mother. That was the point.

It hadn't really occurred to me that Midge Maisel was supposed
to be viewed as a "bad" mother, or that we were supposed to find
anything about her unlikable (after all, she spends the first two seasons charming the pants off literally everyone she encounters, up to
and including famously irascible 1960s urbanist Jane Jacobs). I had
assumed that the erasure of Ethan and Esther was simply the product
of a writers' room that preferred to focus on the will-they-won't-they
dynamic between Midge and Lenny Bruce, rather than the mundane
realities of finding day care and changing diapers. But the more I
thought about it, the more it made sense to me—not that Midge Maisel *was* a bad mom, per se, but that people would view her that way.

---

* In an interview with *BuzzFeed*, Brosnahan herself appeared to align with
  the former view: "This hasn't been a conversation that I've seen surrounding other shows with male leads who are also sometimes self-involved in
  their pursuit of a new dream. And so that's been kind of frustrating,"
  she said. [Julia Moser, "'The Marvelous Mrs. Maisel' Stars Responded
  to Criticism About Midge's Parenting," *BuzzFeed*, June 12, 2019, www
  .buzzfeednews.com/article/juliamoserrrr/marvelous-mrs-maisel-rachel
  -brosnahan-midge-kids-sexism.]

The Marvelous Mrs. Maisel is about a woman who defies social expectations and norms to forge her own pathway in the world, a narrative that resonates with viewers (many of whom were young mothers themselves) who wish they could do the same. But this is something of a Faustian bargain. Midge's kids *have* to be shunted to the side because they would only get in the way; her ambitions can never exist in tandem with her maternal obligations. Both Midge and the *Maisel* writers view her children as antithetical to her success because that is exactly what they are. She is either the spunky self-starter climbing the ladder to pursue her desires, or she is a mother; she can never be perceived as both.

The question is: Why? Why is this the case not just for Midge Maisel but for every ambitious woman with small children in the United States, even today? In a way, the erasure of poor Ethan and Esther serves as a metaphor for the state of working motherhood in general: As a string of complex equations, our ambitions and our children are variables that need to be individually isolated and removed before they can be solved.* It's like that old optical illusion where if you look at the drawing one way, it's a picture of a beautiful young girl; and if you look at it another way, it's an image of an elderly crone. You can see either the girl or the old woman, but you can never see both at the same time.

* * *

This is incredibly embarrassing to admit, but in my early twenties, before I had kids, it never occurred to me that I would have any difficulty balancing work with motherhood. I envisioned myself

---

* At least I think that's how algebra works. I got a 550 on my math SATs. Leave me alone.

beatifically nursing my infant in conference rooms, effortlessly pairing a gauzy maxi skirt with high-tops like other Park Slope moms, barking out orders to my subordinates between singing lullabies. In this fantasy, my hair was lustrous and shiny, my abs taut, and my coworkers in awe of my multitasking powers. *Wow,* I imagined them saying. *We didn't think working motherhood could be easy. But if she can do it, so can we.* The office would be full of breastfeeding, shiny-haired women inspired by my example, taking conference calls and eating free granola in the kitchen.

Of course, absolutely none of this panned out: not the nursing, not the shiny hair, not the abs, none of it. But it wasn't until a few years after becoming a parent, when I was over at my parents' house for Rosh Hashanah dinner, that I finally accepted this was going to be much more difficult than I'd thought. In the midst of ranting about how judged I felt when I left the office at 5:00 p.m., my mother, who worked throughout my entire childhood, rolled her eyes.

"Oh, please," she said. "You think you're the first person to ever realize that being a mother and having a job is hard? It's *impossible.* Everyone knows that. I cried every day after I came home."

This was ultimately the tipping point for me: If my mother—a terrifyingly tough and competent person, a woman who is notorious in my family for intimidating customer service representatives and calling Winnie the Pooh an asshole*—never figured out how to balance work with motherhood, then no one possibly could.

---

* Her exact words, while waiting in line with her infant grandson for the Winnie the Pooh ride at Disney World: "I hate that bear. He's such an asshole. 'I'm so rumbly in my tumbly'? Give me a fucking break." (Toby Axelrod Dickson, December 2017)

For me, it wasn't the judgment or the guilt that was the hardest. I loved my job and I relished the opportunity to leave the house and talk to adults about subjects that had nothing to do with the color red or what sound a kitty made.* It was the sheer logistical struggle of it, the physical impossibility of being asked to do so many different things or use so many parts of my brain at the same time. Every day I would wake up and ask myself a series of administrative questions, each one duller and more soul-crushing than the last: Would I be able to make the interview I scheduled at one if Harry had a doctor's appointment at ten thirty? Could I take that meeting and make Marco his dinner at the same time? It was like an SAT problem: If the train departs at 9:00 a.m. and is traveling at X miles per hour, how fast would it have to go to make it to its destination at Y time, and how could I get there without blowing my brains out?

This is basically all I talk about with my mom friends, though our conversations are mostly limited to saying "Oh my God, it is so fucking hard" over and over again followed by a shoulder shrug.† And there is no shortage of studies supporting this. Working mothers are up to 40 percent more stressed than women who work full-time with no children.[3] They are almost twice as likely as their child-free colleagues to suffer from anxiety or depression.[4] And during the height of the pandemic, they were more likely to binge drink as a means of coping with stress.[5]

The reasons *why* it's so hard are too multifarious to recount in detail here. The lack of infrastructural support available to work-

---

* *Meow* (allegedly).

† In fact, I considered writing a version of this chapter where I just copy-pasted that phrase over and over for ten pages, accompanied by a slew of gun-to-head emojis.

ing mothers in the form of state-subsidized day care or mandated parental leave certainly plays a large role, as does institutionalized sexism, racism, classism, and pretty much every other type of "-ism" you can imagine. It also doesn't help that working moms still do about ten more hours of multitasking per week than our male partners do,[6] a statistic that leads me to wonder how exactly my husband is spending those ten hours. (My best guess? Pooping while watching gardening videos.)

I'm more interested in exploring why the difficulties of working motherhood are still very much part of the cultural conversation, despite the fact that, according to 2023 Bureau of Labor statistics, the number of working mothers has been steadily increasing for the past few decades.[7] Indeed, more than 68 percent of women with kids under the age of six are currently in the workforce, a number that goes up to more than 77 percent for women with kids over the age of six.[8] Working motherhood in the United States is not an aberration—it is, indeed, very much the status quo.

Nonetheless, working mothers are still routinely demonized in mainstream culture, portrayed as frazzled and sexless or as pathological narcissists. From Sarah Jessica Parker's scatterbrained corporate exec in *I Don't Know How She Does It**[*]* to Cynthia Nixon's chronically stressed Harvard Law grad in *Sex and the City* to Anne Hathaway's girlboss CEO in *The Intern*, the struggles of women to "have it all" have served as a plot driver and punch line for women's movies and TV shows for decades.[†] It's a major talking point in

---

[*] Spoiler alert: She doesn't.

[†] I'm not sure why female audiences are supposed to find this entertaining— I personally have a hard time watching movies/TV shows about working moms. I imagine it's how diagnosticians felt when *House* premiered.

the political sphere as well, particularly following the considerable rightward swing in American politics in the 2020s. In addition to famously painting career women as "childless cat ladies," vice president J. D. Vance has suggested that working women are on "a path to misery," referring to options like universal day care that would alleviate parents' burden as "class war against normal people."[9] And with their obsessive focus on pronatalism, the conservative-led effort to increase the national birth rate, billionaires like Elon Musk have repeatedly emphasized that mothers' roles are not in the workplace but at home having children, saying things like "civilization will crumble" if women don't have more kids, while ironically slashing maternal health care via his Department of Government Efficiency (DOGE).[10]

All of this invariably raises the question: If working motherhood is the norm for most parents in the United States, why is it still treated as an aberration? Why do we still view the question of whether a woman can have a job and raise a family as a mystifying puzzle to be solved, rather than acknowledge that it is the reality for millions and millions of people in the United States? Why does Midge Maisel get to run around with a pre-MAGA-era Zachary Levi in tight gray slacks, when most moms have to embark on hours of Camp David–level negotiations with their partners to get ten minutes to take a shower? As the kids say: Make it make sense.

* * *

The demonization of working mothers is puzzling when you consider that, for much of history, working motherhood wasn't unusual at all. In fact, with the exception of those in the aristocracy, most mothers were *expected* to work and were considered unusual if they failed to do so.

In the fifteenth to the eighteenth centuries, middle-class women played a central role in the economy, assuming the bulk of not only domestic labor but also participating in production and bartering goods in the marketplace. Throughout this time, "I often say, men didn't bring home the bacon," notes the author and historian Stephanie Coontz. "Women helped butcher the pig, salt the bacon, and they were the ones who often took it to market."[11]

That began to change with the arrival of the Industrial Revolution, when the emergence of a consumer-driven middle class led to men's and women's roles becoming much more narrowly defined. With middle- and upper-class white men earning more, it was no longer considered necessary for women to earn their own income. "Their role comes to be as the consumer, the person who organizes the family's consumption and comfort," says Coontz. "It becomes the woman's job to make the home a real place of retreat,"[12] a calming, purifying space for their husbands when they returned from the grimy cities.[13]

This shift resulted in the invention of the "Angel in the House," a term taken from an 1854 poem memorializing the ideal housewife: "Man must be pleased, but him to please / Is women's pleasure; down the gulf," the poem by Coventry Patmore reads. "Of his condoled necessities / She casts her best, she flings herself."[14] Depicted as pure, delicate, nurturing, and selfless, the Angel in the House tied husbands to the home with a "silver cord of love" according to Coontz, which would protect them from the corruptions of the industrial world.[15]

This thinking, of course, did not apply to Black, immigrant, or working-class women, who were not presumed to have the spiritually purifying regenerative powers of white women and were expected to continue to be productive members of the labor force. By the turn of the century, Black married women were twice as likely to be in the workforce as their white counterparts.[16,17] But for middle- and upper-class white women of the mid-to-late nineteenth century, there was an emerging expectation that they would stay at home to spiritually nourish the men in their lives. After a long day toiling in the railroads or the factories, trying to avoid their limbs getting amputated or being set on fire or drowning in a pool of molasses,* all men really wanted—nay, deserved!—was a home-cooked meal and the warm embrace of a woman.

"You begin to see, by the mid-nineteenth century, businessmen and professionals stop praising their wives in their diaries for their good business acumen and their shrewdness," Coontz says. "They start praising them for their emotional services to them, and to their children."[18]

With Victorian ideals of white middle- and upper-class women as domestic "Angels in the House" in full swing, married women started dropping out of the workforce. By the start of the twentieth century, only 5 percent of married women were working, according to census data.[19] During the Great Depression, with millions of out-of-work husbands unable to provide for their families, mothers were forced back into the workforce by necessity. This trend continued in the 1940s during World War II,[20] when women served as household breadwinners while their husbands were stationed overseas. As a result, the number of women in the labor force increased by almost 50 percent in the span of just a few short years,[21] and it didn't take

---

* Again, not an exaggeration: This is something that really happened in Boston in 1919. It killed twenty-one people and has come to be known as the Boston Molassacre, a pun that is both stupid and in poor taste and is therefore extremely on-brand for Boston.

long for anxieties to emerge about the newfound autonomy women had assumed in the workplace.

One example of this is the 1945 film *Mildred Pierce*, a domestic drama/noir hybrid directed by Michael Curtiz, starring Joan Crawford as a frumpy housewife raising her two daughters—angelic Kay, and spoiled, slutty Veda—on her own.[22] At the start of *Mildred Pierce*, Mildred is slaving away in a menial service job, trying to eke out just enough of a living to support her kids. At first, it seems like her hard work is paying off: She becomes a wealthy entrepreneur, opening her own chain of restaurants and swanning around in a mink coat and peep-toe pumps.[23] Halfway through the film, you would be forgiven for thinking that *Mildred Pierce* is like a 1940s version of a Tyler Perry film, about a plucky woman who triumphs over sexism and adversity by picking herself up by her bootstraps.

But that is not, in fact, what *Mildred Pierce* is about. *Mildred Pierce* is about a woman whose ambition leads to life kicking the shit out of her. By the end of the film, Mildred has lost everything: her restaurant empire, her younger daughter to pneumonia, and her older child to a life of ill repute as a cabaret singer. Veda ends up having an affair with Mildred's sexy mustachioed new husband, then shooting him in a fit of jealousy, leaving Mildred without a job, a family, or her man. It ends on a definitive bummer note, the 1940s equivalent of *Dancer in the Dark*.

Mildred Pierce was based on an eponymous 1941 pulp novel by James M. Cain set in the Great Depression. Cain's intention was to pay tribute to the grit and temerity of single mothers of this era by depicting their "struggle against a great social injustice—which is the mother's necessity to support her children even though husband and community give her not the slightest assistance," as he told producer Jerry Wald.[24]

By the time *Mildred Pierce* was adapted by Warner Brothers in 1945, however, everything had changed. The war was coming to an end, and with men returning from the front, women would have to leave the workplace and go back home where they belonged. In this context, there was no way that *Mildred Pierce* was going to work as an ode to the self-made woman of the 1930s. So Warner Bros. shortened the timeline of the novel and moved it up to the present-day '40s, adding a murder to the script for good measure, due to Cain's success with the noir *Double Indemnity*, which was a smash hit for Paramount the year prior. The script changes also had the effect of making Mildred's maternal failures seem even more tragic.[25] By the end of the movie, she's right back with her slovenly ex-husband—a fitting punishment for her ambitions.

The message to women is clear: There are consequences to trying to be more than the Angel in the House, to stepping outside the circumscribed boundaries of domesticity. It's the Truman-era version of fuck around and find out: Try to have it all, and you'll end up losing everything.

When the 1950s rolled around, mothers had taken the messaging of *Mildred Pierce* to heart. The United States entered an era of unprecedented economic prosperity, which meant that for some upper-middle-class families, there was no need for both parents to work. While this applied only to a small, privileged demographic, stay-at-home motherhood nonetheless held, and continues to hold, primacy in our conception of what a "good" mom should be.

"The 1950s is this really strange moment in time that we now use as a benchmark for what everything should look like," says Joanna Pepin, an assistant professor at the University of Toronto who has studied the so-called mommy wars, or the rift between stay-at-home and working mothers. "But it is not actually representative of what daily life typically looks like for most families. So even though the labor force departed from that very unique moment, we kind of just keep referring back to that as the reference point."[26]

During the Cold War, the nuclear family unit was also viewed as a major weapon in the United States' arsenal. White, middle-class, perpetually upbeat domestic goddesses like Donna Reed and June Cleaver were viewed as the linchpin of the American family. That didn't mean, however, that mothers were necessarily expected to be emotionally present in their children's lives, as Rebecca Jo Plant, a professor of history at the University of California, San Diego, pointed out to me. Even though June Cleaver from *Leave It to Beaver* is viewed as the archetypal 1950s mom, she doesn't do much actual momming at all on the show. "She's always there in the kitchen. But the really deep conversations, the intimate stuff with the boys—that's always with the father."[27] Still, mothers were expected to be physically present in the home, and those who were not—who worked either out of necessity or for personal fulfillment—were typically pathologized.

With the advent of the women's liberation movement in the 1960s, women's participation in the labor force started steadily climbing again,[28] to the point that by the start of the 1980s, an estimated seventeen million mothers were in the workforce.[29] Perhaps unsurprisingly, it was around this time that conservatives started losing their shit en masse about the dangers of working moms, with the Reagan administration slashing social welfare programs subsidizing childcare,[30] and conservative activists like Phyllis Schlafly lobbying against what she viewed as the feminist-led degradation of the nuclear family.

Such discourse was reflected in the popular media of the time, as writer Susan Faludi documents in her book *Backlash: The Undeclared War Against American Women*. In 1980s and 1990s films like *Fatal Attraction*, *Disclosure*, and *Basic Instinct*, single career women were largely portrayed as morally bereft harridans trying to fill their empty, meaningless lives by seducing hapless men*—who were often already married to, coincidentally, stay-at-home mothers.[31]

As for working mothers in popular culture, they were either vilified as selfish and cold, or viewed through a comic lens of abject incompetence. In the former camp, there was *Kramer vs. Kramer*'s Joanna, played by the flawlessly coiffed Meryl Streep, who leaves her husband and son at the start of the film. Though she's not explicitly identified as a feminist, it's clear we're supposed to attribute her reasons for leaving her family to the feminist movement: In a note she sends to her cherubic son, she tells him she is leaving because she must "find some interesting things to do for [herself] in the world" other than being a wife and mother, and that "being your mommy was one thing, but there are other things, too."

Because the film is largely told from the perspective of her estranged husband (Dustin Hoffman), we are to some degree supposed to view Joanna as self-absorbed and withholding for making this gut-wrenching decision (particularly after she changes her mind and decides she wants to fight for custody of her son anyway). And the scene of Hoffman reading her letter to her son is indeed heartbreaking: I have a very difficult time watching it without feeling tremendous empathy for Hoffman and his son (though he's more interested in watching cartoons than reading the letter). But ultimately, *Kramer vs. Kramer* is a fairly nuanced depiction of the agonizing choices some mothers feel they must make for themselves and their families, and it is far more generous to Streep's character than audiences were. As Faludi notes in *Backlash*, right-

---

* Who, for some reason, are almost always played by Michael Douglas.

wing pundits would come to cite her as a totem for "militant feminists['] . . . negative impact on the family" during the Reagan era, with Gary Bauer, Reagan's domestic policy adviser, telling Faludi that Joanna Kramer was "a symbol of the times" in representing how feminism offered "an excuse for women to run out on their responsibilities."[32]

Even films that were ostensibly intended to offer a more sympathetic take on working motherhood made it clear that they were less than optimistic about women "having it all." In 1987's *Baby Boom*, Diane Keaton plays J.C. Wiatt, a hyper-ambitious businesswoman who shares a spacious co-op with her yuppie, sexually incompetent partner. When she inherits an infant girl, Elizabeth, from a long-lost cousin, she initially resists motherhood with every fiber of her being, literally handing her off to a total stranger at coat check so she can make an important business meeting. But J.C.'s deep-seated maternal instincts suddenly kick in when Elizabeth gets sick, with director Charles Shyer bathing mother and child in warm golden light as she comforts her, thus marking J.C.'s overnight transformation from bad mom to obsessive helicopter parent.[33]

Like *Mildred Pierce*, and like *Maisel*, *Baby Boom* makes it clear that parenthood is incompatible with J.C.'s ambitions. Her partner abandons her, and her boss hands off her accounts to a smarmy male inferior, believing that J.C. is now unable to focus on her job. After she quits in a huff, she resigns herself to a life of complete domesticity in Vermont but finds herself unsuited for that as well. It's only until she combines her new role as a mother with her professional ambitions—a trajectory reminiscent of modern-day momfluencers making bank via the performance of "good" motherhood and domesticity, as we'll discuss later—that she's able to achieve some semblance of equilibrium, launching a gourmet baby food company based on a recipe she made for Elizabeth. (It also helps that she has a rugged boyfriend, played by Sam Shepard, to help her.)

Baby Boom is extremely white and heteronormative and all the things twenty-first-century progressive women deride. But it's also, weirdly, in dialogue with the same issues I find myself struggling with time and again. It was the second act of *Baby Boom*, when J.C. moves to Vermont after quitting her job, that resonated the most, particularly when she has a nervous breakdown over her dilapidated house. "I need to work! I need people! I need a social life! I need sex!" she shrieks. "How much baby food is a person supposed to be able to make in their lifetime? I mean, I am a career woman!"

Having retreated into her fantasy of quiet domestic life (something that virtually any working mother who follows trad wives on social media can sympathize with), J.C. finds it even more frustrating and stressful. Which begs the question: If having ambition is incompatible with having kids, and if having kids is incompatible with having ambition, what, then, are ambitious women with kids supposed to do? Where are we supposed to go? What if we can't afford a beautiful yet ramshackle New England Victorian, or if we have a partner who is less supportive than Sam Shepard? Why is this so hard, and more important, how have we not figured any of this shit out yet?

* * *

There is an argument to be made that today, with most mothers working outside the home in some capacity, women are not "as criticized and stigmatized as they used to be" for doing so, says Linda Seidel, author of *Mediated Maternity*. Seidel believes that even if mothers "are still not getting the support that they need," working full-time is now normative enough that it is largely not viewed as the mark of a bad or neglectful mother.[34]

But if there is, indeed, a lack of stigma attached to working motherhood today, it really only applies to one demographic: wealthy, well-resourced white women. The backlash to Sheryl Sandberg's *Lean In* and Ivanka Trump's *Women Who Work* demonstrates this: Though both books were marketed as universal templates for how to navigate working motherhood, many critics pointed out that the experiences described in such tomes were really only "universal" for women like Sandberg and Trump, with high-powered white-collar jobs and ample access to high-quality childcare.[35] For single mothers working two jobs to scrape together enough money to put food on the table, advice about not using exclamation points in emails in order to be taken more seriously isn't exactly super helpful.

Mothers of color are also much more likely to face actual, material consequences for the stigma surrounding working moms, particularly if they struggle to find affordable childcare. Take the case of Shaina Bell, a twenty-four-year-old single mother who was charged with two counts of child endangerment for leaving her kids at the motel where they were living while she went to work at Little Caesars. (Bell told police that neighbors checked in on the children every hour while she was gone.)[36] Bell was found not guilty at a pretrial hearing, but the sympathetic public discourse surrounding her case and many others like it—namely, what the hell kind of country we were living in that forced mothers to make such decisions in the first place—was short-lived.

In many ways, the question of whether mothers should feel "guilty" for finding it difficult to balance work with motherhood is almost exclusively a white, middle-class concern in itself. A number of Black mothers who I spoke to for this book said they do not dwell as much on these questions as their white counterparts.

"You do have standards to live up to, but they are different" than they are for white mothers, said Donnya Negera, a momfluencer and founder of a diaper bag company. She says that she feels less pressure to present a picture-perfect depiction of working motherhood, and more pressure to speak on issues that affect the Black community: "It feels like people are waiting for our voices," she says.[37]

Jennifer C. Nash, the author of *Birthing Black Mothers* and a professor of gender, sexuality, and feminist studies at Duke, points out that in some ways, the very dichotomy of the good/bad mother is "tethered to whiteness," and many Black women facing institutionalized violence on a daily basis simply don't have the luxury of worrying about "having it all." "Guilt doesn't seem to be the most profound emotion that circulates around mothering," she says. "Black women are concerned with the survival of their children."[38]

Unlike J.C. Wiatt, who is able to transition from a high-powered career to making baby food in a sprawling Vermont fixer-upper, there is no question of whether low-income mothers *can* deftly balance work and motherhood. They just have to. The constant push-pull between work and family life is not an accurate reflection of their lived experiences. And as rising costs of living and high interest rates force more and more women into the workforce out of necessity,[39] the debate over whether we can "have it all" is not an accurate reflection of most women's lived experiences, either.

Every once in a while, a younger woman will ask me whether I think it's possible to have a family and have a career. And my answer to that question is the same one I would give to anyone contemplating going on an ayahuasca retreat and spending seven hours in the jungles of Ecuador with a bunch of strangers puking your guts out. Like, sure, you *can* do it. But why on earth would you want to?

In *I Don't Know How She Does It*, the 2011 Sarah Jessica Parker adaptation of the bestselling novel, Parker's character, Kate, tries valiantly to juggle the pressures of work and family life before a major accident, compounded with her daddy boss (Pierce Brosnan) coming on to her, drives her to a breaking point. The movie ends with Kate promising her husband (Greg Kinnear) she'll stop prioritizing work over family life, with Kinnear vowing to step up at home. It's framed as a happy ending and an equitable trade-off, but one wonders why Kate had to be penalized with a harrowing family emergency and a major threat to her marriage for the two to come to that conclusion (though I suppose not fucking Pierce Brosnan is, in a way, a punishment unto itself).[40]

There's a similar dynamic at play in *The Intern*, the 2015 Nancy Meyers comedy starring Anne Hathaway and Robert De Niro.[*][41] In the movie, Hathaway plays Jules, a terrifyingly competent start-up founder whose husband is a stay-at-home dad. But because she is struggling with her rapidly growing company's workload, and her investors are concerned about her ability to steer the ship, her husband feels neglected and has an affair. As a way to salvage her marriage, Jules agrees to hire a CEO to help manage the company, prompting her elderly intern Ben (De Niro) to encourage her not to set aside her dreams for a man's benefit and her sheepish husband to apologize.

It's a weird ending, in part because it really isn't much of one. The film ends with Jules joining Ben doing tai chi in the park,

---

[*] Full disclosure: I saw this on a plane, so my understanding of the plot may have been impaired by half a tab of Valium.

suggesting she's found some sort of semblance of inner peace. But what has she actually gained? Control over a company whose investors are constantly nipping at her heels, waiting for her to fail? A marriage to a resentful husband, haunted by the shadow of a past infidelity? A BFF-ship with a geriatric employee with boundary issues? It hardly seems worth it.

* * *

The specter of "having it all" continues to cast a shadow over cultural depictions of working motherhood, albeit in less overt ways than the days of *Kramer vs. Kramer* or *Baby Boom*. One major improvement is that working mothers are increasingly depicted less as frizzy-haired, absent-minded oddities and more as a standard, semi-competent presence in any workplace.* In the pilot for the Canadian sitcom *Workin' Moms*, for instance, Kate (Catherine Reitman) returns from maternity leave to her job in advertising, and

---

* It's actually fascinating to watch sitcoms from the early 1990s—when two-thirds of married women with children worked!—to see how much working mothers were treated as a novelty. I've been rewatching *Full House* with my kids, and there's a season 2 episode literally called "Working Mothers" in which Uncle Jesse and Joey get a job writing jingles for a radio station. The whole point of the episode is basically how impossible it is to juggle parenting with a career, with D.J. and Stephanie constantly haranguing the men for help with their extracurriculars and baby Michelle crashing one of their pitch meetings. The episode ends with D.J. and Stephanie essentially guilting Jesse and Joey into asking their boss if their jobs can be remote so they can spend more time at home with them, which the boss readily agrees to. Actually, now that I think about it, *Full House* advocated for flexible remote work policies for caretakers long before any other company did. Maybe Dave Coulier is actually a socialist.

when a client in a meeting asks if she has breast milk on her top, she nonchalantly answers in the affirmative. In the meeting, Kate is neither judged nor mocked for being a mother in the workplace; it's treated as an almost total nonissue, a far cry from the days of *Baby Boom*, when Diane Keaton couldn't even get through a business meeting without having to sing "Itsy Bitsy Spider" on the phone to her baby.[42]

Depictions of working motherhood have also gotten (somewhat) more diverse. Bow Johnson (Tracee Ellis Ross) in *black-ish*, for instance, is an anesthesiologist who is also the mother of four (eventually five) kids, while Lisa Todd Wexley (Nicole Ari Parker) from the *Sex and the City* reboot *And Just Like That . . .* (*AJLT*) is a mom of three and an accomplished documentarian. Both women are Black mothers (albeit very wealthy Black mothers), both are beautiful and accomplished, and both are presumed to be competent at work and parenting, a far cry from traditional depictions of mothers in the workplace.

Yet time and time again, there still continues to be echoes of decades-old discourse about working motherhood. In the pilot for *Workin' Moms*, after Kate's triumph at the pitch meeting, she breaks down after learning she's missed her baby's first word. It's disappointing to watch a woman who had been depicted as self-assured and competent melt into a tear-stained mess the second she starts to feel the pangs of maternal guilt. *Black-ish* has a similarly disappointing moment in the fourth season, after Bow has baby Devante. When her husband, Dre (Anthony Anderson), tells her she should quit her job, she justifiably explodes: "What do you want me to be? A lady of leisure? Sit on the couch and watch *Ellen*? This isn't just a job for me, Dre, this is who I am!"[43] Yet by the end of the episode, following an embarrassing *Workin' Moms*–esque breast milk mishap, Bow decides to stay home with her kids. She frames this decision as wholly hers and not a result of external pressure, but given how vehement she previously was about her job being part of her identity, it rings hollow.[44]

Even Lisa Todd Wexley, the baddest bitch in the *And Just Like That . . .* cast,* is not impervious to the pressures of working motherhood. In a 2023 episode, Lisa finds out she's pregnant, and the show makes profoundly clear that she is not equipped to deal with it: Between parenthood, editing her documentary, and supporting her husband's run for city comptroller, she's burning the candle at both ends. But she doesn't even use the word "abortion" when discussing the pregnancy, merely paying lip service to the idea by vaguely saying, "I'm really grateful that I have that option." The failure of an ostensibly progressive show to discuss the prospect of termination, in the context of a character who almost certainly would have at least considered it, was viewed by many as a missed opportunity, particularly in the wake of the overturning of *Roe v. Wade* (which resulted in many women who are far less privileged than Lisa *not* having that "option").[45]

But for me, Lisa's pregnancy storyline was less disappointing for political reasons and more because it was just so . . . boring. Here was this gorgeous, fabulous, no-bullshit character who had somehow figured it all out: She was happily married, a present and engaged parent, and totally obsessed with her career, *and* she could pull off a chunky cable-chain statement necklace like nobody's business.[46] Yet of all the interesting challenges the *AJLT* writers

---

* Though considering how stupid this show is, that's kind of like saying she's the most socially competent student at a small liberal arts college.

could've thrown at this character, they gave her the most tired one of all: how to balance work with a baby.

In the end, Lisa has a miscarriage, a deus ex machina of sorts that plunges her into a state of guilt, rather than the emotion that many women in her situation are more likely to feel, which is a very understandable sense of relief. It's a cop-out and comes off more as a way for the writers to get out of a storyline they had painted themselves into a corner with than a satisfying conclusion to her narrative. But it also, once again, begs a question that I would think by now we'd all be tired of asking: If fictional women can't figure out how to have it all without leaking breast milk or experiencing a devastating loss or having to pretend to find Carrie Bradshaw tolerable, then who the hell in the real world can?

* * *

A few years after *Maisel* premiered, I started watching another critically acclaimed show about an irreverent female comic who also struggled to "have it all": *Hacks*, starring Jean Smart as Deborah Vance, a Vegas stand-up–turned–QVC shill. Like Midge, Deborah is sharp-tongued and ambitious and figures out how to forge her own unique path in a male-dominated world; also like Midge, Deborah is a mother (albeit to one child, a grown daughter named D.J.). But while *Maisel* largely avoids the question of whether working mothers can have it all by erasing Midge's children from the storyline altogether, *Hacks* is more upfront with its answer: You can't, so don't bother trying.

Deborah is not a good mother in any sense of the word: She's withholding, hypercritical, and she enables her recovering addict daughter. She and D.J. have a loving if not tenuous relationship—but *Hacks* makes it clear that Deborah's ambition was simply too great for her to have been present in her child's life in any real way. The show drives that point home in the second season, when Deborah runs into an old stand-up rival whose career she sabotaged decades ago; though Deborah is plagued with guilt, the woman says she quit stand-up not because of Deborah's interventions but because she saw firsthand how neglectful of a mom Deborah really was. "I saw the sacrifices you were making to have your daughter on the road," her former rival says. "And I just had this vision of the kind of person I'd have to be in order to make it. And you were completely devoted to your work. . . . I couldn't do it. Or I didn't want to."[47]

Though Deborah is taken aback by this withering condemnation of her parenting skills, she doesn't really dispute it. Because for Deborah, shunting her child to the side in favor of her ambition was never really a choice at all: As her protégé later points out, Deborah is constitutionally incapable of not working, "and nothing matters more, even if it should." There is no universe in which her relationship with her daughter would not have been collateral damage to her career, in which she would not have ultimately lost more than she gained.

This is, ultimately, where *Maisel* lands at the end of the show, in a series of flash-forwards showing what has happened to Ethan and Esther as a result of Midge's successful stand-up career. Esther is shown as an adult in therapy who has inherited her mother's sharp intellect but is highly resentful of her success; while Ethan, who has moved to a kibbutz in Israel, is so distant from Midge that he does not even tell her when he gets engaged. All of Midge's dreams ended up coming true—but the show makes it clear that it was at a price.

When the series finale of *Maisel* aired, some fans were disappointed. They did not want to see a world in which Midge's charm and wit and drive and beauty and bottomless wardrobe of A-line dresses would not have won her the day. They did not understand why Sherman-Palladino would undermine her heroine's trajectory of self-realization by showing how her children had suffered as a result.[48]

But I would venture to say that most of the people who felt this way probably did not have children. Because if you do, you acutely understand that every day is a reminder of the things that you give up: the breakfasts you don't eat because you're too busy feeding the kids, the assignments you miss out on because you don't want to travel for work, the cuddles and kisses you miss out on when you're on a string of Zoom meetings. It's a constant back-and-forth between seeing the young girl and the old crone, a tug-of-war between yourself and those you love most in the world. Sometimes you lose, and sometimes they do, but either way, there is always a loser, and that's what *Hacks* and ultimately *Maisel* understand.

Ironically, I first learned this before I had kids at all, when I was fired from my job while four months pregnant with Harry. One day, I got a calendar notification that I had an unscheduled morning meeting. When I got there, I was in a small room with the company's lawyer and the site director, who I'd told about my pregnancy about a month before; I didn't know her well, but I was vaguely aware she'd strongly disliked a piece we'd run ranking Taylor Swift's boyfriends as breakfast cereals.*[49]

With her best sympathetic smile on her face, this woman told me my role was being eliminated and that day would be my last day.

"But I'm four months pregnant," I told her.

"I knowwwwww," she purred.

---

* Taylor Lautner was Cookie Crisp, while Harry Styles was Special K and Jake Gyllenhaal was Apple Jacks.

I remember standing outside my office building, the glare of the midmorning sun on my face, not really knowing what to do. So I took my employee, who had also been fired, to a bar in the Financial District and bought him a pint of Guinness. The second he left, I started sobbing and didn't stop for weeks afterward.

It was an intensely dark period—and it was also the first time that I had ever felt like a bad mother, even though my son was in utero at the time. I had spent my twenties completely reorganizing my entire identity around my career, so when it was put on hold, even temporarily, I totally unraveled. And I blamed it on my pregnancy. How could I not have? Everything had been totally fine, I reasoned, until I had gotten pregnant. I had imagined I would have this baby and absolutely nothing would change; I would continue to climb the ladder, rung by rung, as I always had, because my talent and my drive and my resources would make me the Midge to everyone else's Mildred or J.C., the shining exception to the depressing rule. But the second I'd gotten pregnant, the ladder had been pulled from underneath me. And becoming a mom meant that, to some extent, it always would be. Something would always get lost. Someone will always suffer.

I was extremely lucky: After going on countless job interviews, I was hired by a website run by mothers, targeted at mothers. It was not a perfect fit in the long run, but it was the right one at the time, and I worked alongside some extremely smart, talented women who did not look at me like I had pooped on the floor if I had to leave at 5:00 p.m. It was the closest thing I've ever had to my Converse-and-breastfeeding conference call fantasy, and I'm immensely grateful for it.

Still, it took a very, very long time to unburden myself of the idea that motherhood was, in effect, a steak knife to the heart of my ambitions. It took even longer for me to feel like I was not a bad mother for having these types of thoughts. And I will admit: There are parts of me that still feel this way, sometimes. When my friends ask me about whether they should have kids—which, as we hit our mid-thirties, they are increasingly doing—I usually give some mealymouthed answer about how it depends what their priorities are and what they really want out of life. But really, what I want to say is: There are parts of motherhood that are wonderful, and parts that will obliterate your soul, and you should only have children if you understand that it will feel, a lot of the time, even most of the time, like the things you lose are greater than the things you gain. You will never be able to see the beautiful young girl and the crone. You can never truly have it all, and you will never even come close to feeling like you do. Until, one day, you wake up and realize you've stopped asking yourself the question. This makes you feel sad and tired, and more than a little bit angry. But it also makes you feel free.

2

"Hal, It's About Cats"

The (Relatively Recent) Birth of the "Bad" Mother

Before writing this book, I had assumed that the concept of a "good" mother, like that of a "bad" mother, was basically a constant throughout human history. I thought the "good" mother was like death or taxes or Amy Adams's inability to win an Oscar: unfixed and unchanging, despite humankind's best attempts to ensure otherwise.*

I was shocked to find out, however, that this was not the case. Before the nineteenth century or so, the dichotomy of the "good" mother versus the "bad" mother, with all of its attendant sociopolitical and racial and economic implications, simply did not exist to the extent that it does today. In fact, it's fair to say that the criteria for what constituted "good" mothering was essentially nonexistent.[1] It kind of reminds me of that famous anecdote in which legendary Broadway director Harold Prince describes Andrew Lloyd Webber

---

* As I write this in early 2025, Adams has yet to win her Oscar, despite being an American treasure and probably the best actor working today. Amy, if you are reading this, it is my personal belief you should have won for *Enchanted*.

pitching the famously esoteric musical *Cats* to him: "I . . . said, 'Andrew, I don't understand. Is this about English politics? [Are] those cats Queen Victoria, Gladstone, and Disraeli?' He looked at me like I'd lost my mind, and after the longest pause said, 'Hal, it's about cats.'"[2]

Until relatively recently, being a good mom wasn't about feeding your kids the right brand of organic gruel, or using the appropriate tone of voice to scold them during nine-hour Sunday prayer meetings. It was about making sure your kids didn't die. That was pretty much it. The bar was on the floor. Hal, it was about cats.

That's not to say, of course, that there weren't women in early culture and history who failed to meet this standard. Perhaps the OG archetypal bad mom is Medea, the Greek princess who defies her father's wishes to marry the hero Jason, bearing him two sons. When Jason abruptly leaves Medea for a younger woman, the princess of Corinth, Medea, having sacrificed her youth, beauty, station, and family for this ungrateful fuckboy, kills the princess, then murders her sons before escaping to Athens.

Most contemporary readers view Medea's murder of her sons as the final act of a madwoman, but that reading is largely based on the most famous version of the myth: Euripides's play. Other versions suggest that she does not kill her children at all, and they are murdered at the hands of the Corinthians,[3] or that she accidentally kills them when she tries to make them immortal.[4] Even Euripides's play is to some extent sympathetic toward Medea, depicting her actions not as the product of a deranged woman but as the result of maternal responsibility and love, fearing that they will be captured and brutalized by the Corinthians. "At once will I slay my children and then leave this land, without delaying long enough to hand them over to some more savage hand to butcher," she declares at the end of the play.[5]

In Euripides's version, when Jason finds that Medea has murdered his sons, she escapes on a dragon-drawn chariot, condemning Jason to a violent end for "having seen the bitter result of your marriage to me."[6] Even though Medea commits the most monstrous of monstrous acts, she doesn't face any immediate consequences for it; her actions are coded as legible, even understandable, as those of a woman who, having sacrificed everything for a man who abandoned her, does the only thing she can to level the playing field.

Ancient Roman history is also full of murderous mothers, like Agrippina, who uses her children as tools to further her own ambition—and pays the price for it. As the devious mother of Nero (of "fiddling while Rome burns" fame) and sister of Caligula (of "crazed orgies, incest, and electing his horse to public office" fame),* Agrippina tries to grab power however she can, collaborating with her sister to overthrow her brother (who also, for what it's worth,

---

* As loath as I am to give men the benefit of the doubt, for the sake of accuracy I will point out that many of these details, such as Caligula electing his horse consul, are disputed by scholars and probably did not happen. Unfortunately, future historians will not be able to say the same about our current political leaders, whose decisions are better documented and arguably more baffling, as a horse would probably do a better job as director of Health and Human Services than Trump appointee Robert F. Kennedy Jr. (though the horse's policies would probably be focused less on vaccines and more on the widespread availability of carrots).

was rumored to have been her lover).* She then marries her uncle Claudius to ensure her son will be next in line for succession.[7] Although she succeeds, Nero ultimately becomes resentful of her influence over him and orders her assassination, with one account stating that Agrippina's final act before she died was to strike her womb "for this bore Nero."†[8]

If you look at these examples of ancient bad moms, a common theme emerges. Both are presented as middle-aged women past their reproductive prime, former beauties rapidly losing the only form of currency women had. Rejected by society, they lash out against the patriarchy by weaponizing the only tools they had at their disposal: their children. For these women, being a bad mom wasn't about using the wrong brand of diapers or giving their kids French fries for dinner. It was about trying to reclaim the little power that they had.

* * *

Of course, none of this is to say that it was ever socially acceptable to be a "bad" mother. Murdering your sons to get revenge against your husband or using your children as proxies for your own ambition—these things have historically been, shall we say, frowned upon.

But it is true that women were judged according to an entirely different standard throughout much of Western history—one that had little, if anything, to do with how they raised their children.

---

*   From my cursory perusal of the classics, it seems that for whatever reason—boredom, horniness, a lack of awareness of Mendelian genetics law—the Romans absolutely loved fucking their own siblings. They loved it almost as much as people from California love talking about how much better tacos are on the West Coast. On the whole, the incest is probably worse, but the West Coast people are more annoying.

†   It's giving Livia Soprano, end of season 1.

In the colonial United States, for instance, mothers were not primarily assessed by their parenting abilities, or perceived lack thereof. They were chiefly judged by their work ethic and their ability to contribute to their households. Throughout the first few centuries of US history, says historian Stephanie Coontz, author of *The Way We Never Were: American Families and the Nostalgia Trap*, a "bad" mother may have been defined as "someone who didn't cooperate with her neighbors, who stole, who didn't do her household work, who didn't do whatever work she was supposed to do well." In court records from the sixteenth to the early eighteenth century, there are numerous examples of women being accused of malingering or failing to fulfill their household duties.[9] And instead of townsfolk gossiping about a woman's sex life or such brazen behavior as, say, showing an earlobe on the Sabbath or eating mutton in a suggestive way,* they were more likely to criticize her "diligence, farm skills, and reliability," says Coontz, adding that women defended their reputations in court disputes by "emphasizing their 'industry' or 'industriousness.'"[10]

Puritan women were taken to court over a wide range of seemingly minor infractions[11]—but very rarely were they taken to task for bad parenting. Whippings and beatings were regularly prescribed as acceptable disciplinary measures for children,[12] to the degree that there were few reported cases of child abuse or neglect at this time and there were no specific laws preventing child abuse until the late nineteenth century, as we'll discuss in more detail

---

* This is only kind of an exaggeration. According to court records from Salem, Massachusetts, in the mid-seventeenth century, a woman received a fine for "excess in clothing" and "wearing broad bone lace," while two other unnamed women were penalized for wearing a "silk hood."

later in this chapter.[13] Contrary to our contemporary conception of mother as nurturer and father as disciplinarian, the roles were more complex: The father was viewed as the moral head of the household, "the master of the family, its soul," Stacy Schiff, author of the 2015 book *The Witches: Salem 1692*, writes.[14] Mothers were viewed similarly to how June Cleaver would be in the 1950s: an all-pervasive presence, but at something of an emotional remove. During the Puritan era, "the death of a mother did not mean the dissolution of a family," historian Laurel Thatcher Ulrich writes, "but the death of a father did."[15]

There was a good reason for that: High infant mortality rates, as well as high childbirth mortality rates, contributed to making the mother/child relationship a somewhat detached—even sometimes contentious—one. During the colonial era, approximately 1 to 2 percent of childbirths resulted in the mother's death.[16] Even mothers who did not die during labor would often suffer from complications that would affect them for the rest of their lives. "That pain," says Steven Mintz, a professor of history at the University of Texas at Austin, "had to change their relationship with their child."[17] Indeed, Schiff writes that the mother/child relationship was so cold that Puritan mothers were contemptuous of indigenous women for their relative demonstrativeness, including hugging their children, showing them warmth, and "[weeping] over the children they lost."[18] Perhaps unsurprisingly, it was not uncommon for children who had been taken hostage during Puritan village raids to choose to stay with their Native captors over returning to the colonies.[19]

There were, of course, some standards governing maternal behavior during the Puritan era. During the initial wave of the Salem witch trials, for instance, many of the accused were targeted for deviating from the maternal standards of the day: Sarah Good, for instance, was an impoverished, unhoused mother of two who was well-known for walking around angrily muttering to herself, which was used in court as evidence of her malevolent nature,[20] while Martha Corey, another accused witch, had given birth to a biracial child out of wedlock twenty years prior.[21] Accuser reports that they had witnessed Good and Corey nursing a nonhuman "familiar," such as a bird[22] or a snake,[23] further emphasized their deviance from sociocultural maternal norms, depicting them as inhuman or other.[24]

But for the most part, while mothers were expected to be chaste, pious, devout, and follow the word of their husbands, they were not expected to actually be nurturing or attentive. "This idea we have in the US that children are precious, and we should respond to each and every one of their needs, and they are innocent—this is a rather new invention," says Marga Vicedo Castello, a professor in the history and philosophy of science and technology at the University of Toronto. "Children were abused and mistreated, and nobody paid too much attention to them, until relatively recently."[25]

It wasn't until the mid-nineteenth century, with the onset of the Industrial Revolution, that the standards governing our contemporary understanding of "good" and "bad" mothers really started to emerge. And even then, such distinctions did not, for the most part, arise from genuine concern for the welfare of children nearly as much as they did from the need to reinforce certain economic or racial boundaries: white, upper-class men were expected to labor, while white, upper-class women were expected to tend to the domestic sphere.[26]

Contrary to the whip-wielding schoolmarms of Puritan New England, mothers in the nineteenth century were expected to be warm, nurturing, and, above all else, omnipresent in their children's lives. Even President Lincoln enshrined his mother and stepmother in history as veritable saints, reportedly referring to Nancy Hanks Lincoln as an "angel mother" while demonizing his father as boorish and abusive. "There was a tendency to envelop the mother in veils of sentimentality and direct criticism toward the bad father," says Mintz.[27]

Perhaps the most prominent example of the "Angel in the House" trope is Marmee of Louisa May Alcott's *Little Women*, the almost pathologically selfless matriarch of the March family who, despite the stresses of raising four young girls on her own in Civil War–era New England, has nary an unkind or frustrated word to say about anybody.[28] "I've learned to check the hasty words that rise to my lips, and when I feel that they mean to break out against my will, I just go away for a minute, and give myself a little shake for being so weak and wicked,"[29] she tells her daughter at one point, echoing the sentiments of millions of future Betty Draper–esque housewives who would turn to Valium and vodka gimlets to check the "hasty words" rising to their lips.

The Angel in the House was crucial in shaping our modern conception of the idealized American mother, but it came at a price: With mothers assuming more responsibility for their households, they now also assumed near-total responsibility for the well-being of their offspring. The pressure to live up to the Angel in the House ideal coincided with the birth of the modern parenting advice industry as we know it, creating a climate of intense scrutiny from the very moment of conception.[30] One early-twentieth-century health care manual, for instance, advised pregnant women to avoid "thinking of ugly people, or those marked by any deformity or disease; avoid injury, fright, and disease of any kind"[31] in order to not have a child with deformities or delays. While such advice undeniably set a precedent for how much self-blame and neuroses would come to characterize our modern-day conception of motherhood, it's also kind of hilarious to envision a bunch of pregnant ladies in long skirts and petticoats walking the streets of Victorian-era New York, carefully averting their eyes *Bird Box*–style so as not to glance upon any uggos.

The Angel in the House also came to influence the conception of motherhood in far more insidious ways, says Sara Petersen, whose book, *Momfluenced: Inside the Maddening, Picture-Perfect World of Mommy Influencer Culture*, explores the trope's influence on contemporary Instagram momfluencers. "There's this construction of the ideal American mother as being the angel of the house. And, to get into that club, you had to not only be white, you had to be of a certain social class, [and] you shouldn't be working outside of the home," she explains.[32]

Prior to the abolition of slavery, it was common for enslaved Black women to be tasked with caring for the offspring of their white masters—but not for their own children, who were often sold at auction.[33] "The very idea of ripping Black women's children away from them and selling them as property really underscores how their motherhood was not considered motherhood in the same way that white women's motherhood was considered motherhood," says Petersen. "I think just the starkness of that fact really underscores how deeply embedded racist ideologies still are in how we conceive of a good mother and a bad mother."[34] Even after abolition, in the mid-to-late-nineteenth century, Black women were expected to work, Angel in the House be damned, and as a result the rate of Black married women in the workplace was consistently much higher than that of their white counterparts.[35]

Class and ethnicity also played a tremendous role in our conception of the "good" versus "bad" mother, particularly by the latter half of the nineteenth century, when the United States' very first child abuse case dominated media headlines. The 1874 case focused on Mary Ellen Wilson, a ten-year-old girl who was severely abused by her adoptive mother. Neighbors reported they had heard the girl screaming, prompting a local caseworker to investigate. When the caseworker arrived, she spotted Wilson walking barefoot during a frigid winter, her legs and arms covered in scars from numerous whippings.[36] The caseworker reported the abuse to the American Society for the Prevention of Cruelty to Animals,[37] which brought the case to court. That's because at the time, adults were so profoundly unconcerned about children that there was no official organization devoted to their welfare, meaning that if a horse had a toothache, that horse had more rights than a ten-year-old orphan being forced to walk barefoot in the cold. (As I said: The bar? Low.)

The case of Mary Ellen Wilson had two noteworthy consequences. The press coverage surrounding her adoptive mother's trial drew attention to the plight of abused children, resulting in the formation of the nation's first child advocacy group, the New York Society for the Prevention of Cruelty to Children.[38] The case also coincided with a surge of anti-Irish sentiment within the United States, and Wilson's adoptive mother, Mary Connolly (who ended up serving only a year in prison), was depicted in the press as a slovenly, monstrous, impoverished alcoholic,[39] "a woman whose temper has been embittered by the hardships of tenement life," her face etched with "hard lines and the deviant eye of poverty," as one New York *Sun* column put it.[40] In one newspaper sketch, she's depicted as a corpulent old drunk in the old-school anti-Irish tradition, passed out on the floor next to an empty flask, the wide-eyed Mary Ellen dressed in rags beside her.[41] Such coverage "allowed for all this hostility that can be directed at the poor—not just because they're poor, but also because they're immigrants, they're 'ethnic,' they don't share 'American values,'" says Mintz. "It was the ideal newspaper scandal, because it really played to people's prejudices."[42]

Eventually, the horrific case of Mary Ellen Wilson, Mintz argues, would metamorphose into the widespread surveillance of low-income mothers. With the creation of child protective services agencies in the 1970s, states routinely started "punishing [women] for poverty," says Mintz. The result was a "language of bad moms" tinged by moralism, classism, racism, and judgment that is still "pervasive" to this day.[43]

* * *

"She smokes thirty cigarettes a day, chews gum, and consumes tons of bonbons and petits fours. She drinks moderately, which is to say, two or three cocktails before dinner every night and a brandy and a couple of highballs afterward. She doesn't count the two cocktails she takes before lunch when she lunches out, which is every day she can."[44]

This is Philip Wylie's description of bad moms in his 1942 book of essays, *Generation of Vipers*. Wylie was a polymath who worked as a science fiction novelist before publishing his career-defining work, *Generation of Vipers*, a social critique of American mores. The most controversial essay in the book was "Common Women," in which Wylie coins the term "momism" to describe his theory that the American mother—painted as a middle-aged, chain-smoking, hard-partying, loud-mouthed, sexually repulsive grotesque—was contributing to the downfall of society. In his essay, Wylie chastises the American mother for emasculating her children, accusing her of stunting her son's emotional development under the guise of loving and protecting him. He charmingly concludes that it is the overbearing mothers of America who have "raped the men, not sexually, unfortunately, but morally."[45]

Wylie wrote his book on the heels of the Great Depression, a period when many husbands and fathers abandoned their families because they were unable to provide for them. "Men were marginalized economically. They viewed themselves as failures," says Mintz. "And they weren't able to protect their family from poverty. So the mom became the central figure in the household. They viewed themselves as the ultimate protector of the family."[46] With World War II underway, women were gaining more economic power and fulfillment outside the domestic sphere. So it made sense that the mother would evolve into a target of resentment within the family unit, becoming "the villain for everything that goes wrong," as Mintz puts it.[47]

Wylie was not the first person to proclaim that the "silver cord of love" binding nurturing mothers to their progeny was, in fact, secretly a stranglehold. By the 1920s, child development experts* had started declaring maternal affection to have a stultifying, even castrating, effect.[48] This was a time when people like psychologist John Watson—most famous for his Little Albert experiment, in which he conditioned a nine-month-old baby to nurture an endur-

---

* A field that, in itself, would have been unthinkable a mere forty years earlier.

ing phobia of fluffy animals and Santa beards[*]—were advocating for parents to shake hands with their babies rather than hugging and kissing them. Though to be fair to Watson, he generously allowed for some wiggle room in this regard: "If you must, kiss them once on the forehead when they say good night," he wrote in 1928.[49] So the vitriolic anti-woman messaging of Wylie's tome struck a chord, even among mothers themselves. Although some objected to his misogynistic tone, others found the suggestion that mothers should not be tied *too* tightly to their offspring validating, even empowering.[50]

Momism set a precedent for our modern conception of "good" and "bad" mothers in two important, and arguably quite contradictory, ways. In some respects, Plant says, momism "helps pave the way for women's entrance into the workforce, rather than the other way around."[51] The Great Depression and World War II had given mothers a taste of what life was like when they briefly managed to sever the "silver cord," and Wylie's argument for stay-at-home mothers having "all this energy and pouring it into her kids in ways that can turn pathological" also carried with it a reasonable—dare we say, even borderline feminist—implication: that "women need a more balanced life," says Plant.[52]

But, of course, the rise of momism also set a precedent for a dangerous idea that would become firmly entrenched in our culture: Regardless of how they parented, mothers assumed sole

---

[*] This is obviously a fairly glib summary of what is widely considered one of the most significant, albeit controversial, psychological experiments of all time, but honestly it's not that far off from what actually happened.

responsibility for how their children turned out. Whether they were overly affectionate or withholding, working or nonworking, Black or white, "bad" mothers would be held responsible for everything from homosexuality to schizophrenia to alcoholism[53] to autism. With momism and *Generation of Vipers*, "what starts as a social critique morphs into more of a diagnosis," says Plant, rooted in the idea that mothers and maternal love were "not an unmitigated good, [but] a powerful force that needed to be regulated and held in check."[54]

* * *

It did not take long for critiques about the dangers of overly attentive mothers to give way to those blaming mothers for not being attentive enough. This was largely due to the work of John Bowlby,[55] a British psychologist who, after studying the effects of parental detachment on post–World War II European children, built his life's work on the theory that in order to ensure positive cognitive, social, and emotional outcomes,[56] a baby should "experience a warm, intimate and continuous relationship with his mother (or permanent mother substitute) in which both find satisfaction and enjoyment," as he wrote in his 1951 report on maternal care and mental health.[57]

I first learned about Bowlby and his work in college, when I took a class in developmental psychology.* At the time, I remember hearing about attachment theory—basically, the idea that good mothers

---

*   I remember absolutely nothing else about this class except that I made a reference to Pound Puppies in my final paper, and the professor wrote three (frankly, very aggressive) question marks next to it. I cannot remember the context. I do, however, remember the paper got a C minus.

form strong bonds with their children—and thinking, "Yeah, no fucking kidding." At the time, I didn't understand what was so revolutionary about a British guy saying this, to the degree that his work would be used to torture hungover sophomores at 9:00 a.m. on a Thursday.

What I, as one of those hungover sophomores, did not fully appreciate was that Bowlby's attachment theory came on the tail end of not just Wylie's theories about momism, but also decades of maternal affection being pathologized by (largely male) child development experts like John Watson.* The idea that being a bad mom was synonymous with being present and affectionate was so widely accepted at the time that the countervailing view that mothers should, actually, be *nice* to their children *was* revolutionary.

But Bowlby's work also came at a rather convenient time in US history. By the start of the 1950s, women who had gotten a taste of autonomy with the Great Depression or World War II were catapulted back into their kitchens, once again tasked with being nurturers and caretakers. In this context, the idea that mothers should spend as much time with their offspring as possible, or else run the risk of causing them irreparable harm, was a pretty great way to convince women to quit their jobs and head back home.

This became clear in the 1960s, at the start of the women's liberation movement. In response to the massive popularity of books like

---

* Bowlby himself was raised according to the shake-hands-with-your-baby, stiff-upper-lip school of child-rearing, describing it as deeply traumatizing. [Kendra Cherry, "Biography of Psychologist John Bowlby, the Father of Attachment Theory," Verywell Mind, September 12, 2023, www.verywellmind.com/john-bowlby-biography-1907-1990-2795514.]

Betty Friedan's *The Feminine Mystique*, which argued that women needed to find fulfillment and meaning outside marriage and child-rearing,[58] parenting experts like Bowlby expressed concern about the impact the feminist movement would have on children. "Whenever I hear the issue of maternal deprivation being discussed, I find two groups with a vested interest in shooting down the theory," Bowlby said in a 1965 *New York Times* interview. "The Communists are one. . . . The professional women are the second group. They have, in fact, neglected their families. But that is the last thing they want to admit."*[59]

Over the next few decades, attachment theory would be further weaponized against so-called bad mothers in insidious and horrifying ways, particularly by the medical establishment.[60] Perhaps the most prominent example is the "refrigerator mother," a term for mothers of children diagnosed with autism. Popularized by a 1948 *Time* magazine cover story that characterized autistic children as

---

* An interesting side note about attachment theory is that it forms the basis for attachment parenting, a parenting trend that became in vogue in the early 2010s that advocates for mothers bonding with their infants by spending as much time with them as possible, in the form of babywearing, breastfeeding, and co-sleeping, among other practices. Proponents of attachment parenting argue there is nothing inherently anti-feminist about this ideology, but as the aforementioned *New York Times* quote demonstrates, there certainly was for Bowlby himself. "From the beginning, [Bowlby] meant to use his theory to justify a specific gender role and to justify having the mother in the home," Vicedo told me. [Kate Pickert, "The Man Who Remade Motherhood," *Time*, May 21, 2012, https://content.time.com/time/subscriber/article/0,33009,2114427-3,00 .html and Vicedo author interview.]

"apathetic [and] withdrawn," as if they had been "kept neatly in a refrigerator which didn't defrost,"[61] a refrigerator mother was, in effect, a woman who was viewed as not responding "in a warm way to her children," says Vicedo.[62]

This egregious medical gaslighting would, understandably, cause immense guilt and emotional distress to mothers who were already, as the parents of special needs children, dealing with difficult circumstances. "Imagine you have [an autistic child]. And you take them to a psychiatrist and they say it is your fault," says Vicedo. "For most women of this generation, it was devastating."[63]

Like most tropes related to being a bad mother, the refrigerator mother diagnosis was deeply infused with preconceived notions about race and class. Refrigerator mothers were disproportionately middle- or upper-class women who had achieved some level of higher education, even if they didn't necessarily work full-time.[64] The thinking was that such women had strayed so far from their natural roles as nurturers that they had irreparably harmed their children in the process.[65]

At the height of its popularity, in the 1950s and early 1960s, the refrigerator mother classification was most commonly applied to white mothers, whose children were statistically more likely to be diagnosed with autism.[66] Black children who today would likely be diagnosed with autism were typically diagnosed with schizophrenia instead.[67] The mothers of schizophrenic children similarly faced a tremendous amount of blame and were labeled by psychiatrists as "schizophrenogenic," or causing their child's schizophrenia.[68]

The refrigerator mother theory started falling out of favor around the mid-1970s,[69] as did the idea that bad mothering caused schizophrenia.[70] But the shadow of the refrigerator mother persists to this day. Social media influencers like the alternative health practitioner Joseph Mercola[71] and pediatrician Bob Sears regularly promote the debunked conspiracy theory that the MMR vaccine has been linked to autism.*[72] Though they do not explicitly say mothers cause their children's autism, they do suggest that mothers' unquestioning belief in medical establishment protocols—in this case, adhering to a vaccine schedule—does.

There is also a distinct whiff of mom-blaming in the recent right-wing movement to vilify transgender children and, by extension, the mothers who support them through transition, echoing the medical establishment's efforts in the post–World War II era to link bad mothering to homosexuality.[73] In a 2020 podcast episode, far-right pundit and professional transphobe Matt Walsh attacked NBA star Dwyane Wade for supporting his child's transition, implying that his wife, actress Gabrielle Union, "imposed" this ideology onto him, arguing, "it will never not be weird to see a normal grown man spouting this left-wing gender theory nonsense."†[74] And in June 2023, when failed far-right political candidate Robby Starbuck tweeted a photo of Megan Fox and her children claiming she was forcing them to wear girls' clothes and was guilty of "child

---

*   A pediatrician and the author of *The Vaccine Book*, which has advocated for delayed vaccination schedules, Sears was put on probation in 2018 by the California medical board for doling out fraudulent vaccine exemptions. (The probation ended in 2023.) He is the son of William and Martha Sears, Bowlby acolytes who have written multiple attachment parenting books and received criticism for advocating for mothers to leave the workforce.

†   To which I would respond that it will never not be weird to see a grown man like Walsh have flawlessly trimmed facial hair.

abuse," he tellingly did not include the children's father, Fox's ex Brian Austin Green, in his analysis.[75]

We may be tempted to express horror at the concept of the refrigerator mother, or gasp at Philip Wylie's misogyny, or mock John Watson's advice that infants benefit from little more than a firm handshake and a pat on the head. But the truth is, the contemporary discourse surrounding "good" and "bad" moms is not significantly more enlightened than the days of telling pregnant women not to look at ugly people. If anything, feminism has made the landscape of mom-shaming thicker with minefields than ever before, in that, supplied with more options for how to mother than ever before, we are given more and more opportunities to fail.

Ostensibly, we've developed a more nuanced view of the role mothers play in child development, as well as more diverse perspectives on parenthood. Yet the default for motherhood is still very much white, cisgender, and middle-class, and we continue to penalize women who fall short of this standard. We have yet to bridge the gap between the precolonial and colonial bar for being a good mom— i.e., the ability to ensure your children are not trudging through the snow barefoot or being eaten by wolves—and the labyrinthine, often contradictory, rules governing mothers today. The bar keeps being raised; the standards keep getting higher; the rules of the game keep changing.

More often than not, being a "good" mom feels difficult, if not impossible—and to a large extent, this is by design. Which is why it falls on us to break free of the cycle and keep reminding ourselves that mothering isn't about hugging your kids too much or too little, or whether you should co-sleep or breastfeed or sign them up for tae kwon do or let them play *Minecraft* or any of the other myriad and ultimately less than significant choices you have to make on a daily basis. It's not about any of that, Hal—it's about *cats*. It's about loving your children with every part of your heart and having the resolve to wake up every morning and do it all over again. And if you can keep them alive in the process, that's certainly a plus.

3

"No More Wire Hangers Ever"

Wrestling with the Ghost of Joan Crawford

Joan Crawford saunters into her children's bedroom, her face smeared in cold cream, a white headband bringing her razor-sharp cheekbones and upside-down-parentheses eyebrows into sharp relief. She smiles at her sleeping daughter, ensconced in her bed like a blond angelic sausage, before rifling through her closet. Suddenly, she stops short, her placid expression morphing into a rictus of sheer rage. She plucks out a garment, a pink, tulle monstrosity, and stalks toward her daughter's bed.

"No . . . wire . . . hangers . . . ever," she bellows viciously, holding up the garment. "I work and work till I'm half dead and I hear people say, 'She's getting old,' and what do I get? A daughter . . . who cares as much about the beautiful dresses I give her as she cares about me!"[1] She throws the dress at her daughter, who is quaking with fear beneath the sheets.

Even if you know nothing about Joan Crawford, you're probably familiar with the above scene. "No wire hangers" is from the 1981 movie *Mommie Dearest*, based on a tell-all memoir by Crawford's adopted daughter Christina, a recounting of years of alleged physical and emotional abuse at the hands of her mother. The scene is intended as a harrowing depiction of Crawford's cruelty, but because Faye

Dunaway's performance is so histrionic—and because the impetus for Crawford's rage is so stupid—it's now considered a meme of sorts, and *Mommie Dearest* a cult classic. "No wire hangers, ever!" ranks as one of the American Film Institute's most memorable film quotes,[*2] and there are *Rocky Horror Picture Show*–esque screenings of *Mommie Dearest* at college campuses and queer bars across the country.

Like most cultural artifacts embraced by legions of drunk college students and gay men, *Mommie Dearest* is, objectively speaking, not a good movie. It received atrocious reviews upon its release, most of which focused on Dunaway's unhinged performance.[†] It's also difficult to engage in a good-faith analysis of *Mommie Dearest*

---

* Much to the chagrin of dry cleaners everywhere, who have likely been subject to countless dad jokes.

† For those interested in *Mommie Dearest* and Crawford's life in general, I would highly recommend Karina Longworth's 2016 podcast series *You Must Remember This*, which recounts the production of the film in great detail. According to Longworth's podcast, Dunaway was at the peak of her career during shooting, fresh off winning an Oscar for her performance in *Network*; she genuinely believed that her portrayal of Crawford would garner her a second win. This led to reports of her being something of a narcissistic monster on set, much to the delight of cast and crew members who watched Dunaway get savaged after the film's release. *Mommie Dearest* did irreparable harm to Dunaway's legacy, and she has since stated in interviews that she regrets taking the role. But to me, knowing that Dunaway was so deluded as to think she was giving the performance of a lifetime in *Mommie Dearest* both heightens its tragicomic elements and lends an added layer of poignance to the film. It's a real art-imitates-life moment—you're not just watching Crawford descend into madness in real time, but arguably, Dunaway, too. [Julie Miller, "Faye Dunaway Isn't Sure Making *Mommie Dearest* Was a Good Move for Anyone," *Vanity Fair*, September 1, 2016, www.vanityfair.com/hollywood/2016/09/faye-dunaway-mommie-dearest.]

without acknowledging that its veracity is sharply contested, including by two of Crawford's other children. While Christina's adopted brother, Christopher, who died in 2006, said many of the events depicted in her book rang true,[3] Crawford's two other children, adopted twins Cindy and Cathy (who died in 2007 and 2020, respectively) strongly denied that Crawford had ever been physically or emotionally abusive.[4]

"It makes me very sad," Cathy told a *Vanity Fair* reporter about *Mommie Dearest*. "Every time Mommie's name is mentioned, that book is mentioned. I don't want to give it any more publicity than it's already had. Even when people say or write good things about my mother, that book gets linked to her name."[5] While none of this is meant to discount Christina Crawford's experience, it does suggest that there are aspects of *Mommie Dearest* that are in dispute.

Regardless of the quality of the film or the accuracy of the book itself, one thing is certain: Despite Joan Crawford's decades-long standing as one of the top-earning stars of Hollywood's Golden Age, "most people, when they think of Joan Crawford, think of how she is portrayed by Faye Dunaway in *Mommie Dearest*," Karina Longworth, the host of the Hollywood history podcast *You Must Remember This*, told me. "*Mommie Dearest* has had a longer cultural life than any individual Joan Crawford movie."[6]

And I can't help but feel a little sad about this—not just because I think it's unfair for any one individual to be defined by their worst moments, particularly if they're no longer around to defend themselves, but because Crawford was a much more complex figure than *Mommie Dearest* would suggest. In many ways, both the roles she played on-screen and her public persona helped to popularize a specific type of modern, self-sufficient, career-oriented woman, plucky self-starters who lifted themselves up from their dismal circumstances by sheer force of will. If it weren't for Joan Crawford's acid-tinged turn as the voracious Crystal Allen in *The Women*, or as the ambitious stenographer Flaemmchen in *Grand Hotel*, we probably wouldn't have Samantha Jones or Elle Woods or, God forgive me, Andie Anderson from *How to Lose a Guy in 10 Days*.

But no one remembers Joan Crawford as the gutsy flappers she played in her early career; or the indefatigable middle-aged women she played in *Johnny Guitar* or *Mildred Pierce*; or even as the savage, vodka-drenched wit who'd give bitchy quotes to reporters in her final years.[*7] We don't remember her as sharp-fanged and fiercely driven and nasty and embittered and generous and complicated. Instead, we remember her as how she was portrayed in *Mommie Dearest*: as the craziest psycho bitch mommy of all time.

* * *

Over the past decade or so, there has been a large-scale cultural effort to reappraise previously reviled women. From Monica Lewin-

---

*   Crawford had a lot of hilariously snarky things to say about her Hollywood rivals, particularly her *Whatever Happened to Baby Jane?* costar Bette Davis, a rivalry famously documented in the Ryan Murphy FX series *Feud*. "Working with Bette Davis was my greatest challenge, and I mean that kindly," she said in one 1973 interview. "[She] is of a different temperament than I. She has to yell every morning. I just sat and knitted. [During the filming of *Whatever Happened to Baby Jane?*] I knitted a scarf from Hollywood to Malibu." ["Joan Crawford on Challenges, Bette Davis, and Baby Jane at Her Town Hall Interview (1973)," posted November 4, 2023, by golddust, YouTube, www.youtube.com/watch?v=P54eKzFoVoc.] I prefer her less-well-known (and admittedly, possibly apocryphal) bon mots, such as how she responded to a reporter who asked about a rumor that she'd had an orgy with twenty-five men: "It's an interesting story. But I don't know twenty-five men I'd want to invite."

sky to Paris Hilton to Britney Spears to Tonya Harding, seemingly every widely loathed female celebrity in the 1990s and 2000s has been subject to the redemption arc treatment,[8] be it in the form of a sympathetic biopic (*I, Tonya*) or documentary (*Framing Britney Spears*; *This Is Paris*) or viral TED Talk ("Monica Lewinsky: The Price of Shame").

I have mixed feelings about this phenomenon, largely because I feel it's been too broadly applied: Some of these women, like Monica Lewinsky, a woman who was a private citizen in her early twenties when her sex life became a national joke, are highly deserving of our sympathy, while others, such as Paris Hilton, a woman who has a long history of making racist and anti-Semitic comments, arguably are less so.[9] Not everyone is worthy of an *I, Tonya*–style redemption arc. Some people have done too much harm to possibly be redeemed. Some people are just truly bad people. Some mothers are just truly bad mothers.

If at least half of Christina Crawford's allegations in *Mommie Dearest* are true, Joan Crawford may very well fall into that category. My goal here is not to provide a woman who has been dead for more than fifty years a redemption arc; the harm she did to her child may simply have been too great to render her worthy of one. But if Joan Crawford was, in fact, a bad mother, we have to acknowledge that she probably wasn't for any one specific reason. A bad mother, just like a bad *anything*, is the product of an intricately woven medieval tapestry of a million different threads. And if we're interested in unraveling the picture to assess how it came together,* one of the threads that we invariably have to pull on is mental illness.

---

* To be fair, I don't know anything about medieval tapestries. I assume, however, that many of them feature bears.

This is not a topic that people are eager to discuss. Mothers have historically been viewed as bastions of sanity in an insane world: the shelter from the storm, the hearth in the blizzard, the Angel in the House tethering their husbands and children with a silver cord of love. What's more, there is a prevailing assumption that mothers are innately equipped to serve in this role, that women with children are guided by a biological imperative to provide comfort and stability where it is otherwise lacking. Mothers nurture. Mothers heal. Mothers kiss boo-boos and make them better. And the idea that some women may not be innately well-equipped to do this, or may have unhealed boo-boos themselves, is anathema to many.

It's hard to know exactly how many mothers struggle with mental illness. We can extrapolate from general data, such as the statistic that more than 20 percent of American women struggle with some type of mental health disorder, ranging from depression and anxiety to bipolar or post-traumatic stress disorder (PTSD).[10] In recent years, media coverage has primarily focused on a specific type of maternal mental illness: postpartum and perinatal mood disorders, diagnoses of which have spiked noticeably, with one study showing that they increased by 93 percent between 2008 and 2020 in the United States.[11] Celebrities like Adele, Chrissy Teigen, and Sarah Michelle Gellar have also come forward with their own experiences, leading to increased awareness of postpartum mental health disorders.[12]

But even though heightened understanding of these conditions is undoubtedly a good thing and has led to a rise in screening rates for new mothers,[13] there is an overwhelming sense that we only deem such conversations palatable because these struggles are confined to a finite period. Most postpartum depression narratives are fairly pat recountings from (largely well-resourced, economically privileged) women who had never struggled with mental illness before and were able to quickly clock the symptoms, allowing them to get help in a short period of time. The unifying theme of these stories is that with the right intervention—the right therapist, the right medication—these women are able to go back to being the nurturers, the shelters from the storm. There is little space in the discussion for the less tidy narratives about mothers who do not get better, who recognize that every day they are fighting an uphill battle against their own brain chemistry.

In popular culture, there are shockingly few accurate, nuanced representations of what it actually looks like to parent with a mental illness.* Such depictions usually fall in one of two camps: either mentally ill moms are emotionally disconnected ice queens, their cool glacial exterior hinting at a deep wellspring of rage and trauma (Patricia Clarkson's Munchausen syndrome by proxy mom in *Sharp Objects*, Livia Soprano in *The Sopranos*); or they're comically grotesque Kabuki villains (Piper Laurie's keening Bible-thumper in *Carrie* gives Dunaway's Crawford a run for her money in this regard). Indeed, some of the most interesting portrayals of maternal mental illness aren't in naturalistic film or TV representations at all

---

* I'm using the term "mental illness" quite broadly here, which is by design. There's such a wide-ranging spectrum of mental health disorders and symptoms that it's almost impossible to restrict the discussion here to one specific type. Needless to say, there's a huge difference between the experience of what it's like to parent with a mood disorder like anxiety or depression versus what it is like to parent with a personality disorder like borderline personality disorder. In terms of the cultural perception and the stigmatization of maternal mental illness, however, I think there are more similarities than differences. In this context, I'm using the term to encompass any diagnosis that is considered chronic and is not confined to the period following childbirth.

but horror movies such as 2014's *The Babadook* and 2018's *Hereditary*, in which a mother's struggle to maintain her sanity is rendered literal in the form of battling demonic forces or an ominous gay icon in a top hat.[14]

As a mother who struggles with depression, anxiety, and mood regulation issues, I think there are a few different reasons for this. The first is that the day-to-day reality of living with a mental illness, let alone parenting with one, is stunningly unsexy and difficult to dramatize. There is no dramatic arc, no highly cinematic revelation or redemptive moment; it's just a lot of shuffling around performing mundane domestic tasks, unwashed and messy-haired and bleary-eyed, intermittently mingled with crying bouts in bathrooms. But I think our reluctance to touch on the issue of maternal mental illness also stems from something far more insidious: Culturally, we suffer from a seeming inability to acknowledge women's pain with anything other than flippancy, and that has been the case since the advent of the modern medical establishment.

The inherent misogyny and racism of modern medicine is incredibly well-documented: doctors are more likely to dismiss female patients' reports of pain and deny them pain relief,[15] and Black patients are 40 percent less likely to be prescribed medication for acute pain than white ones.[16] These biases apply to the history of mental health treatment as well. In the late nineteenth century, for instance, physicians regularly characterized female mental illness as a form of "hysteria," a diagnosis they applied to all manners of what was then viewed as aberrant female behavior, from depression to anxiety to PTSD.[17] Cures ranged widely depending on the era and the physician, from a pelvic massage leading to "hysterical paroxysm" (basically, Victorian physician jargon for inducing orgasm)[18] to sexual abstinence[19] to institutionalization.[20] And while the diagnosis primarily applied to single and/or childless women who were thought to have betrayed their biological function by failing to reproduce,[21] it was also sometimes applied to mothers, particularly those who were viewed as resisting their circumscribed domestic roles.

Perhaps the ultimate example of the pathologizing of maternal "hysteria" can be found in the nineteenth-century short story "The Yellow Wallpaper" by Charlotte Perkins Gilman, in which a female writer who has just given birth is diagnosed by her doctor husband with a "temporary nervous condition—a slight hysterical tendency"[22] and confined to an empty nursery to recuperate. Initially published in 1892 in *New England Magazine*, the story was based on Gilman's own experience with what would now likely be characterized as postpartum depression, after giving birth to her daughter.[23] Her doctor prescribed her a "rest cure," forbidding her from writing.

At the time, the "rest cure" was a popular treatment for women with mental illness. But as she wrote in a 1913 manifesto describing the inspiration behind "The Yellow Wallpaper," Gilman chafed against it, writing that refraining from intellectual pursuits for three months brought her to "the borderline of utter mental ruin."[24] Her heroine in "The Yellow Wallpaper" goes over that line. Over the course of an unspecified period of time, she becomes obsessed with a female figure trapped in the room's eponymous wallpaper, gnawing on the bedposts and stripping the walls in order to free her, causing her to descend into insanity.

Today, "The Yellow Wallpaper" can be found on the syllabus of pretty much every intro to gender studies course across the country,[25] and is taught as a condemnation of the medical establishment's infantilization of women. And this is, indeed, how it was intended to be read. As Gilman wrote in her manifesto, her story "was not intended to drive people crazy, but to save people from being driven crazy."[26] She even sent a copy of this essay to the physician who had prescribed her the "rest cure" in the first place, a turn-of-the-century New England fuck-you if there ever was one.[27]

But this was not at all how "The Yellow Wallpaper" was received when it was first published. Literary editors and critics largely dismissed it, with some viewing it as a paltry imitation of Poe's gothic horror genre.[28] Even Gilman's supporters were put off by the work, with one male editor referring to it as a tale too "terrible and too wholly dire" to appear in printed form.[29] In some ways, the nineteenth-century establishment's reaction to "The Yellow Wallpaper" parallels how our culture still views maternal mental illness: either by treating it as a grotesque aberration, a force too terrible and too wholly dire to be viewed as symptomatic of what may be a wider problem, or by dismissing it outright.

Hysteria diagnoses started falling out of favor around the mid-twentieth century, officially disappearing from the *DSM* in 1980.[30] Yet the idea that motherhood could, for some women, be enough of a stressor to trigger a mental health crisis is still difficult for many to wrap their minds around. All things considered, very little has changed since the era of hysterical paroxysms and rest cures; we are still unable to see the mentally ill parent as anything but a source of danger, a psycho mommy clawing at pill bottles and wire hangers.

I remember watching *Blonde*, Andrew Dominik's 2022 Marilyn Monroe biopic, a day or two after I'd given birth to Marco, while I was still in the hospital. I was desperately trying to pump milk, the throbbing of my C-section scar competing with the agony of my uterus violently contracting.* In one scene, Marilyn's mother, Gladys Baker (Julianne Nicholson), frantically dips down the freeway toward a forest fire, weeping as she careens toward the depths of hell, her angel-faced daughter staring helplessly at her from the passenger seat, a hostage to the dizzying eddy of her psychotic mother's emotions. It was too much for me in my hormonal state; I had to turn the movie off.

I get that Dominik's intention in shooting the scene this way was to thrust the viewer into his heroine's nightmarish existence, long before he heaps an endless array of other nightmares onto her.† But as I sat on that bed a mere few hours postpartum, a sore, cramping, weeping mess, Gladys's pain—the all-encompassing, all-consuming scale of it—was too difficult to watch, in that it seemed almost a magnification of my own. And I wondered why we always see such moments from the perspective of the child in the passenger seat or in the bed, coming face-to-face with the blazing abyss. No one, it seemed, wanted to ask what could ever compel a mother to drive her and the tiny, innocent soul she has been tasked to protect, toward the flames. They had to look away, to avoid confronting the enormity of her rage, to avoid being engulfed by the inferno.

Every time I watch *Mommie Dearest*, I try to ask this question of Joan Crawford—why she did the things she (allegedly) did to

---

* The hormones released by nipple stimulation cause uterine contractions and bleeding the first few days after giving birth. It's yet another fun fact about the postpartum human body that everyone conveniently forgets to tell you until it's already happening.

† The movie, which actually features a scene in which a CGI rendering of Monroe's aborted fetus begs her not to kill it, was accused by many critics of being exploitative.

her children, why she was the way she (allegedly) was. I wonder what sorts of corrosive elements were thrown into the fires of her youth to create such a tough and glittering metal. And the answer, I believe, is that Joan Crawford basically emerged from the womb as a fighter, scratching and clawing her way to the life she felt she deserved.

Crawford was born Lucille LeSueur in an impoverished Texas household, her father abandoning her family right after she was born. To support her family, her mother worked at a laundromat. At thirteen, Crawford was sexually abused by her stepfather; though, as dramatized by the Ryan Murphy series *Feud*, she later claimed, with characteristic Crawford bravado, that the abuse was consensual.[31] When she made it to Hollywood, she allegedly subjected herself to the advances of lecherous executives in the hopes of getting bit parts; while this was not uncommon at the time, Crawford spent the remainder of her career plagued by casting couch rumors.[32]

Crawford wasn't the most beautiful woman in Hollywood, nor the most talented. But she was well-known for her grueling work ethic,[33] her generosity toward employees[34] and crew members,[35] and, above all else, her burning ambition. "Her ferocious will to succeed seems a grim version of the life force itself," *New Yorker* critic David Denby wrote.[36] This was reflected in the roles she chose, which were largely hard-bitten, sexy, independent working women with an air of steely indefatigability, an anomalous type in an era where women were largely expected to keep house and spread their legs. In fact, as depicted in *Mommie Dearest*, Crawford's brand was so synonymous with female ambition that when she first tried to adopt her children, she was rejected for being a single woman too focused on her career.* *Mommie Dearest* is not a feminist film by any means, but it is scathing in its condemnation of the adoption agency's misogyny: When Joan bellows "Don't you daaaaaare judge me" at the representative rejecting her for being "unsuitable," we can't help but cheer her on.

That's not to say, of course, that the adoption agency's assessment of Crawford is incorrect. In *Mommie Dearest*, Crawford is emotionally and physically abusive toward her children. Her behavior is erratic, her moods vacillating between periods of alcoholic stupor[37] and wild-eyed mania, her actions stemming entirely from some primal, untrammeled rage rather than any semblance of rationality. And this, I think, is what gets lost in the discussion about the wire hangers scene, and about Crawford in general: Yes, Dunaway's reaction to the wire hangers is outsize and extreme and totally disproportionate to the actual nature of the offense, which is why it reads to many as camp. But it doesn't come off that way to me. It comes off as a pretty accurate representation of what it's like to live with someone with an untreated mood disorder—the way you never quite know what or who will set them off, the way their anger is a life force of its own, burrowed under the skin, simmering underneath and subsiding as rapidly as it burbled up. The way you are a hostage to that anger, the terrified child in the passenger seat, heading toward the flames and waiting for them to smolder and die out. It reminds me of Gladys Baker. It reminds me of my own mother. And if I'm being honest, it reminds me of myself.

---

* Crawford ultimately managed to adopt her children via the black market— something that was, weirdly, not all that uncommon in the 1940s.

* * *

One of my earliest childhood memories is of my mother telling me and my sister that she was going to die. This wasn't something that she would regularly bring up in casual conversation—it was usually while we were having an argument, or if we had done something to make her angry. "You know that I probably have cancer," she'd say. "I don't have much time left. And when I'm gone, you're going to be sorry."

Whenever my mother would say this, or whenever she'd storm into the bathroom and lock the door behind her while my sister and I sobbed and pled with her to come out, I would ask my father why she acted like this. And this was his standard explanation: My mother had been relatively "normal" until six months after I was born, when her older sister, Susan, died of lung cancer at the age of forty. To hear my father tell it, my aunt's death had kickstarted my mother's mental health crisis, making her prone to intense sadness in a way that she hadn't been before. "She wasn't insane," he always said. "And then, after Susan died, she became insane."

I believed this. I also believed my mother when she said she was going to die. How could I not have? I was too young to know what I now believe to be the truth: that Susan, a longtime smoker, had introduced the habit to my mother when she was just thirteen, and that when Susan died, she coped with her feelings of grief and rage and helplessness by telling herself that she would very soon be next. I was also too young to realize just how deeply fucked-up my father's explanation for my mother's depression and mood swings was. This was a woman who, while her sister was slowly and painfully dying in a hospital in Long Island, was taking care of a newborn, without the benefit of long-term counseling or familial support while my father worked grueling hours. I don't know all the elements that went into the fires that forged my mother's own struggles with her mental health, but I'm pretty damn sure it wasn't just my aunt's death, and I'm also pretty sure that constantly hearing my dad attribute them to that did little to help my mother cope.

I want to be clear: There are more differences than similarities between Joan Crawford and my mother. My mom never hurt me and my sister the way Joan allegedly did—she never tried to choke me or made me scrub floors in the middle of the night or took my place at my job while I was hospitalized with ovarian tumors.* But I would also be lying if I said I didn't see parallels. Like Joan, my mother did not grow up with a lot of money—her mother was a homemaker, and her father had a civil service job—and she'd often tell me about the shame of going to summer camps and receiving free underwear. Also like Joan, my mother was fiercely ambitious and competent,

---

* This happens to an adult Christina Crawford in *Mommie Dearest*, when Joan steps in to replace her on a soap opera called *The Secret Storm*. Apparently, this really happened, though accounts differ as to what Joan's motivation for doing this was: While *Mommie Dearest* depicts it as her trying to steal her daughter's thunder, some close to Joan have said that she was terrified about returning to the public eye in her mid-sixties and only did so to ensure Christina's role would not be recast. Per Christina's own recollection, "They asked me about it the day after I was operated on. It was coming to me in a fog, and I couldn't exactly jump up and down in bed about it, but I do remember thinking that it was fantastic that she would care that much." [Robert Windeler, "Joan Crawford Takes Daughter's Soap Opera Role," *New York Times*, October 23, 1968, www.nytimes.com/1968/10/23 /archives/joan-crawford-takes-daughters-soap-opera-role.html.]

attending college and business school on a full scholarship, grad-
uating Phi Beta Kappa, and parlaying her academic success into a
prestigious corporate communications job.

Words fail to describe how much I love and admire my mother.
She was, and is, a generous and funny and smart and relentlessly
supportive parent, and she worked her ass off to give us everything
we wanted. The vast majority of my childhood memories of her are
happy ones: her mellifluous alto singing Jackson Browne and Dolly
Parton; dancing in pajamas to convince my father to get a dog; running to at least three Wendy's at 6:00 p.m. on a Friday, her power
pumps and blazer damp with sweat and rain, to scrounge up a pair
of promotional 3D glasses for me for the TGIF ABC 3D lineup.

But as much as my mother loved us and wanted to protect us,
she still constantly had to negotiate between quieting the angry and
fearful voices in her own head and trying to quiet ours. She had the
unenviable task of fighting two different battles at the same time,
with few resources and little support. It was inevitable that, occasionally, she would end up losing both.

Now that I am juggling parenting two small children with my
own battles with depression and anxiety, I've had my own fair share
of moments when I have said or done things that I know have caused
my children just as much pain as my mother caused me. I've been
both Christina and Joan, Norma Jean and Gladys Baker; the terrified child staring right into the eye of the storm, and the storm itself.
So, naturally, I think a lot about how difficult it must have been for
my mother, who raised me in the nineties, when there was a lot less
support for people who struggled with mental illness in general. I
think about how frustrated and helpless and lonely she must have
felt fending off these demons on top of all the other demands she
constantly faced, and I think about how deeply ashamed she must

have felt when the storm cleared, and the anger subsided, and she looked into our eyes and saw the damage her demons had wrought.

I think about this, and I think about how much I love and admire my mother, and I think about how shitty it would feel to have a handful of your most shameful moments preserved on celluloid for all time, to the degree that they are not just synonymous with your own legacy but with the cultural perception of bad moms in general. And just as I believe it was unfair of my father to dismiss my mother's struggles by saying she was normal until she was not, it feels deeply unfair for the world to do the same to Joan.

I want to be clear: Absolutely none of this is meant to justify the alleged abuse that Crawford inflicted on her daughter. If we take the conflicting testimonies about her at face value, at best, she was a control freak and a hyper-demanding perfectionist; at worst, she was an abuser who did immeasurable harm. Even as we try to make sense of what she did and why she did it, we cannot ever justify it.

But I also want to stress, in a way that *Mommie Dearest* does not, just how much Crawford was also a product of her time, just how high the cards were stacked against her, and just how limited her options were. At the time Crawford was trying to adopt, she was a single woman in her thirties, nearing the twilight of her career. In another era, it's not hard to imagine her turning into a Rose McGowan or an Ashley Judd type, rebranding as a feminist activist or whistleblower.

But all of us are only the products of the resources we have at any given time. Crawford did not grow up in the era of clapbacks and callouts; she grew up during a time when fuckability was the only currency women had. And as *Mommie Dearest* documents, when she started losing that, she was summarily tossed out with the trash. Time and again, Crawford sought salvation in powerful men, like first husband Douglas Fairbanks Jr. (whose silent film star parents did not approve of Crawford, viewing her as a gold digger),[38] or Louis B. Mayer (whose studio, MGM, dissolved Crawford's contract in 1943 so it could focus on younger stars),[39] or Warner Bros. studio head Jack Warner (who initially refused to make *Whatever Happened to Baby Jane?*, deriding Crawford and Davis for being past their sexual prime).[40] Time and again, these men failed her; and time and again, she found that the only form of salvation she had was herself. It's not admirable that her reaction to being rejected by the world was sheer, unbridled rage, but it's also not particularly surprising, either. She had a lot to be angry about.

Honestly, I think most mothers have a lot to be angry about. I think my own mom certainly did. And as much as I feel for Christina Crawford and the younger version of myself and anyone else who has been raised by someone who has had to battle the angry and fearful voices in their head, I think we need to start coming to terms with the fact that many mothers are dealing with issues far weightier than forgetting to bring cupcakes to the PTA meeting. It's not just a matter of acknowledging that mentally ill mothers exist; it's also a matter of admitting that they can, with the right support and resources, actually become loving and capable parents.

We tend to think of the line between bad parents and good ones as fixed and immutable, both groups existing at two distinct poles, too much separating them to ever meet in the middle. But let's assume, for a moment, that it is not. Let's assume that the hanger-wielding psychos—the ones who drive their children to spend thousands of dollars in therapy, to develop pill addictions, to write bestselling tell-all memoirs or share their childhood trauma on morning talk shows—were, at one point, redeemable. Could bad mothers like Joan Crawford, under a different set of circumstances—the right diagnosis, or the right combination of SSRIs and antipsychotics—actually be good?

I am inclined to say, in most instances, yes—not just because I am a firm believer in the value of psychiatric intervention but because I have experienced it firsthand. There is no reason a child has to live as hostage to a mother's emotions, or for a mother to live as a hostage to hers. No one deserves to live in fear of the inferno. The fire can subside; the flames can be extinguished. Both Joan and Christina can be saved.

4

Stifler's Mom Has
Got It Goin' On

Battle Hymn of the MILF

"**A**re ya lost?" Stifler's Mom (Jennifer Coolidge) purrs. She's a statuesque blonde in a skintight lavender sheath, the type of effortlessly sexy nineties minimalist garment you could spend hours trying to find a dupe for on Poshmark. She takes a swig of high-end single malt, lights a cigarette, and exhales, her gaze locked on the nerdy Finch (Eddie Kaye Thomas), who has wandered into her study, having taken a wrong turn at a high school house party.

The two engage in brief repartee, culminating in Stifler's Mom offering Finch a glass of Scotch "aged eighteen years—the way I like it." Though Finch has done little but sweat and stammer in the face of her leonine sensuality, Stifler's Mom is apparently impressed (or bored, or horny) enough to deflower him on a pool table—an adolescent boy's fantasy, or an upholsterer's nightmare, made incarnate.

It's just a few minutes of screen time, but Stifler's Mom in the 1999 teenage sex comedy *American Pie* is permanently ensconced in pop culture history—not just because of Coolidge's indelible performance but because of its association with a now-ubiquitous acronym. Stifler's Mom is described by a minor character in the film* as a MILF, or a "Mom I'd like to fuck."[1]

American Pie did not invent the term "MILF." It appears to have originated from a 1995 post on the online forum Usenet, in a thread about a pictorial from an issue of *Playboy* featuring women at forty. "Boy was I impressed. Those moms are babes," ChiPhiMike wrote.[2] He suggested the feature be retitled "MILFs," or "Mothers I'd Like to Fuck." When I called ChiPhiMike† to chat about his legacy, he couldn't remember exactly where he'd first heard the term, but he imagined it was from one of his fraternity brothers at his engineering school: "We were all used to acronyms," he told me. "It was almost like a secret language, in a way." He only found out his post had gone viral—or at least, the pre-Y2K version of viral—when he saw it cited in a footnote on Wikipedia nearly two decades later.[3]

Its popularization among horny frat bros aside, "MILF" really only became widespread thanks to *American Pie* and its subsequent sequels—*American Pie 2*, *American Wedding*, and *American Re-*

---

*   A young John Cho, literally credited as "MILF Guy."

†   I initially thought the identity of this poster would be difficult to find, but it was not; it took me about twenty seconds. At some point, Usenet's archives shifted over to the (also now-defunct) forum Google Groups, so the post was still available online. ChiPhiMike is currently a father in his early fifties, and he (understandably) requested that I withhold his name for publication. But he was the first to acknowledge that it had perhaps been inadvisable for him to use his name on a horny Usenet comment about MILFs. "Nobody cared about privacy back then," he told me. "If we had the internet back in college, we'd all be in jail."

union, as well as a handful of straight-to-DVD offshoots. It's now a thriving porn subgenre, featuring hot older ladies with taut abs and tearaway yoga pants. It's one of the most popular search terms on Pornhub, and it has not dropped out of the top 10 since 2009;[4] in 2023, it was the second-highest ranking search term globally.[5] It's also firmly integrated into mainstream popular culture, inspiring countless reality TV shows,* big-budget movies, and marketing campaigns, including an unforgettable holiday season ad for the dating app Stir featuring Busy Philipps as the "MILF on the Shilf."[6] The term is so widespread that there is now an entire MILF Cinematic Universe (MCU) of MILF subvariants, including the "GILF" (or Grandma I'd like to fuck), the "yummy mummy" (basically a MILF but in the British Commonwealth), and the "cougar" (an older woman who dates younger men).†

As Stifler's Mom, Jennifer Coolidge was the unofficial progenitor of the trend, the ur-MILF without whom all other MILFs in the MCU would not exist. She established the template for the modern MILF as we know it: a sultry, sophisticated older woman who's horny, wants to fuck, and makes no apologies for it.

---

* The much-reviled TLC reality show *MILF Manor*, which was itself believed to be inspired by a *30 Rock* parody of reality TV competitions called *MILF Island*.

† Academics will one day devote entire theses to the subject of what distinction, if any, there was between "cougars" and "MILFs" in early 2000s popular culture. My best guess is that procreation is not necessarily a prerequisite for cougardom, whereas a MILF by definition must have had a child at some point. But honestly, if I spend more than two minutes devoting mental energy to this question, I will probably just lose the will to live.

In some ways, Coolidge was an unlikely casting choice: a thirty-seven-year-old struggling actor, she'd been working as a cocktail waitress for years before she was cast in *American Pie*, later telling an interviewer she gave props to the Weitz brothers for casting "a normal woman," rather than "a supermodel" as the object of a teenage boy's fantasy.[7] And that's sort of the key to her appeal, as well as that of the MILF in general: Stifler's Mom looks like a *real* mom, albeit one you'd see on the arm of a Goldman Sachs investment banker at Cipriani rather than at soccer practice or a PTA meeting.

As a result of the franchise's huge success, Coolidge became a household name. The movie also marked a "tipping point" for the discourse surrounding female sexuality and motherhood in general, according to a 2007 *New York* magazine piece, which quoted one thirty-five-year-old single mom explaining that she felt "liberated" by the MILF label and its attendant implication that motherhood is, as the authors posited, "more than the death of desirability and the birth of bad haircuts."[8] Thanks to Stifler's Mom, the suggestion that a mom could also be—*gasp*—hot was viewed by many mothers as empowering, even transgressive. Yet the evolution of the trope has proven it is basically anything but.

* * *

MILFs are not, technically speaking, supposed to exist—at least, not according to evolutionary psychology, the study of how survival and reproduction are linked to human behavior.[9] Many evolutionary psychologists have posited that men are more attracted to younger women because they are more likely to be fertile, thus ensuring the propagation of their genetic material, and the reason why men tend to seek out younger partners is because they have biological incentive to do so.[10] This theory has gotten less popular in recent years, in part due to a lack of hard scientific evidence undergirding it,[11] as well as the obnoxiousness of many of the people who promote it.* Still, there's a long-standing cultural assumption that male sexual attraction is predicated on youth—and the popularity of the MILF appears to directly contradict that.

Part of what has fueled this cultural assumption is what Freud famously deemed the "Madonna/whore complex": the idea that women could be perceived either as sexually autonomous beings or as wives and mothers, but never both at the same time.[12] Artistic portrayals of women in early modern culture, for instance, appear to support this, with medieval painters usually depicting women either as the Virgin Mary—a totally desexualized cipher, her curves concealed in heavy robes as the Baby Jesus beams from her lap—or as the wanton nude Eve, the visual representation of original sin.[13] The implications of this dichotomy linger to this day, as does the belief that once women have kids, their sex drive goes into hibernation mode, never to emerge from its wintry caverns again.

The idea that mothers or older women could be viewed in a remotely subversive, let alone sexual, context briefly surfaced in the films of the 1930s and 1940s. Movies like *Stella Dallas* and the aforementioned *Mildred Pierce* featured ballsy, ambitious moms like Barbara Stanwyck and Crawford who parlay their sexuality into improving their economic status. But even in these films, the

---

* Namely, fedora-wearing neckbeards who spend a lot of time on Reddit and pseudo-academic benzodiazepine addicts who sound like Kermit the Frog. [Jesse O'Neill, "Jordan Peterson Says He Was Suicidal, Addicted to Benzos," *New York Post*, January 31, 2021, https://nypost.com/2021/01/31/jordan-peterson-says-he-was-suicidal-addicted-to-benzos/.]

sex lives of the eponymous characters were always in service of their ungrateful children—to advance them socially, or save them from a life of dancing naked for drunken strangers—rather than a product of their own autonomous desires, and both would ultimately be punished for their transgressions. That was in part a function of the mores of film censors of the era—the Hays Code forbade depictions of promiscuity or extramarital sex, and one way directors tried to work around this was to make it clear women could face the consequences for doing so.[14] But it was also a product of a society that steadfastly refused to acknowledge that mothers were capable of having needs or desires outside of taking care of their children.

The 1960s, however, ushered in a notable exception to this trend: Mrs. Robinson, the sultry housewife played by Anne Bancroft in *The Graduate*. If Stifler's Mom is to be considered the ur-MILF, then Mrs. Robinson is her prehistoric progenitor. Long-legged and pillow-lipped, Mrs. Robinson is aggressively, unapologetically carnal, attempting to seduce her husband's friend's aimless son Benjamin (Dustin Hoffman) within the first twenty minutes of the movie. She is defined solely by two things that had previously been viewed in direct opposition to each other: her sexuality, and her status as wife and mother (indeed, like Stifler's Mom, filmmaker Mike Nichols intentionally refrains from giving Mrs. Robinson a first name, with the other characters simply referring to her by the "Mrs." honorific).

Unlike the tireless martyrs of a 1930s working-class women's picture, Mrs. Robinson is narcissistic, manipulative, and vindictive. She grows enraged when Benjamin wants to date her more age-appropriate daughter, Elaine (Katharine Ross), threatening to tell her about the affair in order to dissuade him; when he falls in love with Elaine and confesses he's been sleeping with her mother, Mrs. Robinson alleges to her daughter that Benjamin took advantage of her when she was drunk.*

We are not supposed to think Mrs. Robinson is a good mom, or even a good person. We're supposed to pity her, to some extent—at one point, she tells Benjamin that she ended up in a loveless shotgun marriage after getting pregnant with Elaine,[15] forcing her to give up her dream of becoming an artist—but ultimately, we are supposed to view her as a villainous figure, creepy and grotesque and kind of depressing.

Nonetheless, Mrs. Robinson is by far the sexiest and most memorable aspect of the film. Few people who watch *The Graduate* remember poor Katharine Ross, who played the doe-eyed Elaine. They do remember Mrs. Robinson (as well as the eponymous Simon & Garfunkel song), to the degree that Bancroft's character is still shorthand for a certain type of sexually voracious older woman. Even *American Pie* pays homage to it by having Coolidge's character reference Benjamin's infamous line—"Mrs. Robinson, you're trying to seduce me"—during the party scene.

---

* Honestly, though, it's pretty easy to understand why Mrs. Robinson wouldn't want her daughter to date Dustin Hoffman's character in *The Graduate*. With the possible exception of *Maury Povich* show guests, no mother would be OK with knowingly sharing a sexual partner with their offspring. But more important, Benjamin sucks. He's mopey, unemployed, and like five foot four on a good day. No offense to Dustin Hoffman, but outside of the context of late 1960s/early 1970s American comedies, which framed tiny Jewish men with iron deficiencies as the apex of male sensuality, there's no universe in which a hot mom and daughter would be fighting over him.

Pre–*American Pie*, Mrs. Robinson was by far the most well-known cultural representation of a sexy older woman. But in referencing the character, people tend to forget the complexity of Bancroft's performance, how accurately she captures the quiet desperation of a fading beauty clinging to the vestiges of her youth. What they remember is the image of Bancroft sultrily rolling up her stockings, her leg extended in front of Hoffman's waistline in a clear allusion to an erection. They remember her almost exclusively within the context of the lust she inspires—an object of male desire, rather than the subject of her own story.

* * *

The clip "Hot Stepmom Brandi Love Catches [Stepson] Jacking Off to VR and Helps Him Out" begins with the stepson in question reclining on his bed, stroking his monstrous member while wearing a VR headset. Love, a flaxen-haired, hyper-sculpted adult performer in her late forties, walks in on him. Instead of reacting with horror, as virtually any parental figure (step- or otherwise) would do, she smiles gamely and strips down, shaking her butt in front of his face. Approximately three minutes into the clip (which is, all things considered, way too long to not realize someone's butt is in your face), he finally registers her presence, right as she's kneeling between his splayed legs. "Mommmmmmmm," he says petulantly, like a kid who's angry their Switch has been turned off before dinner.

"Sssssh," she says pointedly. "*Step*mother." This is, apparently, a compelling enough argument; and the rest of the clip proceeds as you'd expect.

Love is one of the reigning queens of what is commonly referred to as "MILF porn" and is frequently ranked among the most searched-for performers on the tube site Pornhub year after year.[16]

She specializes in what is commonly referred to as "fauxcest," a portmanteau of "faux" and "incest" that refers to the pornographic depiction of staged, semi-incestuous relationships.* Fauxcest videos follow a specific template, as implausible as it is invariable: a busty stepmother in yoga pants and a tight tank walks in on her stepson or stepdaughter masturbating or having sex and feels the need to "correct" their technique (even though, in most cases, they seem to have been doing fine on their own). There is no context, no preamble, no postcoital unpacking of whether this will make next year's Thanksgiving awkward. It's just forty minutes of expertly lit pelvis-banging.

Fauxcest has inexplicably exploded in popularity over the past decade,[17] even though many people, including Love herself, find the implications of the genre disturbing. "At first I didn't get it, I was like, 'What? You want me to say what?'" Love once told me about shooting fauxcest scenes. "But then I got into it, because my job is to be an actress and have fun and make that fantasy believable. It doesn't have to be mine."[18] She attributes the rise of fauxcest to the inherently forbidden nature of the dynamic. "The more taboo something is, the hotter it's gonna be. It's fantasy," she says.

This is a commonly accepted explanation of fauxcest: that it's arousing to people because it violates social norms. "There is this allure of the untouchable, and what's untouchable to us is often the

---

* This distinction is mostly emphasized for legal reasons: Many porn companies won't produce even fictionalized versions of blood relations having sex, for fear of violating obscenity laws. [Natasha Vargas-Cooper, "What Do Women Want? To Have Sex with Their Stepbrothers," *Jezebel*, July 7, 2015, www.jezebel.com/what-do-women-want-to-have-sex-with -their-stepbrothers-1714291638.]

most appealing," director Jacky St. James told the *Daily Beast* in 2017.[19] But to me, this explanation doesn't quite explain why the stepmom specifically has so much prominence in the cultural imagination, as opposed to other stepfamily dynamics (in 2015, for instance, "stepsister" ranked much lower on Pornhub's list of most popular search terms than "stepmom" did).[20] I'd argue that people don't enjoy watching Brandi Love's fauxcest content because it's taboo; or at least, that's not the *only* reason why. It's because she is a mother—and it's because, like Stifler's Mom, her behavior is a radical departure from what we'd expect from a *good* mother—that people find her content so arousing.

I realize that asking whether fictional porn MILFs are "good" or "bad" moms is kind of like asking whether Darth Vader ever took out insurance on the Death Star: dumb, pedantic, and totally beside the point.* Still, I was curious how actual adult performers felt about this question, so I decided to ask the former MILF porn star Eva Lovia if she ever considered whether the moms she played in porn were good or bad.

"Honestly, they're probably terrible," she said, laughing. "They're always really stern and yelling and authoritarian. It's funny because you'd think with moms, that you'd want their nurturing side. But the MILFs in commercial porn are always very aggressive and telling you what to do."[21]

---

* It is also, apparently, a topic that has been covered by at least one insurance podcast that I'm aware of. [Peter Mansfield, host, *Insurance Coverage*, podcast, "Star Wars Special: The Insurance of the Death Star," May 9, 2024, www.rpclegal.com/thinking/insurance-and-reinsurance/star-wars -special-the-insurance-of-the-death-star/.]

And this seems pretty obvious, right? In real life, a "good" step-mom wouldn't accidentally walk in on her stepson masturbating and immediately start sitting on his face. She'd let him have some privacy and head back to her room to watch *The Great British Baking Show*.

But this is precisely the point of MILFs: They don't watch *The Great British Baking Show*. They don't have any hobbies or interests outside of fellating Zoomers and folding laundry while wearing lacy lingerie.

"'A wife who is also your mom' is something I think a lot of men unconsciously want," a male friend told me when I asked him why he thought MILFs were popular. "Not only will she cook and clean up after you, but she'll never complain and also sexually gratify you for the honor." The MILF exists entirely in service of other men's desires—and in this sense, she's just as subservient to the patriarchy as the stereotypical "good" mom is.

This was obvious to me when I rewatched *American Pie* before writing this chapter. Given how indelibly Coolidge's performance is, like Bancroft's, engrained in the cultural imagination, I was struck by how little Stifler's Mom actually appears on-screen. One moment, she's there, smoking a cigarette and crossing her legs; the next, she's deflowering Finch on a pool table. That's it. We're not given any insight as to whether this woman is married or single, or why this sophisticated lady with great taste in top-shelf liquor is interested in a stammering teenager in the first place. We don't even know her first name, because Finch doesn't bother to ask. (In *American Pie 2*, he finally does: It's Jeanine. But we never hear it again, because when the two have sex again, she creepily demands that he call her "Stifler's Mom" mid-coitus—which, again, raises far more questions about her interior life than it answers.)

The movie also raises a question that nobody really asked at the time, but post-#MeToo and age-gap discourse, seems obvious in retrospect: What kind of irresponsible, amoral adult woman— nay, what kind of terrible mother—would have sex with her son's eighteen-year-old friend? This is a question that I actually had the opportunity to pose to the screenwriter of *American Pie*, Adam Herz, who has spent the past few decades grappling with the legacy of the MILF trope. When I asked Herz whether he considered Stifler's Mom a "good" or "bad" mother, I figured he, like Lovia, would laugh in my face—but apparently, this was, indeed, a question that had come up during *American Pie*'s development process.

"We did actually talk about [whether Stifler's Mom was a good mom or a bad mom]," Herz told me. According to Herz, the creative team wanted the party scene to take place at Stifler's house, prompting them to ask themselves: What kind of mother would allow that?

"Obviously she's permissive to an extent—she's semi-supervisory, but also absent," Herz explained. "She's the kind of mom who's going to be like, 'Well, XYZ is going to happen, so I'd rather it happen in a way that is at least controlled and safer'"—sort of like Mrs. George in *Mean Girls*, admonishing a roomful of high school girls that "if you're going to drink, I'd rather you do it in the house." We're supposed to view Stifler's Mom as a self-obsessed, inattentive parental figure—which is reflected in the fact that she raised a kid who's as big an asshole as Steve Stifler (Seann William Scott).*

---

* Stifler also has a little brother, Matt, played by Eli Marienthal in the first two films and Tad Hilgenbrink in the spinoff *American Pie Presents: Band Camp*. Apparently, Jeanine Stifler did just as bad a job raising him as she did with her elder son: He's arguably an even bigger prick than Steve.

Rewatching *American Pie* more than two decades later, there's also an obvious question here about consent and the power dynamics at play in the Stifler's Mom/Finch relationship, as well as the Freudian implications of the character demanding that Finch call her "Stifler's Mom" during sex. When I spoke to Herz, it was clear that these issues were not discussed at length.

"It was just a pure, brainless joke," he said. "[There's] that saying—analyzing humor is like dissecting a frog. Nobody's that interested, and the frog dies."[22]

At the risk of breaching one of the so-called immutable rules of comedy, it makes sense that no one involved with *American Pie* would raise an eyebrow at some of the more problematic elements of the MILF scenes. That's kind of why the character works: because probing too deeply into these questions would require us to acknowledge that Jeanine Stifler is written as a shitty mother, as well as a shitty all-around person. I'll put it this way: If a forty-year-old woman had sex with an eighteen-year-old boy on a pool table at a high school party in real life, we'd probably ask what the hell was wrong with her. But the fact that Stifler's Mom is written as a caricature prevents us from asking these types of questions, just as we don't ask them about the characters played by Brandi Love or Anne Bancroft. We are given permission to fetishize her without thinking too deeply about the implications of her actions.

I realize that demanding nuance and three-dimensionality in a movie where a teen fucks a pie is something of a lofty ask. And it's a testament to Coolidge's prodigious comedic skills that her performance had as much staying power as it did; had she not been cast, it's easy to imagine the MILF trope being limited to the occasional fratty thread or porn search (and *American Pie* itself being relegated to the Walmart $5 DVD bin). For what it's worth, Coolidge herself appears to have tremendous gratitude for the franchise, telling *Vanity Fair* that she "got a lot of play" from her appearance in *American Pie*, in terms of both her career opportunities and getting "a lot of sexual action."[23] So I don't want to begrudge Coolidge (or her former partners) their feelings about the film.

But I also don't think the MILF trope has been good for women in general, and for mothers in particular. Sure, it's a reclamation of sexual agency for a figure that has traditionally been robbed of it. But it's also fundamentally quite restrictive—not just in terms of how the MILF is supposed to act but how she is supposed to look as well. Rarely will you see the term "MILF" applied to anyone other than a specific type of woman—namely, a thin, fit, white, cisgender, conventionally attractive mother. This is especially true in porn, where it's not uncommon for women who have never had children, or even women in their late teens and early twenties, to be cast as "MILFs."

"Mainstream pornography presents a very, very narrow view of what a woman is supposed to look like once she has kids," said Lovia. "They don't have fat where it's not supposed to be, or have dimples. They always have their makeup on, [they're always] in heels. They always look like JLo."

As a mother who does online sex work, primarily posting on the subscription-based platform OnlyFans, Lovia is uniquely attuned to the cultural stigma surrounding motherhood and sexuality. She is often forced to confront the societal perception that any woman who is openly sexual cannot also be a good parent. "For a lot of the actual moms playing MILF roles, a lot of the criticism online is: 'Your poor kids; you're a terrible mom; you're a terrible wife. I can't believe you're in sex work,'" she told me.

That stigma is something Brandi Love, the queen of the MILFs, also has direct experience with: In 2006, she founded the organization Parents in Adult after a family member, irate at her choice of profession, called local police on her to search her house and try to take her then-four-year-old daughter away.[24]

"When I started to talk to people in the industry about it, they'd say, 'I'm fearful of my ex-husband,' or 'I'm fearful of my parents,' even though what we're doing is legal," she told me. "Just because we're porn stars doesn't mean that we're doing inappropriate things at home."

Even if, from certain angles, the MILF can be viewed as a departure from conventional depictions of motherhood, she doesn't represent a departure from patriarchal norms that dictate a woman's body belongs to everyone but herself—nor can she exist in reality without being summarily punished for her sins.

At the end of the day, Jeanine Stifler gets off easy. For the crime of refusing to go gently into the good night of sexless motherhood, she doesn't lose her husband and her daughter, as Mrs. Robinson did; nor is she subject to a police investigation. In exchange for being objectified by millions of late Gen Xers and millennials, Jeanine Stifler gets two seconds of screen time and a bout of mediocre sex with the guy who played Rosenberg in *Harold & Kumar Go to White Castle*. All things considered, it's a pretty good deal.

* * *

When I started writing this chapter, I didn't find the term "MILF" particularly offensive. In fact, I kind of loved it.

I've been called a MILF a few times—mostly in a winking, semi-ironic context by my female friends, not in a lewd or objectifying way. And every time, I found it both amusing and flattering, to the degree that I probably would've preferred it to being labeled a hard worker or a clever person or even a good mom. For whatever reason—internalized misogyny, low self-esteem, or some combination thereof—being lauded for keeping it tight, against the seemingly insurmountable odds posed by motherhood, struck me as the highest form of achievement.

Which is why I was surprised to learn, while I was writing this essay, that most of the mothers I know categorically loathe the term. "It's annoying the norm for women past thirty-five is to be seen as unfuckable and we need some word to be the exception," said my friend Jess Machado,[25] who has a ten-year-old. "It [also] feels particularly like a white-man thing. I'm not sure other cultures view moms or aging women with such disgust."

My friend Annie, whose daughter is three, also takes umbrage with the term, particularly when it is used by men. "It's just another way they put you in a bucket of being solely identified as a mom," she said.[26]

Even ChiPhiMike, the horny frat boy who inadvertently coined the term thirty years ago, hates it. "I've got daughters. I've been married. I know a lot of strong, successful women, and I have a lot of respect for women," he said. "With MILF, that respect maybe wasn't a part of that. You're objectifying someone and not looking at the whole person."

On the surface, these seem like very obvious points. Of course, the MILF objectifies women. Of course it's a figment of the patriarchal imagination, alongside stereotypes like the Angel in the House or the psycho mommy or any other by-product of a male hive mind that runs on a cocktail of horniness and contempt. Of course, it's yet another construction designed to make mothers feel inadequate, penalizing us whether we are deemed too sexy, or not sexy enough. But when I told

American Pie screenwriter Adam Herz, for instance, that I had spoken to mothers who were offended by the term, he seemed genuinely surprised that women over the age of thirty-five being considered unfuckable was a thing to begin with.

"The joke of *American Pie* was, you have these guys, and whatever they're in a room with, they're probably going to try to fuck it," he said. "So when you say that the term 'MILF' upsets some women because it implies they're not desirable, it's like, trust me, that's not what most guys think. Straight men are attracted to women—period."

Later, I asked Herz specifically why he thought MILF was such a popular genre, given how much our culture prioritizes feminine youth and beauty over age and experience. He took issue with this premise.

"What are you talking about?" he said. "For the love of God, there's pregnant porn. There's something for everyone. So the idea that motherhood makes a woman sexually unattractive—I don't know where that came from."

I don't know if Herz was being perfectly honest with me or with himself here. I will say that it seems disingenuous that a well-educated man in his fifties would be unaware of the role ageism and sexism play in cultural beauty standards. (At the very least, it makes me think that he has never read a single issue of *Redbook* magazine.) But ultimately, Herz inadvertently made a greater case for the MILF being problematic than *American Pie* or *The Graduate* or porn featuring twenty-year-olds in an apron and heels ever could.

Even if Herz were correct that the patriarchy does not marginalize women above a certain age (which he is not), and even if he were correct that the audience for MILFs is comparable to that of another niche fetish like pregnancy porn (which it is not), he's right about one thing. Women are not the final arbiter of what constitutes

MILFdom: straight men like him are. And once that ceases to be true—once a woman ages past a certain point, and goes from being a MILF to just being a plain old M—then from the perspective of a straight male audience, she ceases to exist as well.

I became more aware of this when I gave birth to my younger son, Marco, and transitioned from being an active MILF to another member of the MCU, the MILF emeritus. When I had Harry, I was able to "bounce back," as the saying goes, fairly quickly. It took about six months or so to lose the baby weight, and once I did, people acted as if I'd won an Academy Award. "A mom? No way. I never would have guessed," strangers at bars would say. "Seriously. I don't believe you. Show me your C-section scar." It was inappropriate and bizarre, and I hate that I loved every second of it.

This was not the case, however, after I had Marco. He is now three years old, and I'm still about eight pounds past my usual weight, and I've given up trying to lose it. I don't do my hair or wear much makeup, and I'm too poor to get Botox or manicures or filler or any of the other routine self-maintenance procedures favored by the hot and over thirty-five. When I look at photos of myself, I feel I'm objectively less attractive than I was three or four years ago, and I can definitely tell the difference in how strangers perceive me. Before, men on the street looked at me with unvarnished interest; now, the best they can muster is faint curiosity, as if they'd just seen an intact, unpeeled banana on a mailbox. *Where'd the banana come from? How'd it get there? Why did the person unpeel it before abandoning it?* I can see these questions flickering in their minds for a nanosecond, before they shrug and go about their day. This is not me being self-deprecating; it's the truth. A switch has been turned off; a plug has been pulled. My sexual capital has plummeted.

I have extremely complicated feelings about this. On one hand, I'm not Brandi Love or Eva Lovia or Jennifer Coolidge; I'm not a model or an actor or an influencer or anyone else whose body serves as currency. Being viewed as fuckable—even fuckable with the caveat of also being, ugh, a *mom*—doesn't benefit me in any material way. I have other needs than male validation, other priorities than getting free drinks. And because I am in a monogamous relationship with a man who is just as exhausted and stressed-out and unconcerned with being hot as I am, that significantly reduces the pressure to keep it tight on my end.

But I'll be honest: losing my MILFdom has also been difficult, in part because it makes me feel like a cliché. Since having kids, I've been resistant to the idea that motherhood automatically renders one exhausted, frumpy, and sexless, and being hot felt like one way to combat that, a dam I could build to avoid being swept up and swallowed whole by the raging currents. When the dam broke, it felt, in a way, like an admission of defeat. I'd promised myself I would never lose myself entirely in becoming a mother, and I'd failed in at least this specific respect.

Mostly, though, it's forced me to come to terms with just how much being conventionally attractive had given me a strategic advantage. It wasn't so much that I started losing out on material rewards like free drinks at bars or admission to exclusive clubs—because let's be honest, I was cute, but I wasn't Australian wellness influencer–level. It was more that I could no longer get a pass for the type of weird, borderline antisocial behavior that was easier for people to overlook when I was younger and better-looking.

For instance: I have a folder on my phone consisting of about two dozen photos of dead rats that I've seen on the street over the past few years.* When I was in my twenties, if I walked around a party telling people about this photo album, some of them would have been weirded out—but more often than not, particularly if the person I was talking to was male, they found it quirky and compelling. Now that I'm a mother of two in my thirties, however, they find it deranged. They immediately excuse themselves to talk to someone more normal, and honestly, who can blame them? Objectively speaking, whether you're a young, hot twentysomething or a haggard elderly woman, telling a complete stranger at a party about your dead rat photo album is an absolutely fucking insane thing to do.

To be clear, it's undoubtedly a good thing that my life no longer revolves around my sexual value. I am by far a more interesting and stable and well-rounded person than I was in my twenties. It's just unfortunate that it took actually losing my sexual value to understand that.

When I spoke to Eva Lovia, who now has three children, I shared with her that being a mom in my mid-thirties made me feel sexually invisible. She had absolutely no idea what I was talking about. In fact, she says, when she used to post custom clips on OnlyFans, none of her fans wanted to see her as the type of ultra-manicured, pristine MILF role popularized by mainstream porn. They wanted to see her as she really was: a mom.

---

* When I tell people about this folder, they (very reasonably) ask me why I do this, and to be honest, I've never been able to come up with a good explanation. I'm terrified of rats, so it's possible it's an exposure therapy–type thing, but admittedly there's also probably a weird frisson I get when I see people's faces start to register that they're looking at a dead rat. I should probably talk about it with my therapist, but to be honest, when it comes to the things I need to unpack in treatment, the dead rats folder ranks pretty low on the list.

"When I posted content after having a child, you would have some people who were like, 'Oh my God, your boobs are disgusting,' because they look different after you've been breastfeeding," she said. "But the vast majority of people are like, 'You look so sexy.' I think there is something about a woman who has surrendered her body to motherhood that summons up nurturing and comfort and safety. And I think men really crave that."[27]

I am not a professional adult performer, and people don't pay $30 a year for the privilege of seeing me naked, so I don't know if Lovia and I are necessarily coming at this from the same vantage point. But my hope for myself is that one day, I will be able to. Because as exhausted as I am by some aspects of the MILF trope—the one-dimensionality of it, the subservience to male desires, the suggestion that folding laundry in one's lingerie is a fun and cool thing to do and not a one-way ticket to getting a yeast infection—there are some things about it that I still find aspirational. Because, like a MILF, I also don't want to always put myself last. I also don't want to lie in bed after a long day of chasing after my kids, too exhausted to do anything but watch *The Great British Baking Show*. I also desire more for myself than a life of servitude to others, even if such an admission puts me in danger of being labeled a bad mother. And that's the one good thing you can say about MILFs, and about bad mothers in general: They never, ever apologize for their desires.

5

"Give 'Em Love and What Does It Get Ya?"

Why We Love to Hate (and Hate to Love) Stage Moms

When I tell people that I'm working on a book about bad mothers, they usually ask if I have a favorite one. Usually, I'll tell them no, largely because it strikes me as a bizarre question. I mean, sure, to an extent, this project is about reassessing historically maligned women, but still—a "favorite" bad mom? That's like asking someone if they have a favorite maritime disaster,* or a favorite tyrannical despot.†

But as the great Dakota Johnson famously opined: "That is not the truth, Ellen." I do, in fact, have a favorite bad mom. And it is Momma Rose, the ur–stage mother from the iconic Broadway

---

* Though if I had to pick, it would probably be the one that Quint talks about in *Jaws*.

† A young Joseph Stalin, for reasons that will be obvious if you have access to Google Image search.

musical *Gypsy*, with a book by Arthur Laurents and songs by Jule Styne and the musical theater legend Stephen Sondheim.*

Gypsy is based on the memoirs of Rose Hovick's elder daughter, Louise Hovick, who recounts her iterant childhood as she and her sister, June, a precocious kiddie star, traveled across the country seeking fame on the vaudeville circuit in the 1920s. Ostensibly, the musical is the origin story of how the shy and awkward Louise became the glamorous and world-famous burlesque dancer Gypsy Rose Lee. But the undisputed driving force behind the musical, the star of the show, is Rose. She's an irrepressible figure—a pushy, tight-fisted, middle-aged broad who swans around vaudeville stages in wide-brimmed hats and sweeping overcoats, imposing her will on theater owners in order to ensure her kids take center stage. She's amoral, manipulative, and controlling, wrapping weak-willed men around her finger, smuggling teen chorus boys into motel rooms, and swiping silverware from Chinese restaurants. Above all else, she's indefatigable; her drive, her ambition, cannot be killed by traditional means.

Her personality is most thoroughly exemplified in her legendary number "Everything's Coming Up Roses," in which she has a breakdown after her younger and more talented daughter runs away to elope with an older boy; and it reaches its apex at the end, when she

---

* Though the character is colloquially known as "Momma Rose," no one actually calls her that during the play; the other characters either call her "Rose" or "Momma," and she's credited as "Rose" in the original libretto. "Momma Rose" appears to be a by-product of the cultural imagination rather than Sondheim or Laurents themselves; sort of like how everyone thinks the Berenstain Bears are actually called the Berenstein Bears.

encourages a terrified Louise to strip onstage, to the horror and disgust of her long-suffering boyfriend/agent. Through it all, Rose gives not one single solitary fuck about anything other than her overarching goal: making June, and then Louise, a star, regardless of whether they want to be or not. And she doesn't care if she loses everything in the process—which she of course ultimately does.

Rose has been referred to as the King Lear of musical theater; and like King Lear, she's a deeply complex and tragic figure. Unlike King Lear, however, Rose is often referred to—usually by men—as a "monster." This is what Frank Rich calls her in his 1989 review of a Broadway revival starring Tyne Daly, referring to her as a "tyrannical stage mother" who both "champions and cripples" her children.[1] And though she's been played with varying degrees of sympathy by grand dames of the stage—from Ethel Merman to Bernadette Peters to Patti LuPone—this is kind of always how she's perceived: as a terrifying force of nature who will stop at nothing to thrust her children into the spotlight.

This is how everyone views Momma Rose—seemingly everyone, that is, but my own mother. In early 2025, I took her to the latest Broadway revival of *Gypsy* starring Audra McDonald: We watched the 1962 film adaptation starring Rosalind Russell and Natalie Wood all the time when I was a kid, and *Gypsy* is one of her favorite shows. But I didn't know why until after the production ended, and I told my mom how much I loved McDonald's performance as an unhinged stage mom whose obsession with fame renders her incapable of being a good parent.

"Oh, I totally disagree with you," she said. "That's not what the show's about. It's about a mom who worked hard and sacrificed and tried her best to do everything for her children, and they weren't grateful for any of it. She's a good mother. That's what good mothers do."

When she said this, I had two reactions. The first was: "Holy shit, I really wish I had recorded this as a voice memo so my therapist could hear it. I think it could explain a lot." But the second was: "OK, well, she's also not wrong." Not in the sense that Momma Rose was a "good" mother, per se, or that forcing your child to strip in front of inebriated strangers so she can get star billing at a burlesque house is anything other than an abhorrent thing to do. But she wasn't wrong in the sense that what Rose does throughout the show is, pretty much *exactly*, what our culture tells good mothers to do.

At the end of the day, Rose's greatest offense is not so much that she fails to love her children (though she certainly falls short in understanding them, particularly Louise). It's that she is a mother who works relentlessly to champion her children and encourage them to succeed, in precisely the way we expect good mothers to—except she doesn't live up to her end of the bargain, because she demands something, anything, in return.

That's clear by "Rose's Turn," the harrowing final number of the show and the apex of Rose's psychic meltdown, when she stands onstage abandoned by her partner and children, musing aloud: "Why did I do it? / What did it get me? / Scrapbooks full of me in the background?" Like all of Sondheim's lyrics, Rose's words are supposed to be ironic: She's so delusional that she is incapable of viewing her isolation from her kids as the consequence of her own actions and can't see it as anything other than a totally unwarranted slight against her.[*] But she is also not articulating anything that mothers haven't

---

* Again—this is extremely Livia Soprano–esque.

thought since time immemorial, particularly as they have suffered through viola recitals or 4:00 a.m. swim practices or any number of activities intended to enrich and support their kids. What *does* it get you? Why *did* you do it?

At the end of the day, Rose's greatest offense is that she refuses to fade away into the background of the scrapbooks, that she insists on being seen and heard as a middle-aged mother who is expected to be neither. She offers conditions for the one thing that is meant to be unconditional, demands recompense for the one job on earth that asks everything, and offers nothing material in return. It's that demand—not her exploitation of June, not her neglect of Louise, not her sublimated desire to take center stage herself—that makes her a monster.

* * *

I have a soft spot for stage mothers, in part because, if you hew to a strictly technical definition of the term, my own mom (kind of) was one. I was a theater kid in every sense of the word: I did school plays, took acting and tap and voice lessons, and demanded attention wherever I went. When I was eight years old, my mom enrolled me in a kids' acting workshop run by a former 1960s stage actress who gave lessons out of her Upper West Side studio. At the end of each semester, Monica May held a student showcase, and afterward, my mom told me she had gotten a call from an agent who had been in the audience who wanted to represent me. The agency was called—I shit you not—Lil Angels.

Lil Angels was not particularly glamorous or prestigious. Its office was in Yonkers, about an hour from where we lived in New York, and when the agent sent me to a photographer to get headshots, he and my mom ended up styling me like a middle-aged stenographer from Staten Island named Linda. Still, I was excited, and I think my mom was, too. She'd harbored her own performing arts aspirations in her youth, and I think part of her felt like she would be depriving me of a valuable opportunity if I didn't give it the old college try.

So, for about four to six months of my childhood, Lil Angels became a part of my life. Every two weeks or so, I'd be pulled out of school to schlep to auditions, where I'd be asked to read for things like toothpaste or laundry detergent ads, or, in one case, a production of the all-Black musical *The Wiz*,* before the casting director, who was always either an older woman with red-rimmed glasses or a young white gay man who smelled really good, politely thanked me for coming in and then I'd never hear from them again. And while I'm not sure exactly how my relationship with Lil Angels ended, I do remember that after a while, they just stopped calling.

My time as an aspiring child actor was relatively uneventful. At worst, it was a waste of time and money on my parents' part (and hair spray on the part of the photographer who tried to make me look like a woman who wore pantyhose and rode the tram to work). But even though I'm sure some people would sniff at my mom's decision to sign me to a kiddie talent agency, I completely understand why

---

* This is 100 percent true. I don't remember which production it was or even if it ever went up, but I do remember the director was very nice and taught me some of the choreography for "Brand New Day" to make up for the time we'd spent traveling down there.

she did it. I think she correctly assessed that even though there was a very small chance that I would be cast in anything, it was a chance that I would've regretted not taking. And yes, I'm sure there was a part of her that thought it was a chance *she* would've regretted not taking, too.

For this reason, I've always been drawn to stage moms, from Momma Rose to "momager" Kris Jenner, long rumored to have leaked her daughter Kim Kardashian's sex tape to further her career,* to the eponymous housewives in *Dance Moms*, who are regularly depicted guzzling wine and slinging insults at each other while wearing an extraordinary amount of bedazzled denim.

It's not so much that I relate to these women, or that I understand precisely why they're so deeply invested in their children's vaudeville or reality TV careers or, in the case of *Dance Moms*, whether they take

---

* For years, *Keeping Up with the Kardashians* (*KUWTK*) fans have made it seem as if Jenner was complicit in the tape's release, often using a quote from the first episode of *KUWTK* as "evidence": "When I first heard about Kim's tape, as her mother, I wanted to kill her. But as her manager . . ." This quote, however, has been taken out of context. What Jenner actually said was: "When I first heard about Kim's tape, as her mother, I wanted to kill her. But as her manager, I knew that I had a job to do, and I really just wanted her to move past it." In a 2022 appearance on *The Late Late Show with James Corden*, Jenner denied releasing the infamous sex tape while hooked up to a lie detector test, an answer that was determined to have been truthful. That same year, however, Kardashian's ex-boyfriend, Ray J, who also appeared in the sex tape, went on Instagram Live and accused Jenner of having brokered the release of the video—a claim that, to date, she has never publicly acknowledged.

first place in expressive jazz performance at nationals.* It's more that I sympathize with the general impulse to do whatever it takes to carve out the best life for your child, whatever that may look like for them. If one of the primary tenets of good parenting is wanting your child to have more opportunities than you did—and I think we can all agree that this is an admirable, if not always achievable, goal—then it stands to reason that if a parent senses exceptional talent or ability in a child, they will want to foster it.

I also just admire stage moms for their chutzpah. Women like Rose and Jenner demand to be seen, demand to be reckoned with, and demand, in some ways, to be hated. It's so easy for women to become invisible when they become mothers that I can't help but respect the fact that stage moms refuse to do so.

Of course, this is not the predominant cultural perception of stage mothers in general. We are expected to view these women as terrifyingly unhinged. We're supposed to gasp at Jenner's craven

---

* I watched *Dance Moms* for years, mostly because I imagine that watching it perfectly replicates the experience of what it feels like to have your prefrontal cortex removed. The undisputed star isn't a dance mom at all but instructor Abby Lee Miller, who seemingly thrives on psychological torture and verbal abuse to pit her small pupils against one another. And that's to say nothing of her treatment of the mothers, whom she is actively antagonistic toward and treats as if they are boils on her ass that she needs to get lanced. One of her most effective attempts at psychological terrorism is the "pyramid," a weekly ranking of Miller's students devised by *Dance Moms* producers to heighten tension in the show and is often used by Miller as a retaliatory weapon against students and parents who displease her. Every week, the moms sit around and bicker over who's at the top of the pyramid, and it's like, who fucking cares? Mackenzie was on the top of the pyramid this week, and she's going to be on top next week. Stop rhinestoning your daughters' curling irons and go get a massage or, better yet, a bachelor's degree.

disregard for maternal norms such as protecting her children or being concerned for their welfare or making them wear a bra at Paris Fashion Week.[2] We're supposed to laugh at the dance moms' eagerness to throw a punch at Miller when she puts their kids at the bottom of the pyramid, and we're supposed to condemn Rose for seemingly prioritizing her own ambitions over the well-being of her children.

"There's a difference between parents who push their children, ones that hold them to high standards, and ones that are complicit in their child's misery," Margaret Lyons, then a TV critic at *Vulture*, wrote in 2012. The lessons *Dance Moms* teaches its young charges is an "acutely sad one: that their moms won't protect them."[3]

But there's another irrefutable truth about stage mothers that people are loath to acknowledge: Often, they get results. The Kardashians and Jenners are household names, as are Maddie Ziegler, Miller's star pupil whose big break involved dancing in Sia's "Chandelier," as well as her *Dance Moms* costar JoJo Siwa, aka "JoJo with the Bow-Bow." Even Rose Hovick's children, as marred as they were by their mother's aggressive pursuit of fame, carved out prominent careers in entertainment: Gypsy Rose Lee as one of the most famous burlesque artists of the twentieth century, and June as the actor June Havoc, a Broadway star who appeared in the Oscar-winning classic *Gentleman's Agreement.*

If you look at shows like *Dance Moms* and *Gypsy* and *Keeping Up with the Kardashians* in aggregate, two wildly contradictory messages emerge. Yes, *Dance Moms* and *Gypsy* and *Keeping Up with the Kardashians* should be viewed as condemnations of stage parenting, as well as a testament to the psychic harms inflicted on children who have been pushed at an early age to succeed in adult fields. On the other hand, as loath as we may be to admit it, they can also be read as endorsements of their methods. To paraphrase Jenner herself: As mothers, we know these women are glaringly deficient. But we also know that, as managers, they have a job to do.

So why, then, do we loathe stage mothers? Is it because we're genuinely repulsed by the extremes to which they go to ensure their children are successful, often at the cost of their emotional development or mental health? Or is it because we know, on some level, that they are getting something right—or that their dark and unhinged behavior reveals something equally dark and unhinged about our parenting priorities in general?

Lyons is certainly correct that there's a line between parents who hold their kids to high standards and parents who are complicit in their child's misery. But I'm not sure if we've reached a universal consensus on where that line is. Certainly, there are behaviors that most of us can agree are over that line: physical and emotional abuse, for one, or blatantly disregarding a child's own expressed boundaries and desires. But it's also, shall we say, interesting that this line tends to shift when it is mothers encouraging their children toward stereotypically feminine pursuits, like dance or theater; versus fathers encouraging their children toward stereotypically masculine pursuits, such as sports or politics or, I don't know, competitive fly-fishing.*

Over and over again, the stories of men like Richard Williams (father to Venus and Serena), Earl Woods (father to Tiger), and Mike Agassi (father to tennis pro Andre) teach us that the role of the father is to instill children with the self-discipline and fortitude needed to achieve great things, even if that entails making great

---

* I don't know what heterosexual men do with their free time. It's not really any of my business.

sacrifices. I can't help but wonder why such commendations rarely apply to women like Maddie Ziegler's mother, Melissa Gisoni, or Jenner or Momma Rose—mothers who have also raised extremely high-achieving children, albeit in less culturally acceptable fields.[*]

As obsessed as modern parents are with raising high-achieving children, few are willing to probe too deeply into what "high-achieving" actually means—or, more to the point, what raising such kids actually entails. Doing so would force us to acknowledge that we do not live in a meritocracy, and the cards are heavily stacked against the marginalized, regardless of how talented they may be. It also forces us to acknowledge the truth: that the Tiger Woodses and Serena Williamses and, hell, even the Maddie Zieglers, do not spring forth from the sea like Aphrodite, inherently equipped to take over the world. Behind every prodigy there is a parent who has or parents who have cultivated their gifts and encouraged them to keep going where others would have quit. And because women assume the lion's share of parenting in our culture, it follows that more often than not this parent would be female.

To further complicate matters, not every mother in the position of raising an exceptional child is pushy or neglectful. For every Jaid Barrymore (who notoriously brought her then-nine-year-old daughter, Drew, to party with her at Studio 54),[4] or Teri Shields (mom of Brooke, who famously performed nude in 1978's *Pretty Baby* when she was just twelve years old),[5] there are probably

---

[*] I mean, look—I'm sure there are people who think that Tiger Woods's being extremely good at hitting a small plastic ball into a hole is far more impressive than Kim Kardashian building out Skims, a $4 billion shapewear brand. I am no Kardashian apologist by any means, but I am not one of those people.

about one hundred examples of mothers who fly completely under the radar, who support their kids' ambitions and do their best to ensure their experiences in the spotlight are as nontoxic as possible.

I recently watched the Hulu documentary *Child Star*, in which Christina Ricci (best known for playing Wednesday Addams in the Addams Family franchise) credits her mother with creating a safe and nurturing environment for her on set. Ricci says her early film career was an outlet for her and her mom to escape her allegedly abusive dad and that she received nothing but "positive reinforcement" and support from her mother.[6]

The former Nickelodeon kid star Keke Palmer also told me that while she feels her mother, Sharon, could have done a better job protecting her from feeling the pressure of being the family breadwinner, she ultimately felt she did the best she could with the resources she had at the time. "I hated my parents for a long time," she said. "[Then] you come around to the reality [of] who your mother is, that she's a nuanced person, and you don't have to like everything about her to still love and respect her for what she did. . . . I wasn't driving myself to the auditions. I wasn't making sure I learned my own lines. I wasn't negotiating my deals and my contracts. My family did that for me."[7]

Of course we rarely hear about these women. Why would we? Their existence runs counter to the narrative that "good" mothers encourage their children to become the best versions of themselves, without having a stake in the outcome. We only hear about stage mothers when their behavior is so extreme as to be classified as "monstrous," because to acknowledge that a mother can take care of a child while also monetizing their gifts—or cultivating them to the point that they can one day become monetizable—crosses a line. We don't want to acknowledge that the line between exploitation and nurturing, between motivation and force, is often much more amorphous than we would like to think. We don't want to acknowledge that mothers who drive their children to 4:00 a.m. practices, or prepare their green juice for three-hour tennis drills, may be doing it for reasons other than out of the kindness of their hearts. We are so deeply invested in the concept of motherhood as an act of total self-abnegation, as a journey women undertake to complete the cycle of self-erasure and ensure that our lives and bodies belong to anyone but ourselves, that to concede otherwise for even a moment is anathema. So we use one side of our mouths to praise the children and the other to admonish the monsters.

* * *

The idea that a parent's job is to instill children with the self-discipline and fortitude to achieve great things, even if that means pushing them to the brink or forcing them to make sacrifices, is, like the concept of a "good" mother itself, a relatively new one. It largely stems from the rise of "intensive" parenting, or the idea that parents need to invest significant time and money to ensure their offspring's future success. The term originates from social scientist Sharon Hays's 1998 book *The Cultural Contradictions of Motherhood*, which describes how Bowlby's research about early childhood development being linked to maternal behavior led to heightened parental anxiety. Because parental labor falls on women, Hays argued, mothers started spending exponentially more time and money on their children, resulting in parenting becoming "child-centered, expert-guided, emotionally absorbing, labor intensive and financially expensive."[8]

Over the past twenty or thirty years or so, intensive parenting has become de rigueur among the more privileged ranks, to the degree that raising a child who achieves conventional metrics of success is one of, if not the most, reliable marker of "good" parenting. For many parents, there is no limit to the amount of money they are willing to spend on Mandarin lessons and SAT tutors and lacrosse camps and violin intensives, as long as it ensures their child has a semblance of an advantage.

The belief that intensive parenting is tantamount to good parenting dominates to this very day—even though we know, pretty much for sure, that none of this is good for kids' mental health. Studies show that constant parental pressure results in a higher likelihood of kids developing depression and anxiety, as well as aggression and anger-management issues, and there is no shortage of angry Reddit threads[9] and TikToks[10] and Pixar movies[11] demonstrating the horrific impact of helicopter parenting. That's to say nothing of how deleterious intensive parenting is for parents themselves, particularly mothers, who are more likely to report feeling anxious, stressed, and depressed.[12]

Yet despite mounting evidence that intensive parenting benefits no one, there is still this prevailing cultural idea that it is normative, even laudatory. There is, however, one caveat: This applies only if the intensive parent in question is pushing children to compete in areas that have been culturally sanctioned as legitimate, such as sports or academics or industries that are considered financially lucrative, such as finance or tech. If the by-product of intensive parenting is, say, a child getting into Harvard, or becoming a tennis prodigy, the reaction among other parents isn't repulsion; on the contrary, it's closer to envy. But if a parent pushes a child toward a field that is not viewed as legitimate (such as dance, or acting, or, God forbid, beauty pageants), or is too honest about the methods they use to ensure their children are successful, or if the child buckles under the pressure and rebels in some way, the parent is deemed monstrous— even though, in many cases, they are simply taking cultural scripts about the lengths one must go to achieve success to their logical conclusion.

Probably the best example of the weird amount of jealousy and disgust inspired by "successful" helicopter parenting is Yale law professor Amy Chua, who in 2011 published the memoir *Battle Hymn of the Tiger Mother*.[13] In the book, Chua describes her extreme disciplinarian tactics in raising her two daughters, Lulu and Sophia, banning them from participating in school plays and having sleepovers and forcing them to practice piano and violin for up to six hours a day. At one point, she describes threatening to give away her youngest daughter's dollhouse if she doesn't master a piece for an upcoming recital, making her practice hours into the night.

To hear Chua tell it, her book was intended to be self-deprecating rather than prescriptive. "I do feel a little pang [of regret]," she said in a 2023 interview. "I made a lot of mistakes and went to the brink."[14] She also characterized the book less as a parenting manual and more as an exploration of cultural differences between the more lenient Western school of child-rearing and Chinese parenting, which focuses on achievement, discipline, and respect.[15]

But when *The Wall Street Journal* ran the excerpt with the headline "Why Chinese Mothers Are Superior," there were two reactions: Readers either freaked out, barraging Chua with death threats and accusing her of abusing her children;*[16] or they seemed weirdly inspired by her parenting methods. Some of the criticism was a bizarre amalgam of both: "Amy Chua's new book will make her readers gasp—with horror and with envy," read the deck of one representative *Slate* review.[17]

More than a decade after the book was published, the reaction to *Tiger Mother* is complicated by the fact that, on paper, at least, it's hard to argue Chua's parenting methods weren't successful—albeit according to a very limited metric. Sophia is a Yale Law School graduate and former US Army attorney, while Lulu is a Harvard graduate and a judicial law clerk in Miami.† And though she has expressed regret over some of her behavior,[18] Chua still maintains

---

* Perhaps unsurprisingly, little of this scrutiny was afforded to Chua's husband, the Yale Law professor Jed Rubenfeld, who had presumably endorsed or consented to these child-rearing tactics. Interestingly, in 2021, Chua defended her husband [Irin Carmon, "The Tiger Mom and the Hornet's Nest," *New York*, June 7, 2021, https://nymag.com/intelligencer/2021/06/amy-chua-jed-rubenfeld-yale-law.html] when he was placed under investigation at Yale Law School for alleged sexual misconduct, which he denied. He was suspended from 2020 to 2022; at the time of this writing, he is currently back in the classroom teaching.

† Chua's career over the past decade has taken a much weirder—yet inarguably incredibly influential—turn. She is close with the right-wing Supreme Court justice Brett Kavanaugh, whom she publicly praised in a *Wall Street Journal* op-ed before he was accused of sexual assault in 2018, which he vehemently denied. (Following his confirmation, Chua's elder daughter, Sophia, clerked for Kavanaugh.) She also notably mentored both Vice President J. D. Vance and former GOP nominee Vivek Ramaswamy when they were her students at Yale Law School, which has led to her becoming something of a darling of the right-wing press.

a positive relationship with her daughters—and by and large stands by her methods. "I still believe achieving excellence can bring a lot of benefits, and I'm glad I instilled a sense of grit in my kids," she said in the same 2023 interview, adding she feels "most of it was worth it." If one assesses Chua's tiger mom methods according to purely superficial standards of achievement, one is forced to conclude that the juice was, indeed, worth the squeeze.

For most parents, this is a very uncomfortable takeaway, and one that explains our squeamishness with stage parents in general. It's hard to come to terms with the idea that raising children (arguably the most self-sacrificial thing a person can do) can, under certain conditions, be transactional; that treating children as canvases for our own ambitions, as little bits of clay to be molded and massaged and pinched and prodded toward our own goals, can be successful, depending on your definition of the term. No one asks whether we need to move the goalposts in terms of how we define successful parenting, or eliminate them altogether. No one questions why we continue to characterize an Ivy League education and a six-figure salary as proof of good parenting, rather than using broader, arguably more important metrics such as a child's overall health and happiness, or whether they grow up to become a podcaster. Instead, we demonize those whose children fall short of these arbitrary metrics, as well as parents like Chua who take this hyperaggressive yet culturally sanctioned approach to child-rearing to its logical conclusion.

There's more than a little bit of sexism at play here as well. It's helpful to compare the critical response to two very different Oscar-winning movies about abusive and domineering parental figures: 2014's *Whiplash* and 2017's *I, Tonya*. In *Whiplash*, Miles

Teller's jazz drummer Andrew endures months of psychological torture and humiliation at the hands of Fletcher (J. K. Simmons), his teacher at a conservatory. Fletcher is a sadistic demon: He throws chairs at students' heads, slaps them, pelts them with vicious ethnic and homophobic slurs, and even drives one student to take his own life. Yet at the end of the movie, he justifies them by telling Andrew they are necessary to motivate his pupils to greatness: "There are no two words in the English language," says Fletcher, "more harmful than 'good job.'"

In the Tonya Harding biopic *I, Tonya*, Harding's chain-smoking, parrot-toting mother/coach LaVona Golden (played by Allison Janney) is similarly abusive: She berates Tonya for her performance, forces her to practice till she pees her pants, and beats her with a hairbrush if she fails to land her jumps perfectly. (In real life, LaVona admitted to spanking Tonya with a hairbrush once, but denied being consistently physically abusive.) When an adult Tonya confronts LaVona about her behavior, she defends herself in much the same fashion, characterizing her abuse as a small price to pay for Tonya's success. "I made you a champion, knowing you'd hate me for it," she yells, echoing Fletcher's own defense. "That's the sacrifice a mother makes. I wish I'd had a mother like me instead of nice."*

Both LaVona and Fletcher are unequivocally verbally and physically abusive; though they intermittently display glimpses of humanity (both Simmons and Janney won Oscars for their performances), we're not supposed to admire them or even try to understand them; we are supposed to view them both as monsters. But

---

* To be fair, my mom says the same thing to me, though it's usually in the context of her telling me to straighten my hair.

there is a suggestion, by the end of both films, that for better or worse, both LaVona's and Fletcher's methods "work," in that they have produced something akin to real greatness: Tonya makes it to the Olympics, and Andrew turns in a performance that finally earns Fletcher's respect.

In describing both antagonists, however, the language used by (mostly male) reviewers was subtly quite different. When *Whiplash* premiered, many viewed it similarly to how some critics viewed *Tiger Mom*, conceding that Fletcher's methods were effective in the same breath as admonishing him.

"We're in an era of praise, where encouragement is the teaching tool and every kid gets a medal for participation," Brian Tallerico wrote for RogerEbert.com. "Have true talents been left to wither because they were over-watered?"

The Guardian's Mark Kermode had a similar takeaway, citing an apocryphal story about Charlie Parker reaching greatness only after his bandmate threw a cymbal at him: "[T]he message is familiar: only from great suffering—and great fear—comes great art."[19]

One Google reviewer seemed to view the film as a buddy comedy of sorts, characterizing Fletcher as "aggressive to [Andrew] but is later revealed to be of the noblest intentions with some heart-rendering affectionate scenes between the two."[20]

The consensus seemed to be that there was a kernel of wisdom buried in Fletcher's abusive treatment of Andrew, a much-needed counternarrative to the era of overly permissive parenting, where everyone gets a hug and a medal for participation. Sometimes, these reviewers seemed to imply, "good job" was truly the most harmful phrase in the English language.

Weirdly, in late 2024, *Whiplash* made the internet rounds again when Vivek Ramaswamy used it as a reference point for a rant he posted on X about how Americans prioritized "mediocrity" over achievement. He urged parents to instill discipline in their kids by introducing them to "more movies like *Whiplash*, fewer reruns of *Friends*." Many on X mocked Ramaswamy for his thread, saying he'd entirely missed the point of Simmons's terrifying *Whiplash* performance—but he didn't, really. He was just articulating a sentiment that most people who watched the movie when it came out were too scared to say explicitly: that with high achievement comes high cost.

Reviewers were not nearly as nuanced toward Janney's LaVona. One critic referred to her as "grotesque";[21] another as "a graduate from the *Mommie Dearest* school of parenting."[22] There is very little mention of what LaVona's intentions may have been, no elaborate justification for her cruelty, no suggestion that the end may have justified the terrible means. Fletcher is credited for both Andrew's trauma and his greatness;[23] when it comes to her Olympic athlete daughter, LaVona is merely assigned responsibility for the former.

I don't bring this up to justify either Fletcher's or LaVona's actions—they are both objectively horrific, abusive people—nor am I trying to say that anyone who was somehow inspired by *Whiplash* and repulsed by *I, Tonya* is a misogynist. But the diverging audience reactions underscore how much gender plays a role in our perception of what constitutes "good" and "bad" parenting. By the end of *Whiplash*, we're supposed to conclude that while Fletcher may have pushed his young charge to the brink of sanity, he did so for a noble reason; that an adult putting a college student through agony is not only justifiable but also laudable if the end product is deemed interesting or culturally valuable.* But stage mothers do not benefit from this assumption. There is no suggestion that the means, however horrifying, may have contributed to the ends, or that there was even any rationale behind the means at all.

At the end of the day, LaVona Golden's training methods aren't all that different from Andre Agassi's father, Mike, allegedly giving his son speed before a match[24] and forcing him to hit 2,500 balls a day when he was just seven years old.[25] Nor is Amy Chua threatening to donate her younger daughter's dollhouse significantly more abhorrent than Tiger Woods's father, Earl, reportedly calling his then-eleven-year-old son a "little shit" or a "dumb motherfucker" as a motivational tactic before he teed off.[26] Yet we have been led to believe that Tonya Harding made it to the Olympics *despite* having an abusive parent, while Tiger's or Andre's or Andrew's extraordinary achievements are *because* of it. Bad fathering, we are told, is a prerequisite for greatness, while bad mothering is a prerequisite for trauma.

* * *

None of this is to say, of course, that trauma does not result from this type of parenting style—it invariably does, more often than not.

---

* One of the most fascinating things about Damien Chazelle, the director of *Whiplash* and *La La Land*, is his singular obsession with jazz music, specifically how he views jazz musicians like Teller's character and Ryan Gosling's Seb Wilder from *La La Land* as somehow representative of the apex of hypermasculinity. As someone who attended a college with a prestigious jazz conservatory, and thus has spent an inordinate amount of time with jazz musicians, I feel uniquely qualified to dispel this notion. There is nothing hypermasculine or sexy about jazz musicians. They are basically like Trekkies, except more likely to use the word "killin'" in casual conversation.

Tonya Harding buckled under her monstrous mother's expectations, getting mixed up in a scheme where a hired goon clobbered her opponent's knee, destroying her career and relegating her to nineties late-night talk show punch lines. Many *Dance Moms* alumni have spoken about how much they suffered under maternal pressure as well as Miller's tutelage,[27] to the degree that some of them,[28] most notably Maddie Ziegler,[29] no longer speak to her.* Even Chua's flawlessly pedigreed daughters concede that they suffered under their mother's parenting regime, despite ultimately harboring positive feelings toward her. "It was maybe a less carefree childhood than a lot of other people's," Chua's younger daughter, Lulu, admitted to the *Daily Mail* in 2023. "I lost that childhood innocence, that sense of joy and wonder, and I definitely felt a lot of stress."[30]

That's essentially the realization that Louise comes to by the end of *Gypsy*: The show ends with June as an accomplished stage actress and Gypsy as a world-famous burlesque star, luxuriating in her dressing room and instructing her staff to keep her mother out.

---

* A stint in prison for bankruptcy fraud, coupled with racism allegations from a former student in 2020, has rendered Miller persona non grata within the *Dance Moms* community. In a 2020 statement, Miller apologized for past racist remarks, writing in a statement that "I genuinely understand and deeply regret how my words have effected [*sic*] and hurt those around me in the past." But that hasn't stopped her from being absolutely unhinged on TikTok, making videos where she photoshops herself into pictures with her former students. Notably, one *Dance Moms* alumnus who does still regularly speak to Miller is Siwa, who herself was recently accused of exploitative behavior toward minor contestants on her reality show *Siwas Dance Pop Revolution*. (Through a representative, Siwa denied the allegations.)

When Rose bursts in anyway, Louise is cold and dismissive, and Rose returns the favor by lashing out, demanding Louise let her run her bath or help her get dressed; when Louise refuses, Rose insults her for being a "cheap stripper." But Louise stands resolute in her power: "I'm having the time of my life, because for the first time, it's my life," she shouts. "And I'll be damned if you're gonna take it away from me!" It's cathartic and emotional and campy as hell, and it's hard not to root for Louise as Rose slinks off like a kicked dog out of her dressing room.

It's at that point that Rose breaks down, unleashing her resentment in the fervent "Rose's Turn," envisioning her name in her daughter's place on the marquee. When Louise finds her onstage, she takes pity on her, but also can't help but marvel at her mother's indefatigability. "You really would've been something, Mother," she muses. "If you had had someone around to push you like I had."

This is one of the last lines of the show, and when Louise says it, it's rarely played as winking or ironic or self-referential, a twist of the knife in the gut of the monster mother. Usually, it's played in earnest, and the audience is kinda forced to agree: Rose could've really been something, if she had had someone to push her like she did with her own daughters. And while the crux of the show is Rose's failure to see Louise for who she really is, at that moment, you get the sense that both mother and daughter see each other with perfect clarity. And for all the trauma and chaos and anger that Rose's delusions have wrought, Louise is able to see her as a mother who worked hard and tried her best to give her children what she thought they wanted. Rose's fundamental error, at the end of the day, was certainly not that she didn't try hard enough to do that, nor was it that she wanted some demonstration of gratitude for all that she had sacrificed. It was that she didn't try to see her daughters for who they were until much, much too late.

* * *

My stint with Lil Angels was brief enough that I will never know whether I would have, at some point, felt similarly to how Louise did about her mother, and I suppose I am grateful for that. I always viewed it as something of a blip, a fun little factoid to pull out at college orientation sessions or when the movie *Riding in Cars with Boys* aired on premium cable.* Until my son Harry turned eight—the same age I was when I was "discovered" at Monica May's showcase—it had never once occurred to me to ask my mother what her memories of that time period were and why she had agreed to devote significant time and financial resources to sign me to the agency.

"You were a beautiful little girl, and you were very talented, and most importantly, it was something you really, really wanted to do," she said.

"Was there a part of *you* that wanted it as well?" I asked her. "Like Rose?"

"No, not really," she told me. "I had terrible stage fright. You were much braver as a kid than I was. And again, you really wanted to do it. I would've felt guilty if I hadn't at least let you give it a shot."

---

* Aside from *The Wiz*, young Drew Barrymore in *Riding in Cars with Boys* is the only other role I remember specifically reading for. I must have been about nine or ten years old. I remember being certain I was going to get the role, despite having zero experience and looking absolutely nothing like Drew Barrymore. Then I saw the trailer for the movie a year later and realized they had probably gone in a different direction.

I know there are probably people who will read that and think that my mother is not being totally honest about her intentions, and that she should have "known" better than to pull her eight-year-old daughter out of school and parade her in front of middle-aged casting directors with red-rimmed glasses. But she was also right: I *did* really want to be a Lil Angel. I did want to sing and dance and act and punish the American public with how much of a little attention-seeking shit I was, the same way I punished the teachers and friends and family members who had to deal with me. And if my own children ever came to me and said they harbored similar ambitions, and someone wanted to help make them come true, I *absolutely* would feel compelled to at least give it a shot. And if they were successful, and it reached the point where I would have to put my life and my priorities aside to help them fulfill their dreams, I would not hesitate for one moment to do so—and I would be lying if I said I would not be disappointed if, after everything I did and all the work I put in, they suddenly announced they wanted to stop, or harbored resentment toward me for putting my own ambitions aside to make theirs come true. I would probably wonder the same thing Rose does at the end of *Gypsy*: *Why did I do it? What did it get me?* Perhaps that is uncharitable or unattractive, but it's the truth.

When a mother says what Rose does—that everything she has put her child through is for *her* benefit, to give her the opportunities she never had—we recoil at the self-aggrandization and martyrdom on display. We assume they are being disingenuous, that their actions are motivated by their own sublimated desires and not what they deem best for their children. We are repulsed by the idea that anyone could possibly view motherhood as transactional, at the expectation mothers should be rewarded for pushing their children toward something they never asked for.

But now that I am a mother, I know the truth: Children do not ask for nothing. Children demand everything: our bodies, our time, our space, our attention, our sanity.* And most moms, in reality, do not get anything in return for this. Instead, we are asked for more: to devote ourselves to our children's successes, only to be blamed entirely for their failures; to teach them that hard work and discipline and sacrifice are key to achieving one's dreams, only to be punished if we take that lesson further than we should. We're asked to give up everything for our children, without any support or assistance or expectation, even if we have the sneaking suspicion that with a little push in the right direction, we, too, could have been really something. And that's the reason why we hate stage mothers: because they have the balls to ask for something, anything, in return.

---

* Literally as I was trying to finish this draft, Harry was eating lunch and asking me the following questions: "Where and what is Albuquerque?" "Is Sharpay Evans from *High School Musical* still alive?" "Can I watch *Sonic the Hedgehog*?" "Why doesn't the cat like me?" And frankly, the fact that I answered each and every one of them makes me eligible for canonization.

6

Peg, It Will Come Back to You

At Home with the Bundys

My husband and I have wildly diverging tastes in TV. He loves Criterion Collection classics, Formula 1 documentaries, and YouTube gardening videos featuring whimsical elderly British men. I love Netflix dating shows, soapy teen dramedies, and early-aughts sitcoms about neurotic white men looking for love in the big city. He watches TV to be educated; I watch to feel lobotomized. As you can imagine, this causes conflict.

Fortunately, there are a few moments of respite, when my husband's attentions are otherwise occupied, and I can blissfully enjoy a terrible show on my own. One of these opportunities is Knicks basketball season, when he and Harry are so distracted for such a long period of time that I could probably murder someone or host a 1970s-style key swap party in our apartment without anyone noticing.* It was during one such Knicks season that I decided to watch all eleven seasons of *Married . . . with Children* on Hulu.

I don't remember how I decided that this would be a good use of my time. I vaguely remember that I'd watched *Married . . . with Children* when I was a kid with my dad—who, it's fair to say, is kind

---

* This is particularly true if the Knicks are losing (which they often are).

of like a Jewish, more erudite Al Bundy—and that I'd found it funny. Mostly, what I remembered was Christina Applegate's crop tops and the fact that the Bundys had a talking dog, both of which were as good reasons to rewatch as any. What I did not realize was that the sitcom, which focuses on disgruntled working-class shoe salesman Al Bundy (Ed O'Neill), his garish wife Peg (Katey Sagal), their promiscuous teen daughter (Christina Applegate), and their horny son (David Faustino), aged horribly.

Married . . . with Children is racist, misogynistic, homophobic, and fatphobic; occasionally, watching it makes me physically recoil, such as during the early seasons, when the audience regularly catcalled a then-sixteen-year-old Applegate.[1] In the years since the series was canceled in 1997,[2] some of the show's female stars, including Sagal and Amanda Bearse (who played the Bundys' neighbor, the shrill feminist stereotype Marcy), denounced *Married . . . with Children*, with Bearse referring to it as "misogynist"[3] and Sagal alleging the women on the show were "completely exploited."[4] Still, I kept watching—mostly because I had nothing better to do, but also because there was something about the virulently anti-PC spirit of the show that struck me as quaint, almost charming. As someone who had been reared on the warm-and-fuzzy, feel-good ABC Family sitcoms of the nineties, it was refreshing to watch a TV family that just didn't give a flying fuck about each other's feelings. In a way, it kind of reminded me of my own.

Unlike the Cosbys and the Keatons and the Tanners, the Bundys don't eat yogurt or wear sweaters or talk through their problems. They eat microwave dinners and wear cheap nylon and constantly probe at each other's insecurities, like a meaner version of the Simpsons or a Midwestern version of the Costanzas. Peg in particular is a marked contrast to the Elyse Keatons and Clair Huxtables of the era, the warm, nurturing, touchy-feely mothers of prime-time TV. I can think of no other mother in sitcom history who is less interested in her kids. Her daughter is borderline illiterate, and her son is a sociopath, but Peg is remarkably unconcerned with their development, spending most of her time at the hairdresser or the mall or watching daytime talk shows. Peg is also profoundly slothful, refusing to cook or clean[5] or work full-time[6] despite the family struggling with its finances throughout the show's run.[*] As she says in one season 3 episode: "Why should we age or sweat or die early? That's what men are for."[7] Her self-absorption makes her a bad mother, and her laziness makes it so she doesn't even try to pretend to be a good one.

But despite this, I have to say—when I rewatched *Married . . . with Children,* I *loved* Peg Bundy. I loved her style—how much she nods to the 1960s housewife aesthetic of big hair and pedal-pusher pants and curve-hugging prints, while not actually mimicking any 1960s housewife behaviors. I loved that she wasn't a typical harried working mom on the self-improvement hamster wheel, who read parenting books or attended La Leche League classes or lectured on the benefits of positive affirmations for kids' self-esteem. Unlike most sitcom moms of the 1980s, there was never any question that Peg Bundy was going to set out on the work/life balance high wire, that she would attempt to have her cake and eat it, too. Why should she go to the trouble of making a cake when there's a perfectly good package of Twinkies in the house?

---

[*] There are a few episodes where Peg gets a job, such as the season 1 episode "Peggy Sue Got Work" where she works part-time at a clock store to try to afford a VCR (so she can tape *Phil* while watching *Oprah,* natch). But she quits after overhearing two housewives gossiping about a particularly juicy *Oprah* episode involving "transsexuals." ["Peggy Gets a Job," posted February 21, 2022, by *Married with Children,* YouTube, www.youtube .com/watch?v=QRWzKMlP5po.] Really, this show did not age well.

I don't typically view laziness as an aspirational trait. But in Peg's case, I have to say: I kind of do. Because I am someone who is constitutionally incapable of not caring about anything. I have spent hours writing and rewriting Yelp comments. I regularly fume over things teachers said in conferences and report cards six years ago. I still hold a grudge against my cousin for allegedly cheating during a 1997 game of Battleship. There is virtually nothing too small and insignificant for me to get myself into a lather about.

So seeing a woman care so little about two roles she's supposed to care an awful lot about—being a wife and being a mother—is kind of delightful. I like to think of Peg as someone who clocked the insane expectations placed on her, to somehow alchemize her shitty husband and shitty kids and shitty life into a middle-class suburban fantasy. And instead of killing herself trying to live up to them, she chose to bow out entirely. To paraphrase the comedian Ali Wong, instead of leaning in, Peg Bundy lies down.[8]

But this is not how *Married . . . with Children* viewers, or those within the world of the show, saw Peg Bundy. They saw her as the butt of the joke, her retro style trashy and déclassé, her leopard slacks and beehive hairdo coding her as frumpy and asexual.* One of the recurring jokes on the show, in fact, is how desperate Al is to avoid having sex with his wife, at one point locking her in the basement in order to escape it.[9] For the mostly male audience, Peg served as an outlet for

---

* Someday, graduate students will write theses about the period of American popular culture when unattractive schlubs complaining about how much they hated having sex with their hot wives was considered the height of comedy (e.g., *The King of Queens*, *According to Jim*, etc.). *Married . . . with Children* was kind of the precursor to this trend.

their frustration about spoiled housewives who had it so damn good eating bonbons all day while their husbands slaved away in the factories or corporate America, working to put food on the table.

This frustration often manifested itself in disturbing ways. In one episode, Peg hits her head and develops amnesia, prompting her husband to turn her into a Stepford-esque automaton who cooks, cleans, and performs sexual services for his benefit;[10] in another, Peg walks in the door asking Al if he missed her, prompting raucous laughter from the audience, which only intensified when he retorted: "With every bullet so far."[11]

Given that it premiered in the eighties, *Married . . . with Children* viewers didn't see Peg as clever or transgressive. They saw her as slovenly and manipulative, a drain on her poor, put-upon husband and flailing kids. They saw her as her neighbor Marcy describes her in one episode: as "a horrible wife, a worse mother, and proud of it," and "the laziest bitch in Chicago."[12] They saw her, as one 1996 *Newsweek* op-ed put it, as "white trash."[13]

* * *

At the height of *Married . . . with Children*'s popularity in the early-to-mid 1990s, the nation was gripped by an obsession with the so-called white trash aesthetic. Shows like *Cops* and *Jerry Springer* dominated the airwaves; the rural Texas-born former exotic dancer and single mother Anna Nicole Smith appeared on the cover of *New York* magazine in cowboy boots with the headline "White Trash Nation";[14] and an Arkansas native nicknamed "Bubba"[15] was in the White House.

Critics frequently invoked the term "white trash" in describing *Married . . . with Children*, and not always in a negative context.

In 1994, *Entertainment Weekly* praised the show's "white trash ethos," lauding its "brutish, dark, etiquette-free, politically incorrect manner,"[16] while the *Arkansas Democrat-Gazette* column cited the Bundys as "white trash chic" and "the most uncouth [couple] on TV."[17]

In truth, the designation is not quite accurate. By most measures, the Bundys are firmly working-class; they live in a relatively well-appointed home in the Chicago suburbs, with a patriarch who is consistently employed. When critics referred to the Bundys as "white trash," they were saying more about their own biases than they were saying anything about the Bundys' actual socioeconomic status. What led critics to label the Bundys "white trash" was less their income and more their—or, specifically, Peg's—refusal to pull herself up by her bootstraps and strive to rise above her station. And this was not perceived as a good thing. Because as much as Americans may have loved watching *Saturday Night Live*'s Phil Hartman as Clinton housing McDonald's cheeseburgers on the campaign trail,[18] or slobbered over the fashion line Guess's cheesecake photos of Smith chewing on a piece of straw,[19] the term "white trash" wasn't an ironic reclamation by any means—it was an insult.

The concept of "white trash" is as old as America itself. According to Nancy Isenberg, professor of history at Louisiana State University and author of *White Trash: The 400-Year Untold History of Class in America*, the term was coined by wealthy white English landowners to differentiate themselves from lower-income, non-landowning whites, or the "idle and unproductive" settlers dispatched by the monarchy to colonize the New World.[20] This hierarchy was solidified in the first half of the nineteenth century, when non-landowning poor in the colonies were viewed as morally degenerate and the "offscourings"—literally, an English term for "fecal waste," per Isenberg—of society. [21]

Over the past two hundred years, "white trash" evolved into a broader catch-all for low-income white Americans. "White trash was what you became when you fell out of the working class and into disrepute," columnist Philip Martin wrote in the aforementioned *Arkansas Democrat-Gazette* piece. "It always bespoke an attitude that respects nothing and no one, that believes nothing matters and so what if it did."[22]

But the elitist core of the trope has always been the idea that poor white people are inherently less driven and productive than wealthier ones, and that their failure to ascend up the economic ladder can be attributed to their supposed unwillingness to enter the labor force. "Work is entirely central to this concept," says Lisa R. Pruitt, a professor at UC Davis Law who studies rurality, class, gender, and whiteness. "The heart of the white trash trope is the [perceived] laziness."[23]

Women are particularly vulnerable to this critique. As guardians of the house and home, women have historically been held responsible for reinforcing their families' social positions, serving "as a mediator between different cultures and races," explains Isenberg. "They're viewed as dangerous because they can disrupt the social order by marrying outside their class [or race]. And white, poor women are often seen as the most likely to do that."[24] Those who fail to marry well enough to enter the middle class are more likely to be deemed "white trash" as retribution for what is considered their poor social choices, as well as their failure to adhere to the overall social order.

This was very much a source of concern for conservatives in the late 1980s, when *Married . . . with Children* premiered. By 1988, the percentage of single-parent families had more than doubled, from 13 percent in 1970 to 27 percent.[25] Many Republicans attributed this trend to Black "welfare queens," which we'll discuss in the following chapter. But data at the time showed that Black women were not leading the trend toward single-parent households. In fact, a 1989 census report found that almost two-thirds of single parents were white,[26] with rising rates of single motherhood sparking panic among so-called family values pundits and politicians.[27]

Conservatives proposed a wide range of explanations for these numbers, from the trickle-down effect of the Sexual Revolution[28] to the pernicious influence of the CBS sitcom *Murphy Brown*.*[29] But overall, right-wing pundits seemed less interested in figuring out *why* low-income women were having children they couldn't afford, and more interested in figuring out how to punish them for doing so.

---

* In 1992, Vice President Dan Quayle made headlines for a campaign speech blaming out-of-wedlock motherhood on *Murphy Brown*, the CBS sitcom featuring Candice Bergen as an ambitious broadcast journalist who gets pregnant and chooses to raise the child on her own. In his speech, Quayle accused the sitcom of "mocking the importance of fathers, by bearing a child alone, and calling it just another lifestyle choice." Everyone, including many Republicans, thought this was a stupid claim for many reasons—but in my opinion, it's primarily because most of the women having children out of wedlock in the early 1990s probably only vaguely knew who Murphy Brown was. It's hard to imagine a sixteen-year-old girl in the South contemplating whether to have sex with her boyfriend after a Def Leppard show, then tuning in to *Murphy Brown* and saying, "Oh, well, this neurotic fortysomething feminist with whom I have absolutely nothing in common can handle single motherhood, so I may as well not use a condom tonight." It would be like blaming the American opioid crisis on the 1996 Scottish art house movie *Trainspotting*.

"Bringing a child into the world is the most important thing that most human beings ever do," conservative commentator Charles Murray wrote in a 1993 *Wall Street Journal* op-ed. "Bringing a child into the world when one is not emotionally or financially prepared to be a parent is wrong. The child deserves society's support. The parent does not."[30] Murray then went on to argue that all social support systems, including welfare and food stamps, be abolished to disincentivize low-income women from becoming single mothers, or else risk America lapsing into an "unrecognizably authoritarian" state.

Murray does not acknowledge that most women in the agonizing position of having to apply for meager public benefits to put food on the table do so as a last resort, not out of a desire to avoid labor; nor does he acknowledge how, say, safe and accessible reproductive health care would significantly reduce the burden on the welfare system, or the possibility that maybe, just maybe, men who either can't or are unwilling to support a family should wear a condom during sex. But that didn't stop a lot of conservatives, particularly our current president, from finding many of Murray's ideas persuasive.[31] To date, he is credited with being one of the most influential thinkers shaping contemporary public policy,[32] his work cited by such figures as Vice President J. D. Vance.[33]

The obsessive focus on low-income mothers reliant on public benefits is part and parcel of what author Susan Faludi deemed a right-wing-driven "backlash" against women.[34] In the late 1980s and early 1990s, politicians and pundits treated low-income mothers as punching bags; even ostensible liberals, such as Clinton secretary of health Donna Shalala, publicly decried the media "condon[ing] children born out of wedlock."[35] This animus showed up in the media as well. The success of franchises like *Cops* and daytime TV talk shows like *Donahue* and *Oprah*—the ones Peg would frequently reference on *Married . . . with Children*—ushered in a wave of imitators framing maternal poverty as spectacle, with paternity testing segments on *Jerry Springer* putting the perceived promiscuity, idleness, and self-indulgence of low-income single mothers on full display.[36]

Such segments adhered to a specific template: As the host revealed the results, the camera would cut between the mother on-screen, the defensive prospective father, and the angelic infant whose paternity was in dispute. Each time the host dramatically intoned "you are *not* the father," the exonerated man would do a victory dance, while the camera zoomed in on the mother (and even, sometimes, her child) weeping with shame. Each time, the message was clear: A lazy, uneducated woman had made poor choices, and now she and her child had to pay the price on a public stage.

Meanwhile, the middle-class housewife watching at home felt reassured that she had made the right choices to uphold her own role in the social order. She had worked hard. She had married well. And now, vacuuming her kids' playroom while watching trash TV, she could reap the rewards. No matter how dissatisfied she might be, no matter how much she wished things in her own life might have turned out differently, at least she had done better than the women on *Jenny Jones* and *Springer*. At least she *was* better.

* * *

Married . . . with Children ran for eleven seasons, from 1987 to 1997.[37] Its run coincided with that of another, more critically acclaimed show about a lower middle-class Midwestern family led by a brassy matriarch: *Roseanne*, the hit ABC sitcom created by comedian Roseanne Barr. Both shows were frequently cited in trend pieces zeroing in on the rise of the so-called white trash aesthetic in popular culture.*[38] Yet in most respects they could not have been more different. Unlike the slothful, self-indulgent Peg Bundy, the on-screen Roseanne Conner was painted as self-sacrificing and industrious, cycling through menial low-income jobs to help put food on the table. Though she could be caustic to her husband and kids, unlike Peg and the slutty single moms of *Springer*, there was never any question that Roseanne Conner was a good mother willing to do anything to provide for her family.

For this reason (and because it was an objectively better-written show), *Roseanne* was critically acclaimed in a way *Married . . . with Children* was not. Many in the media viewed it with reverence as an almost documentarian portrayal of the underclass,[39] with *Nickel and Dimed: On (Not) Getting by in America* author Barbara Ehrenreich viewing the courageous Roseanne Conner as emblematic of "the neglected underside of the American female experience,"

---

*   Essentially, the arguments of many of these pieces boiled down to "poor people exist, and there is also popular entertainment about their lives and their struggles that exists." Occasionally, there would be a point-of-view hidden in there, which fell into one of two subcategories: either that this is a good thing or that this is a bad thing contributing to the overall degradation of the culture. But mostly, in perusing such cultural criticism, I am reminded of how some print journalists earned $5 a word in the 1990s, and I am struck by just how much more these men were paid than me for being boring.

which she characterized as marked by "poverty, obesity and defiance."[*40]

This was not, however, the public perception of Roseanne Barr herself. Barr, who based the sitcom on her own experience raising her three children,[41] was at one point in the early 1990s among the most hated celebrities in America,[42] with late-night TV talk show hosts regularly making misogynistic jokes at her expense.[43] There were various reasons for this: Barr's public persona was unreservedly brash, and the fact that she was a larger woman who had the audacity to appear in public, let alone on television, probably didn't help. In 1990, she mangled the national anthem at a Padres game, prompting conservatives to flip out and then-president George H. W. Bush to deem her performance "disgraceful";[†44] her ability to elicit wildly disproportionate reactions from the right by being mildly subversive was akin to that of Chappell Roan or Lizzo today.

---

* Barbara Ehrenreich died in 2022, but I do sincerely wonder if she ever thought about having written this and cringed. That said, considering I once wrote a column, earlier in my career, about the best ways to dispose of semen after coitus, I'm not really one to talk. [Ej Dickson, "There's One Post-Sex Problem That Nobody Talks About," Mic, July 16, 2015, updated June 28, 2021, www.mic.com/articles/122372/post-sex-problem-spillag.]

† At the time, Barr's performance, which involved her shrieking the lyrics with her fingers in her ears, was viewed as disrespectful and unpatriotic, even though she would later say it was not intended as such and she was just trying to block out the delay from the mic. [Dan Snierson, "Roseanne Arnold's national blunder," Entertainment Weekly, July 23, 1999, https://ew.com/article/1999/07/23/roseanne-arnolds-national-blunder/.]

But the public perception of Barr as vulgar and nasty was also inextricably intertwined with the view that, by virtue of her socioeconomic background, she was an unfit mother. Part of Barr's lore was that she had grown up poor and at one point lived in a trailer park in Colorado,[45] something that helped lend credence to her on-screen persona but was used against her whenever possible by the media.

Barr's affair with fellow comic Tom Arnold, who became her second husband, also fueled intense criticism about her mothering abilities. In a 1990 *Vanity Fair* article, an anonymous source cited her daughters' hospitalizations for mental health struggles as evidence that Barr "seems much more concerned about her relationship with [Tom Arnold] than her relationship to her kids."[46] The story painted Barr as cheap white trash who had thrown her maternal responsibilities to the wind to have sex with a sleazy guy; an accompanying cover photo of a peroxide-blond Barr straddling Arnold did little to change this view. "They [the media] write about me like I'm a murderess, and all I do is a little fucking comedy show on TV," she said in the story.[47]

Ultimately, the widespread loathing for Barr in the nineties would, to some extent, be proven to have merit. In 2018, Barr would be fired from a reboot of *Roseanne* for posting wildly racist tweets comparing Obama adviser Valerie Jarrett to an ape. Over the past few years, Barr seems to have been red-pilled even further. She has espoused election fraud[48] and QAnon conspiracy theories,[49] as well as Holocaust denialism,[50] and she regularly takes to social media to rant about Democrats and "the Deep State."[51]

But while most available evidence would suggest that Barr is not a great person, at least one individual close to her—her daughter,

Jenny Pentland, who wrote a memoir in 2022 about her complex relationship with her mom—disputed the media's contention that Barr was a bad mother, or at least offered a more nuanced view. Though Pentland acknowledged her childhood was traumatic for a number of reasons, she arrived at the view that, in light of what her mother was dealing with at the time—newfound fame, a partner dealing with cocaine addiction (Arnold is now sober), a highly public divorce, and being widely loathed by the rest of the world—she did the best she could with the tools she had. "It occurred to me when I was writing that: Could I have survived this?" she told *Vogue*. "And it was pretty clear to me: No. . . . I was like, Jesus Christ—both my parents deserve gold medals or something. I couldn't have survived a day in my mother's shoes—and how could you be angry when you know that?"[52]

That same question, it seems, could apply to virtually all the mothers who watched *Roseanne*, and seemingly saw something of themselves in her struggles to get through the day with a family and their sanity intact: waking up at 5:00 a.m. to stuff a Thanksgiving turkey you can't afford, struggling to help a child with abuse or addiction or another problem too big to understand, summoning up the courage to quit a demeaning job and hoping that things will get better—even if experience has taught you, time and again, they probably won't. It must have felt good to see someone like Roseanne ascend to the top of the Hollywood elite—and it must have felt terrible to see them try to tear her down again.

* * *

Earlier, I wrote that critics characterized *Married . . . with Children* as a show about poor white trash, even though the Bundys were solidly middle-class. And that is true for Al, who was a star fullback in high school[53] and is (somehow) able to support the entire family on a shoe salesman salary.* But that's actually not the case for Peg. Part of Peg's lore is that she grew up on a pig farm in Wisconsin,[54] trading in her rural roots for an ostensibly more comfortable life as a housewife in the Chicago suburbs.

Peg's upbringing as an impoverished farm girl is the source of many of the jokes the show makes at her expense. (To wit: her last name is "Wanker," named after the Wisconsin county she was born in, and one of the running gags is that her dad is a shotgun-wielding hick and her mom is a morbidly obese crone.[55]) Instead of the sleek, shoulder pad–heavy 1980s working woman wardrobe, she opts for tawdry, ill-fitting animal print; unlike her adversary Marcy, who wears her hair in a sensible blond bob, Peg rocks a sky-high, bright red, absolutely iconic beehive. She may live in a respectable middle-class neighborhood, but there's nothing respectable or middle-class about her, and there never can be.

In theory, unlike the paternity test–seeking single mothers of *Springer* and *Maury*, Peg has done everything "right": She married well, had kids, and used her position as mother and housewife to achieve the American dream of upward mobility. But in practice, the show makes it clear that you can take the girl out of the pig farm

---

* Al is an objectively terrible shoe salesman. He barely sells any shoes; he spends most of his days meeting with his anti-feminist group and leering at mall teens and insulting his female customers. In general, the economics of the show don't make much sense, and there are Reddit threads with dozens of comments trying to assess what the Bundys' income was. ["Al Bundy's Finances," Reddit, http://www.reddit.com/r/marriedwith children/comments/1glimcr/al_bundys_finances/?rdt=56425.]

but you can't take the pig farm out of the girl. She's trash, through and through. The audience is aware that she's never going to ascend beyond that, but there's an assumption that she should at least adopt the pretense of trying. And Peg just doesn't have any interest in doing any of that shit.

The social and economic prospects for working-class women are arguably even bleaker today than they were thirty years ago. As rent and living costs have skyrocketed, middle-class families like the Bundys are becoming increasingly rare,[56] to the point that it is basically not feasible for many families to survive on just one income.[57] *Married . . . with Children* wouldn't make sense today for many reasons, not least of which is that it's almost impossible to imagine Peg Bundy getting away with not working outside the home at all. We'd like to think we have come a lot further than the days of the landowning elite or even the days of *Springer* and *Maury*, when the desperation of the poor was a spectacle to be savored. But as the middle-class collapses, so, too, does the distinction between the housewives vacuuming at home and the struggling single mothers they watch on TV.

It is a bleak situation—which is perhaps why I find myself so delighted by Peg, despite the politics of the show itself being so gross. I'd like to think Peg knows, in her trashy, petty little heart, that having a job and working hard isn't going to get her the VCR. Cooking delicious, nutritious meals or keeping a clean house isn't going to get her the respect of her dirtbag husband. Dressing in tasteful, tailored Banana Republic neutrals isn't going to garner her any esteem from the feminist who thinks she's the laziest bitch in Chicago, anyway. Nothing she ever does is going to change the world's perception of her as a failure of a wife and mother, the tacky, stupid, morally reprobate, high school drop-out daughter of pig farmers from Wisconsin. And she knows it. When the cards are stacked against you, only an idiot would try to play to win.

7

One Very Bad Day

Linda Taylor, the Welfare Queen, and the Monster of Our Making

The School for Good Mothers, the foreboding 2022 bestselling novel by Jessamine Chan, opens with Frida Liu, the protagonist of the novel, having "a very bad day." Overwhelmed by having to balance work with single motherhood, one day Frida leaves her toddler daughter in her ExerSaucer to pick up some papers at work—a serious, though isolated, offense. A neighbor reports her to the police, and a judge rules for her to spend a year at a rehabilitation center for women who have been deemed "bad" mothers by the state, where she must "demonstrate her capacity for genuine maternal feeling and attachment" and "show she can be trusted" to raise her daughter.

Many of the bad mothers at the rehabilitation center are, like Frida, single women of color,[1] and most are of low socioeconomic status. Their crimes range widely in terms of seriousness—one woman is sent to the center for letting her kid play in the backyard alone, while another is sent there for posting a video of her child throwing a tantrum on Facebook. They are forced to undergo a series of increasingly impossible tests to prove they are fit to raise their own children; that their "very bad day" does not define them. Ultimately, few of them pass—which is, of course, exactly the point.

Chan's novel is a chilling read; its depiction of a dystopian future in which mothers are held to impossibly high, constantly shifting standards has been compared to Margaret Atwood's *The Handmaid's Tale*. Yet perhaps the most shocking thing about Chan's novel is that, even though it is ostensibly a work of speculative fiction, the events documented in the book are far from theoretical. As Chan herself has said in various interviews, many of the things that happen in *The School for Good Mothers*—the court-mandated parenting coaches and counseling sessions,[2] the intense surveillance,[3] the criminal charges resulting from seemingly minor infractions[4]—have happened to women like Frida and the other bad mothers in reality.[5]

The real-life inspiration for *The School for Good Mothers*, according to Chan,[6] was the story of Niveen Ismail, a single Kuwaiti mother who immigrated to the United States and permanently lost custody of her three-year-old son after she left him alone in his crib for ninety minutes before police arrived.[7] But it could have easily been inspired by Jerri Gray, who was charged with criminal neglect in 2009 when her fourteen-year-old 550-pound son was reported to the authorities, leading to him being placed in foster care.[8] Or Tanya McDowell, an unhoused mother who was charged with first-degree larceny and sentenced to five years in prison for using a babysitter's address to register her six-year-old son for school.[9] Or Samantha Mungai, a Kenyan immigrant whose parental rights to her daughter were terminated when she left her four-year-old alone in the apartment while she went to work.[10]

All of the women listed, as well as the majority of the women enrolled in the fictional School for Good Mothers, are Black and brown women. Black children in particular are overwhelmingly represented in the child protective services (CPS) system, to the degree that a staggering 53 percent of Black children will be subject to a welfare investigation before they turn eighteen.[11] This is in spite of the fact that only a relatively small percentage (17 percent) of investigations are found to involve actual instances of physical abuse.[12] The vast majority of cases investigated by CPS—75 percent—stem from instances of neglect, which is defined in New York state as inadequate supervision,[13] failure to provide sufficient food or shelter, or a lack of adequate medical care[14]—all of which often result from cases of extreme poverty, not necessarily lack of care.

These statistics are damning—not just because they demonstrate the inherently racist practices of CPS but also because they reflect the extent to which race and class are central to the state deciding who is a "good" mother and who is not. This book documents the myriad ways in which our culture inculcates women with the belief that they are bad mothers, thus resulting in an insurmountable amount of social pressure and internalized anxiety. But for a sizable percentage of women in this country—specifically, those who are Black and brown—the fear is far from theoretical.

Black and brown mothers in the United States are subject to intense surveillance and policing, to the degree that there is an argument to be made that "the quintessential bad mother in the United States is a Black mother," says the legal scholar Dorothy Roberts.[15] In her 2022 book *Torn Apart: How the Child Welfare System Destroys Black Families: How Abolition Can Build a Safer World*, Roberts argues that our inherently racist conception of "good" and "bad" mothering in the United States—influenced in part by the Angel in the House trope, as we discussed in chapter 1—has resulted in such cruel policies and the erosion of the welfare state, as well as the systemic removal of Black children from their homes. "These policies persist in large part due to these stereotypes associated with Black mothers and how risky and dangerous they are," she says.[16]

One prominent example of this type of policing that Roberts cites is the case of Vanessa Peoples, a mother who was taking her two young sons on a picnic when one of them briefly scampered off to catch up with a family member (something that any mother of young children knows happens about thirty to forty times a week). Though Peoples never lost track of her child's whereabouts, within minutes a passerby had called the police; three weeks later, cops arrived at her house unannounced for a child welfare visit. When Peoples, who was undergoing chemotherapy for leukemia at the time, protested, they hog-tied her on her lawn, dislocating her shoulder in the process, and charged her with child endangerment and police obstruction.[17]

Unable to afford a lengthy legal battle, Peoples ultimately took a plea deal and was sentenced to a year's probation for child endangerment. "Because my son wandered away for less than a minute, I have issues finding work and housing," she wrote on her GoFundMe page.[18] "[I] can't get a job in many areas with this conviction on my record. I also have trouble getting housing. I am stuck in a cycle I can't get out of on my own." A momentary act of disobedience from her toddler—not even a very bad day, but one split-second bad moment—had, effectively, cost Peoples her livelihood, her home, and, temporarily, her freedom.

In discussing the state of modern motherhood, it's helpful to think about the panopticon, a circular prison design originated by the eighteenth-century architect Jeremy Bentham that is frequently cited as a metaphor in academic writings about surveillance. A panopticon consists of individual cells surrounding a central guard tower. Though prisoners can't see into the guard tower, they can see into the other prisoners' cells, giving them the constant feeling of watching and being watched. The idea is that everyone can watch each other at all times as a means of regulating one another's behavior and regulating themselves.[19] Even if they're not familiar with the concept itself, to some extent most mothers have had the experience of parenting within a panopticon. But as much as middle-class white women may constantly feel enmeshed in the push-pull of judging and being judged and fearing judgment from others, for those who do not fall into the above category, the reality is far worse. For women like Frida Liu or Samantha Mungai or Vanessa Peoples, it is largely assumed that you are not good enough until you can prove otherwise; and until you can, there may be horrifying, tangible, lifelong consequences.

* * *

If the default for the "good" American mother is the beatific Victorian ideal of the Angel in the House, the self-sacrificing, flaxen-haired nurturer beaming in the doorway, then it follows that the default for the "bad" American mother is anyone who deviates from that model. This applies to virtually any woman who does not adhere to American maternal norms (i.e., any woman who is not white, middle-to-upper-class, heterosexual, and cisgender). But it is especially true for Black women.

"The category of good mother is one that has been constructed to exclude Black women," says Jennifer C. Nash, professor of feminist studies at Duke University and author of *Birthing Black Mothers*, an examination of the figure of the Black mother in American history and culture.[20] "The ways in which the state has been fundamentally preoccupied with breaking down Black families, pathologizing Black [women], stigmatizing Black mothers, policing Black children at schools—it all works to ensure that ideas about good mothers are primarily a space that white women can access."

As Nash argues in her book, the dehumanization of Black women has been embedded within our conception of American motherhood since the days of slavery,[21] when as many as two-thirds of Black mothers were forcibly separated from their own children at auction;[22] some of these women were forced to raise (and often, if they had just given birth, nurse) enslavers' white children as if they were their own.[23] This system was intended as a brutal method of control, and underpinning it was the belief that Black women were incapable of caring for their own children,[24] but inherently malleable enough to exploit their labor for the benefit of white children.[25] The image of Black motherhood in the South during the mid-to-late nineteenth century was a deeply bifurcated one: on one end, there was the slatternly, promiscuous "Jezebel" popping out babies left and right;[26] on the other, the grandmotherly, nurturing "mammy" stereotype seen in films like *Gone with the Wind*.[*27]

---

* Objectionable as we find the "mammy" stereotype today, the reality of what life was like for Black female slaves in domestic roles was arguably more horrifying. Because only 10 percent of Black female slaves during the antebellum period lived past the age of fifty, and because those who worked as "wet nurses" had to be of childbearing age, most of the Black slaves who cared for white children were not grandmotherly types but very young women. African American studies scholar Patricia Turner has argued that the cultural conception of the "mammy" as an older, more asexual figure is a fabrication, intended to obscure the reality that many of the young Black women tasked with caring for white children were also being raped by their enslavers. [Patricia A. Turner, *Ceramic Uncles and Celluloid Mammies: Black Images and their Influences on Culture*, Chapter 3: Back to the Kitchen, pgs. 43–45, https://archive.org/details/ceramicunclescel00turn/page/44/mode/2up.]

The effects of this systemic dehumanization linger to this day. Black single mothers are more likely than their white counterparts to live below the poverty line.[28] They are more likely to experience postpartum depression and other maternal-related mental illnesses[29] and are less likely to get treatment for it. They are also three times more likely to die from a pregnancy-related cause,[30] a disparity that persists even when you control for factors such as socioeconomic status. "Class is no inoculation from experiences of violence when you deal with medical providers," Nash says. "That really illuminates for me how this category of good mother is tethered to whiteness."*[31]

Nowhere is white America's contempt for Black mothers more apparent than in the trope of the "welfare queen," the racist stereotype that has, for the past sixty years, virtually dominated both progressive- and conservative-led discourse regarding Black motherhood.† The welfare queen stereotype is intended to evoke "a lazy

---

* As just one example of how deeply engrained racism is into the medicalization of Black mothers, Nash told me a horrifying story about when she was pregnant and saw an ob-gyn, an older white man in his seventies. "He's like, 'You know the rules, right? There's no alcohol. And of course, you can't smoke crack,'" she recalled. "I was like, excuse me?" The fact that Nash was thirty-five years old at the time and a PhD did little to dissuade her doctor from speaking to her with such naked contempt: "He didn't even really register my horror. He just kind of laughed it off as a joke." [Author interview with Jennifer Nash, September 9, 2023.]

† Though there is a great deal more to say about the intersection between racism and perceptions of Black motherhood in America, I've chosen to focus on the welfare queen trope because of how insidious its influence has been in shaping culture and public policy, and how direct of a causal relationship there is between its initial usage in the 1970s and the subsequent policing of "bad" Black and brown mothers in America.

woman—implicitly Black—who continues to have children in order to increase the size of her welfare check" and "lives high on the hog at the expense of hardworking American taxpayers," according to a 2016 paper by UC Davis legal scholar Lisa R. Pruitt, titled "Welfare Queens and White Trash."[32] There are clear similarities between the two tropes—primarily, the shared emphasis on state dependence as synonymous with laziness. But the demonization of the welfare queen has cast a larger shadow on public policy and cultural perceptions of Black motherhood at large.

Much of this stigmatization has been driven by ostensibly well-meaning progressives. Perhaps the most notable is Daniel Patrick Moynihan, the former Democratic New York state senator who in 1965 published a now-notorious document about the state of the Black family. The report was titled *The Negro Family: The Case for National Action*, but today it is better known as the Moynihan Report.[33]

Prior to the 1960s, the vast majority of welfare recipients were single white women.[34] But Moynihan was deeply concerned about the then-rising rates of single Black mothers,* particularly those receiving government aid.[35] Moynihan attributed this to Black Americans being unable to achieve equal economic footing with middle-class whites, which he blamed on (surprise, surprise) "a matriarchal structure which, because it is [so] out of line with the rest of the American society, seriously retards the progress of the group as a whole."[36] Moynihan argued that it was "dominant" Black mothers who pushed away their

---

* Birth rates for unmarried Black women actually started falling around 1970 and have continued to decline ever since. [Ta-Nehisi Coates, "The Math on Black Out of Wedlock Births," *The Atlantic*, February 17, 2009, www.theatlantic.com/entertainment/archive/2009/02/the-math-on -black-out-of-wedlock-births/6738/.]

male partners by making them feel "inadequate," and thus were in part responsible for the "disintegration"[37] of the Black family unit.[38]

The Moynihan Report is difficult to read, and not just because of Moynihan's stilted prose. Though his goal in writing the report was arguably laudable—Moynihan at the time was trying to get more funding for anti-poverty efforts—the paternalism drips off the page. Many leftists and civil rights activists were highly critical of the report, arguing that it was overly simplistic in its near-exclusive focus on slavery and glossed over the damage wrought by systemic racism and oppression. Further, by blaming Black poverty on the scourge of "broken homes" headed by single Black mothers, Moynihan effectively positioned the targets of centuries of oppression as somehow bearing responsibility for perpetuating it."[*][39] Black feminists were particularly critical of the report, accusing Moynihan of promoting racist and misogynistic stereotypes by presenting Black women as domineering.[40]

"What Moynihan was getting at was how the afterlife of slavery has shaped how Black families operate," Nash says. "But it doesn't mean that there's something pathological happening. It's

---

* There are many historical explanations for what Moynihan perceived as the "disintegration" of the family unit—some of which he refers to in his report, some of which he does not. The report does mention that in the late nineteenth and early twentieth centuries, many Black men ventured up north to find viable employment, which led to many Black women effectively raising families on their own. But what he perceived as a "matriarchal structure" was, in fact, Moynihan pathologizing a deeply rooted historical tradition of Black women taking a more communal approach to child-rearing than their white counterparts, often sharing the burden of childcare with sisters, aunts, and grandmothers. [Author interview with Jennifer Nash, September 9, 2023.]

that Black families have been under siege from the state since its inception."[41] Such a discussion, however, would necessitate having in-depth conversations about contemporary poverty policy and the need for, say, increased federal funding to job creation programs—something that conservatives like columnist George Will,[42] who often quote approvingly from the Moynihan Report, have little interest in.[43]

Nonetheless, Moynihan's ideas gained significant purchase, prompting right-wing academics to direct their scrutiny toward the figure he positioned as responsible for the disintegration of the Black family: the Black mother.[44] And thanks to the virulent racism of the Republican Party, as well as the political ambitions of a guy who was at that point best known for costarring with a chimpanzee in a movie called *Bedtime for Bonzo*, the paternalistic handwringing generated by the Moynihan Report would ultimately metamorphose into something closer to contempt.

* * *

The term "welfare queen" originated from a *Chicago Tribune* news story that Ronald Reagan frequently mentioned in a stump speech during his first presidential run.[45] In his speeches, Reagan would refer to an anonymous woman in Chicago who had been arrested and charged with welfare fraud, bilking more than $150,000 from various government programs in a year[46] by registering for state benefits using dozens of names, addresses, and Social Security numbers.[47]

Reagan's "welfare queen" was a real person: Linda Taylor, a woman who was charged with welfare fraud in Illinois in 1974. The details of her past are murky, but we know she was born in poverty in the rural South around 1926[48] to a white mother* and an unknown man who was believed to be Black[49]—which would have been, at the time, a violation of the state's laws prohibiting interracial marriage.[50] Taylor lived on the margins of the margins of society, getting expelled from school at the age of six[51] and getting pregnant with her first child around the age of fourteen.[52] Rejected by her white family members due to her mixed race,[53] she moved out west to seek her fortune, where she, like her mother before her,[54] quickly racked up a criminal record for "vagrancy" due to laws targeted at controlling "loose women."[55]

Taylor was a deeply complicated figure, as documented by Josh Levin's true crime deep dive *The Queen: The Forgotten Life Behind an American Myth*. She undoubtedly committed systemic welfare fraud, collecting benefits under various different names and reporting fictitious children to get additional money for childcare. She also may have been a career criminal in other respects as well. Throughout her life, she was suspected of bigamy,[56] kidnapping,[57] and even the murder of a former neighbor (though she was never charged with the latter two crimes, and the bigamy charge was ultimately dropped).[58]

On the campaign trail, Reagan regularly trotted out Taylor's story with his own embellishments, accusing her of stealing "hundreds of thousands of dollars" from the state (she was only

---

* Taylor's mother, Lydia, was arrested multiple times for "vagrancy"—an extremely broad charge that was often weaponized against low-income women of the era (or really, anyone who didn't conform to existing social mores) to give police unlimited power to arrest them. [Josh Levin, *The Queen*, Little, Brown and Company, 2019, 196.]

charged with stealing $8,000, though prosecutors suspected her of stealing more).[59] The national media seized on the story, regaling middle-class readers with tales of Taylor's exorbitant purchases while simultaneously framing her as a bad mother, citing an arrest report noting that her "dirty" apartment had only one cot for her and her two grandsons to share, both of whom were malnourished and dressed in ragged clothes.[60]

Though Reagan failed to win the presidential nomination that year, Republicans instantly seized on the image of Taylor as a greedy and neglectful parent who bought fur coats and luxury cars for herself instead of taking care of her kids. It wasn't enough that Taylor was found guilty of welfare fraud; in order to fully demonize her and other women like her, she had to be found guilty of being a bad mother as well. She was a perfect antagonist for nice white middle-class Republican women, who saw themselves as having made the responsible choice to marry well, have children, and play by the rules.

Though the media framed Taylor as a monster, her children seemed to have a much more complicated perspective. According to Levin, who interviewed Taylor's son Johnnie for his book, they viewed their mother's cruel and neglectful treatment as part of a larger cycle of the abuse that she herself endured: "At times, they saw themselves and their mother as victims of an unjust world," Levin writes. "At others, they felt as though they were getting lashed around by an unstable woman's cruel whims."[61] But such analysis was not reflected in media coverage of Taylor's case, nor was there much discussion of the cycle of racism and poverty that had kept her and her family in such dire circumstances. The response was

almost totally characterized by righteous indignation toward Taylor, who was perceived as having the gall to expect hardworking
taxpayers to support children she never should have had in the first
place.

Taylor's story sparked a statewide investigation into "welfare
cheaters." The state of Illinois set up an anonymous tip line to report
suspected cases of welfare fraud; most of the calls, unsurprisingly,
centered on low-income women of color suspected of having babies
in order to receive state aid. "She came into this apartment with two
children and now she has four and [she's] driving a big Chrysler,"
one Karen reported in a 1975 call.[62] It didn't matter that the majority of the people who receive welfare benefits were (and are) white,
or that the majority of those sentenced for welfare fraud are men.[63]
The damage had already been done. Thanks to Reagan, the slovenly,
system-cheating welfare queen was established as a fixture in the
American imagination.

For decades, the welfare queen trope would be resurrected
by politicians to justify slashing funding of state benefits programs,* including former president Bill Clinton, who evoked the
welfare queen trope during his reelection campaign to appeal to
racist white middle-class voters. In 1996, Clinton campaigned on
"ending welfare as we know it," promising to curb spending and

---

* Reagan himself spearheaded this in 1981, slashing the Aid to Families with Dependent Children by more than a sixth after taking office.
[Dylan Matthews, "'If the Goal Was to Get Rid of Poverty, We Failed':
The Legacy of the 1996 Welfare Reform," *Vox*, June 20, 2016, www.vox
.com/2016/6/20/11789988/clintons-welfare-reform.]

make the requirements for eligibility more stringent.[64] Despite intense resistance from members of his own party—including, ironically, from Moynihan, who predicted the legislation would result in "children sleeping on grates, picked up in the morning frozen"[65]—Clinton passed his reform bill, the Personal Responsibility and Work Opportunity Reconciliation Act, in 1996.[66]

By his side at the bill signing was a woman named Lillie Harden, a single Black mother from Arkansas. Harden had clearly been selected to speak because, to the attendees, she was supposed to serve as an anti–Linda Taylor; she was there to perform the role of the self-sufficient, "good" Black mom who, after being on welfare for two years,[67] had tired of leeching off the generosity of the government. Thanks to then–Arkansas governor Clinton's welfare-to-work reform program,[68] she said, she got a job at a supermarket, getting her off welfare and giving her a sense of "independence" and pride.[69]

Harden's sad fate, however, underscores the failure of Clinton's initiative. In 2002, she suffered a stroke; under Clinton's plan, she was denied access to Medicaid and could not afford to pay for her medication. She died in 2014 at the age of fifty-nine.[70]

* * *

Today, the welfare queen trope has fallen somewhat out of favor in political discourse—in part because most people consider it deeply retrograde and offensive,* and in part because, to some extent, the damage has already been done. Clinton's legislation, as well as broader economic changes, resulted in a massive decline in the number of adults and children receiving welfare.[71] While overall poverty rates have declined following Clinton's welfare reform legislation, the number of households with children living on $2 or less a day increased by 153 percent between 1996 and 2011.[72] Black and Latinx single mothers are by far the most represented demographic, with 31 percent of Black single mothers and 33 percent of Latinx single mothers living in poverty, as opposed to 24 percent of white single mothers.[73] The vast reduction of the public benefits system

---

* Strong emphasis here on "most people": As recently as May 2024, then–presidential candidate Trump trotted out the welfare queen as a talking point, telling a roomful of GOP donors, "When you are Democrat, you start off essentially at forty percent because you have civil service, you have the unions, and you have welfare. And don't underestimate welfare. They get welfare to vote, and then they cheat on top of that—they cheat." [Shane Goldmacher, X, "Trump, per audio: 'When you are Democrat, you start off essentially at 40 percent because you have civil service, you have the unions and you have welfare And don't underestimate welfare. They get welfare to vote,'" May 4, 2024, https://x.com/ShaneGold macher/status/1786937806251495775.] Though Trump did not specify who "they" referred to, the dog whistle came across loud and clear. "You would think that by now there would be a less Reaganesque way to rally Republicans than to rail against the mythological 'welfare queens,'" the syndicated columnist LZ Granderson writes. "Perhaps with all of his court appearances, Trump didn't have time to come up with new material." [LZ Granderson, "Granderson: Trump's Racist 'Welfare' Dog Whistle Is Nonsense Just Like Reagan's," May 27, 2024, www.yahoo.com /news/granderson-trumps-racist-welfare-dog-100053223.html.]

has overwhelmingly impacted Black and brown women, primarily Black and brown women with children—and it is largely thanks to both conservatives and progressives alike buying into the welfare queen trope, primarily for cynical political reasons.

Still, even though the welfare queen trope is not explicitly invoked in the public arena as often as it used to be, the ghost of Linda Taylor frequently rears her ugly head in contemporary culture. One individual who has arguably built an entire career off demonizing low-income Black mothers, for instance, is Judge Judith Sheindlin, a.k.a. Judge Judy.

Prior to her TV career, Sheindlin was a judge at New York City Family Court, where she gained a reputation for openly berating people in her courtroom, who were quite often (though not exclusively) low-income Black and brown women. In a 1993 *Los Angeles Times* article, Sheindlin is quoted as telling a crack-addicted mother whose infant broke open his skull after she gave birth on a bathroom floor, "Can we do anything about this woman? I know she's on the streets, but can we stop her from populating half the planet?" This remark— essentially, a joke about forcible sterilization—prompts the writer to praise Sheindlin's "tart" and "tough-talking" demeanor, lauding her for bringing "intelligence, compassion, and healthy skepticism" to the courtroom.[74]

Sheindlin would later credit this profile with kickstarting her career on syndicated television,[75] as *Judge Judy* aired from 1996 to 2021. Her attitude toward low-income Black mothers did not soften when she landed her own TV show. In one viral clip, she admonishes a twenty-one-year-old mother of three for having too many children;[76] another clip praises Judge Judy for berating a woman who spent some of her welfare money on rent and bail for her partner. The clip's titled "Judge Judy Gives Greedy Welfare Queen PERFECT

Punishment After How She Spent Stolen Benefits."[77] Over the years, a handful of Sheindlin's critics have pointed out that Sheindlin's brand is built on exploiting and mocking the vulnerable and poor;[78] Sheindlin's longtime executive producer Randy Douthit himself has also faced allegations of racist and sexually harassing behavior, including calling a Black guest a "ho" and instructing staffers not to feature too many Black litigants on the show, because it would make it look "ghetto." (He's denied the allegations.[79]) Yet none of this controversy has mitigated Sheindlin's success: Her show continues to live on in syndication and spawned a spinoff on Amazon Freevee. As of 2024, she was worth an estimated $560 million.[80]

The success of *Judge Judy* has also spawned countless courtroom show imitators such as *Divorce Court*, *Lauren Lake's Paternity Court*, and *Support Court with Judge Vonda B.*, all of which similarly alchemize maternal poverty into entertainment. Such shows have found a second life on social media, where featuring impoverished women seeking recourse from the court system routinely goes viral. "Terrible mother wants to party instead of taking care of kids," reads the caption for one viral clip from *Support Court with Judge Vonda B.*,[81] while another clip from the same show features the caption "Lazy mother refuses to pay child support and [criticizes] judge's job."[82]

It's largely thanks to Sheindlin that our culture has such an appetite for this type of content. Also thanks to Sheindlin, there is little room in such narratives for discussion of the factors that actually contribute to such cases in real life, such as systemic poverty, racial inequality, and lack of access to support systems such as universal childcare. Such an acknowledgment would make it much harder for viewers at home to feel superior to the women on their phone screens, or better yet, ask themselves what kind of dire situation they had to be in to end up on such shows in the first place.

* * *

The moms who show up in my TikTok feed from bite-sized excerpts of courtroom TV shows are usually anonymous, their stories nonspecific and easy to scroll past. But Mary Johnston, the chain-smoking, physically abusive tyrant portrayed by Mo'Nique in Lee Daniels's 2009 film *Precious*, is not nearly so easy to dismiss. The mother of the titular character, Mary displays no empathy for her daughter or her grandchildren, using them only to receive a benefits check; she relentlessly berates Precious (Gabourey Sidibe), forcing her to cook and clean, and she is horrifically, brutally violent, at one point attempting to drop a TV on Precious's head from the top of a staircase.[83]

Precious premiered to critical acclaim, and Mo'Nique won an Oscar for her spine-chilling portrayal. But if you look at initial reviews, it seems there was something of a split in the consensus between the largely white and male critical establishment and Black reviewers. While most critics seemed to take it for granted that *Precious* was holding up a mirror to the millions of Preciouses hiding in plain sight, a few Black reviewers accused the film of furthering stereotypes of "exaggerated Black depravity,"*[84] most notably with

---

* Nowhere are these objections made clearer than in the 2023 film *American Fiction*, in which Issa Rae plays the critically acclaimed author of *We's Lives in Da Ghetto*, a fictional book clearly inspired by *Push*, the novel *Precious* is based on, that the film's main character, a frustrated Black novelist, deems catnip for "white publishers fiending Black trauma porn." [Joey Morona, "'American Fiction' Is Smart, Self-Aware, and Funny as Heck: Movie Review," Cleveland.com, January 9, 2024, https://www.cleveland.com/entertainment/2024/01/american-fiction-is-smart-self-aware-and-funny-as-heck-movie-review.html.]

Mo'Nique's portrayal. "One of the problems with 'Precious' and Mo'Nique's character is not that we get a view of the monstrous mother," the film historian Donald Bogle said at the time, "but that African Americans think the white audience thinks she is representative of Blacks."[85]

Indeed, it's clear that, when viewed through a certain lens, Mary in *Precious* serves the exact same role for white audiences that Linda Taylor did in the 1970s: as a boogeyman intended to reinforce the perception that low-income Black women are inherently bad mothers and thus undeserving of public assistance. The Black academic Charlene Regester underscores this by analyzing *Precious* less as a naturalistic depiction of the Black experience and more as a literal horror film, in the same vein as *Psycho* and *Carrie*. Much like Norma Bates and Margaret White, Regester argues, Mary Johnston is more symbolic of the "perverse social relations that breed monstrosity."[86]

I have no doubt that mothers like Mary Johnston exist outside the realm of fiction, simply because evil and brutality exist in all corners of the world and in all forms. It feels glib to conceive of her as just a caricature, and the world of *Precious* purely as fictionalized trauma porn.* But I think there is some truth to the suggestion that white critics in particular had a vested interest in viewing *Precious*

---

* That's especially true considering that Mo'Nique herself has said that she based the character of Mary on her brother Gerald Imes, who sexually abused her when she was just seven years old. Gerald later went on *The Oprah Winfrey Show* and admitted that the allegations were true. He reportedly was sentenced to twelve years in prison for molesting another child. [Janet Taylor, "Commentary: Not Buying Mo'nique's Brother's Apology," *Essence*, October 29, 2020, https://www.essence.com/news /monique-abuse-oprah-winfrey-show/.]

as a slice-of-life portrayal of the Black experience, rather than as a metaphor for the systems of poverty and oppression that give birth to the cycle of abuse.

Because it's relatively easy to accept the reality of a monster like Mary Johnston—a woman so evil that she literally attempts to drop a TV set on her daughter's head. It's easy to conceive of her as a singular individual, an aberrant product of a system we otherwise believe to be functional. It's much harder to accept that the aberrance may lie in the system itself, and harder still to confront the role that we may have played in creating such a monster.

* * *

In *Torn Apart*, Roberts argues that thanks to the media and politicians' demonization of welfare recipients, the model for government assistance has effectively been replaced by a system of policing and surveilling Black mothers. She writes that the child welfare system should actually be referred to as the "family policing" system,[87] because it is predicated less on concern for families' welfare and more on the need to control and regulation.

But she also argues that this punitive system doesn't just have implications for low-income Black and brown women, even though it is they who are overwhelmingly affected by it. "How Black mothers are punished is how we are all punished, because we have this terrible system of care in the United States where you have to consent to being surveilled or give up custody in order to have your motherhood supported," she told me. "[The absence of support] is true in general about motherhood. You're supposed to do it on your own—if you can't, you are punished."[88]

This is, of course, true to an extent (otherwise, I wouldn't have been able to write an entire book about it). But in reading Roberts's book as a companion text of sorts to Chan's novel, it's chillingly clear that some of us are given more chances than others to evade this punishment.

As a chronically stressed-out working mother, I, too, have certainly had my own very bad days. Though I have never left my children unattended, that doesn't mean I can't possibly conceive of a situation where I would for a moment or two: to run to the pharmacy downstairs to get medicine or diapers, for instance, or to take the dog out if he was scratching at the door and I couldn't get in touch with a neighbor to watch the kids for five minutes. I could see myself making the exact same calculus that many of these women probably made: how long it would take me to get them dressed and ready to go out versus the much shorter amount of time required to simply place Harry in front of the TV, Marco in his crib, and walk out the door and back.

I can very clearly conceive of a situation in which I would make the same decision that Frida, Samantha Mungai, and probably countless other mothers have done. Most likely, it would be fine. If someone asked questions, I am fairly certain that they would accept any explanation I gave, which would be the truth: that I was just gone for five minutes, that it was an emergency, that I'd never done anything like that before.

But it is not lost on me that if I was anything other than a middle-class white woman, people might not extend me the grace of believing I was telling the truth. It's not lost on me that they might not extend me the grace of listening to an explanation at all. There would be no benefit of the doubt, no sympathetic word, no "we've all been there," no comforting hand on the shoulder. There would just be me, guilty until proven innocent, forced to stand in front of a judge to prove that I can be trusted to love and care for my own children. But why should anyone believe a monster?

Casey Anthony
Is in the Book

On True Crime and Motherhood

In his book *I Wear the Black Hat: Grappling with Villains (Real and Imagined)*, which analyzes famous villains throughout history and popular culture, author Chuck Klosterman makes it clear there is one notorious villain he will not be addressing: a certain toothbrush-mustachioed, possibly one-balled genocidal maniac.

"So here is my problem: I was not going to write about Adolf Hitler," he writes,[1] before enumerating the various reasons why: He doesn't feel like he has anything new to say, he doesn't want to run the risk of somehow being perceived as defending him, and he sees no benefit to doing so. Yet as Klosterman recounts, every time he told people he didn't want to write about Hitler, they acted as if it was a tremendous oversight. This was particularly true of Jewish acquaintances, one of whom told Klosterman during a casual dinner, "Hitler is in the book."

"'No,' I responded. 'You must have misheard me. I said Hitler is not going to be in the book,'" Klosterman writes. "'Then you're doing it wrong,' he said. '*Hitler is in the book*.'" Thus opens Kloster-man's essay about Hitler, titled "Hitler Is in the Book."[2]

This is all a convoluted way of saying that I really did not want to write about Casey Anthony.

It feels strange to have to explain who Casey Anthony is, con-sidering how omnipresent she was during the early aughts. But for those who did not grow up watching *Nancy Grace* at the dentist's office, Anthony was the mother of Caylee Anthony, a two-year-old girl who was reported missing by her grandmother (and notably not Casey herself), and found dead in the woods near the family's home.[3] Police immediately zeroed in on Casey as a suspect. Initially, she told police that a babysitter had taken Caylee,[4] which turned out to be false; moreover, to many, her behavior appeared inconsistent with that of a grieving mother whose daughter had been missing for a month. After she was charged with first-degree murder, pros-ecutors would show the jury photos of Anthony partying at a club during that time period, with one witness testifying that she had participated in a hot-body contest.[5]

Such behavior, compounded with the fact that Anthony was young and conventionally attractive, contributed to a perception of her as a party girl who had murdered her daughter in cold blood so she could continue maintaining her self-indulgent lifestyle. There were elements of this perception that were undoubtedly influenced by sexism and a paternalistic view of how good white middle-class mothers "should" behave, but for the most part, it was totally war-ranted. She *had* lied—a lot. Her behavior *was* weird. And she didn't seem particularly interested in learning about what had happened to her daughter. So, when her trial began in May 2011, it prompted a media feeding frenzy, with HLN TV show host and former prosecutor Nancy Grace leading the charge with her obsessive coverage of the "tot mom."*[6]

As of this writing, it is unclear how Caylee Anthony died. An autopsy proved inconclusive, determining that the cause of death was "homicide by undetermined means";[7] though duct tape had been found on Caylee's mouth and skull, the defense argued that this was part of an elaborate cover-up, and that George, Casey's father, had staged the burial after Caylee accidentally drowned in the family's swimming pool (he was never charged).[8] Casey herself did quite a bit to promote this theory, alleging that her father had molested her as a child, something he has staunchly denied.[9] Due in part to the ambiguity of the circumstances surrounding Caylee's death, Casey Anthony was ultimately acquitted of first-degree murder, something many still believe was a miscarriage of justice (though a minority believe that there was enough reasonable doubt to warrant her acquittal).[10]

If someone were to ask me whether I believe Casey Anthony killed her daughter, I would say: "Probably." If someone were to ask if Casey Anthony knew more about her daughter's death than she told the police, I would say: "Yeah, almost certainly." But the truth is, prior to writing this book, I knew nothing whatsoever about the Casey Anthony case. The only reason why I have a semblance of an opinion about Casey Anthony's guilt or innocence is because for the

---

*   Grace, who started her career as a prosecutor before gravitating to cable TV, became a huge star as a result of her coverage of the trial. She did not shy away from openly proclaiming her bias in covering the case, declaring after Anthony was acquitted, "The devil is dancing tonight." By the time the trial ended, Grace's viewership had increased twentyfold. [Linda Seidel, "Nancy Grace and the Motherhood Critics," in *Mediated Maternity* (Lexington Books, May 9, 2013), 3.]

past few years, when I have told people (particularly women) I was working on this book, 90 percent of them asked if I planned on writing about her. And when I said no, they seemed almost disappointed. "Why not?" they would say. "She's the quintessential bad mom. Who's a worse mom than Casey Anthony?"

I didn't know anything about Casey Anthony—I had, in fact, actively tried to ignore coverage of her case when it happened, and I continued to avoid it when it came up in cable retrospectives and true crime podcasts. The few details I had heard over the years, such as Caylee being buried with a Winnie the Pooh baby blanket, were simply too horrifying for me to comprehend; there was no way I could hear stories like that and not immediately think of Marco, clutching his own blankie in his tiny fist.* So, when people asked why I wasn't writing about Casey Anthony, I didn't know how to answer. I just knew that the prospect of writing about mothers who are accused of harming their children, particularly in the context of a book that essentially argues that the "bad mom" is largely a social tool designed to control women, seemed . . . hard. Like, really hard.

It wasn't that I was concerned that simply writing about accused killer moms would be perceived, somehow, as a defense or an exoneration of their actions. In our postliterate age, I'd like to think that anyone willing to purchase this book—or any book, really—wouldn't be that stupid. Plus, even if that were my intent, it would

---

* He calls it his "nyah nyah," but really there are three different nyah-nyahs: a blue-and-white one; another blue-and-white one, which has a giant hole and the first nyah-nyah was purchased to replace; and a white-and-yellow one that is covered in taxi cabs. It is impossible to predict which nyah-nyah Marco prefers at any given time. One may as well try to guess what the weather will be in a country you've never visited, months from now.

be pretty damn difficult to argue that a woman who took the life of her own child was actually—surprise, bitch!—a good mother after all. The truth is, I just didn't want to do it.

I didn't want to spend my one precious life thinking about women intentionally causing harm to their children, especially since the fear of my own children being harmed consumes me on a near-daily basis. I am an anxious mother prone to worrying about her children's safety, the type who will pack a jacket for their toddler on the off chance they may be cold, even when it's eighty-five degrees and sunny outside. I didn't want to try to make sense of something I saw no hope of rendering legible, or try to understand what would drive someone to do the thing I most feared. It didn't strike me as an interesting psychological exercise, or a useful experiment in testing the limits of empathy. It seemed like torture. I would rather have superglued my hands to the broad side of a radiator than try to reach a place of even minimal empathy and understanding for a woman accused of hurting her own child. I wasn't even sure I wanted to think about the true crime fans who found themselves drawn to such stories, who struck me as depressing in their own right. I saw zero benefit to trying to conjure any understanding for anyone on any side of this.

Which, I suppose, is why I had to do it anyway.

* * *

I am not a fan of the true crime genre. This wasn't always the case: Like practically everyone else in America, I listened to *Serial* and watched *The Jinx* and *Making a Murderer* at the peak of the true crime wave in the mid-2010s. But after I gave birth to Harry, I realized I no longer had any tolerance for it. I'd listen to podcasts like *Crime Junkie* while he napped, and as the hosts girlishly oohed and aahed and gasped over the lurid details, I knew it was no longer possible for me to do so along with them—not when the victims they were talking about had once been tiny little babies like the one in the bassinet right next to me. The idea of something terrible happening to my child, and a bunch of chirpy former marketing majors using it as an opportunity to hawk electric toothbrushes, made me absolutely incandescent with rage. It still does.

For a while, I thought my aversion to true crime was fairly common, and that every new parent felt the same way I did. A few years later, however, I downloaded TikTok and learned how wrong I was. I was inundated with videos of women in their early thirties doing their makeup or their nighttime skin-care routine while gleefully recounting lurid details of rapes and murders and kidnappings. This was especially true during the height of the pandemic, when social media swarmed with conspiracy theories about Hillary Clinton drinking kids' blood[11] and Wayfair smuggling infants in overpriced cabinets[12] and sex traffickers attempting to abduct little girls from Target.[13]

Most of these conspiracy theories, I would later learn, were shared on social media by middle-class mothers.*[14] And I think they were so

---

* As a journalist, I'd spent years studying the reality of sex trafficking and the myths surrounding it, so I knew that these stories were likely bullshit (most sex traffickers aren't strangers hiding in parking lots, but are trusted friends or loved ones of the victim). But I did not understand why the women spreading these conspiracy theories were not asking themselves very basic questions about the stories they were promoting. For instance: Why were these traffickers always at Target? Did they have a preference for Sonia Kashuk–branded beauty products? What did they have against Costco or Walmart? And why did they want to abduct my kids so badly, anyway? It's basically impossible to find someone willing to accept $20 an hour to watch my children for an afternoon. Am I to believe there are thousands of strangers lurking in the home goods aisles willing to take them for free?

quick to believe these stories in part because decades of consuming true crime content had primed them to do so. When you spend hours upon hours listening to horrific stories about women and children being raped and abducted and murdered, you will, perhaps unsurprisingly, become a bit paranoid. And with the sex trafficking panics of the early 2020s, that paranoia manifested itself writ large.

It's no secret that women constitute much of the true crime fandom. A Pew Research study from 2022 found that women are twice as likely to consume true crime podcasts than men,[15] and Amanda Vicary, an associate professor at Illinois Wesleyan University who has extensively studied the genre, estimates that three-quarters of true crime podcast listeners are female.

"It's sort of counterintuitive, right?" she told me. "Think about everything true crime is; it's bloody, it's gory, it's sad, it's aggressive, it's violent. It's everything that you'd stereotypically associate with men, and men are the ones killing ninety percent of the time. So, what is it about this genre that's so appealing to women?"[16]

Vicary published a paper on precisely this subject in 2010, a few years before the *Serial*-led true crime boom. In a series of studies, she investigated which types of stories male and female true crime consumers were drawn to and why they found them appealing. She concluded that the vast majority of women were interested in stories about male killers targeting female victims, particularly when those stories contained psychological profiles of the perpetrators.[17]

"It seems to me like we are turning to true crime, whether we're consciously aware of it or not, because we're looking for tips and tricks to keep it from happening to us," she said. "So if we know what set the killer off, or what's in his background, we know what to look out for."[18]

When true crime fans talk about why they are drawn to the genre, this is one of their talking points: that consuming so many stories about women getting murdered is not lurid or exploitative but instructive in some way. Even though the likelihood of being attacked by a serial killer is extremely low,[19] and even though the majority of murder victims in the United States are not, in fact, female,*[20] there's a widespread perception that if women hear enough stories about female victims, and the tactics used by predators to ensnare them, we can avoid becoming victims ourselves.

But what if the perpetrator in question is not a man, but a woman? And what if the victim is a child, someone even more vulnerable than women are? What, exactly, is the appeal of such stories then?

* * *

---

*   This is true—2022 FBI data shows that men are four times more likely to be the victims of homicide than women [M. Lederer, "140 Women and Girls on Average Were Killed by a Loved One Every Day Last Year, UN Finds," Associated Press/PBS News, November 25, 2024, https://www .pbs.org/newshour/world/140-women-and-girls-on-average-were-killed -by-a-loved-one-every-day-last-year-un-finds], though women are more likely to be the victim of sexual assault [Cal Poly Humboldt, "Sexualized Violence Statistics," accessed July 20, 2025, https://www.humboldt.edu /supporting-survivors/educational-resources/statistics] and they are more likely to be murdered by an intimate partner or someone they know. [Erica L. Smith, "Female Murder Victims and Victim-Offender Relationship, 2021," Bureau of Justice Statistics, December 2022, https://bjs.ojp .gov/female-murder-victims-and-victim-offender-relationship-2021.]

It is perhaps a testament to the unthinkability of the act itself that there is no specific word in the English language for a mother murdering her child. When a parent takes a child's life, it is known as filicide. But there is no semantic distinction made for gender, despite the fact that when mothers and fathers kill their own offspring, they do so very differently.

Men, for instance, are more likely to murder older children;[21] women, by contrast, are more likely to kill their children during infancy.[22] Men who commit filicide are more likely to be unemployed, or abuse alcohol and drugs. Women are more likely to be single and have limited access to childcare.[23] Men are more likely to use so-called active methods of violence, such as stabbing, shooting, or shaking. Women are more likely to resort to methods such as drugging, drowning, or suffocation.[24]

Generally speaking, filicide is extremely rare. Out of the 25,000 or so homicide cases reported in the United States per year, there are only about 450 reported cases of parents killing children.[25] But Michelle Oberman, a professor of law at Santa Clara University School of Law and coauthor of the book *Mothers Who Kill Their Children: Interviews from Prison*, believes this number is actually higher, particularly when it comes to cases of neonaticide (the killing of a newborn). These are the so-called dumpster baby cases that were subject to extensive coverage in the 1980s and 1990s, in which a young mother—usually a teenager who had been concealing a pregnancy, or didn't even know she had been pregnant—would give birth and dispose of the baby, most often in a trash can or dumpster.* "The discovery of the body is often quite random," she told me. "For everyone that turns up in the dumpster, well, how many didn't turn up in the dumpster? Sorry," she said, after I let out an involuntary groan. "I always forget how this sounds."[26]

Oberman is used to this reaction: She is one of a very small handful of researchers willing to probe into the phenomenon of mothers killing their own children. She started in the early 1990s, when she was working at Chicago's Loyola Law's health law institute and received a call from a public defender, asking her to consult on a case of a fourteen-year-old girl who had given birth to a baby on the toilet. The girl claimed to not have known she was even pregnant in the first place; prosecutors later determined she had likely conceived after being sexually abused by a bunch of boys in her grade. She pled guilty to involuntary manslaughter, though the charge was dropped after an autopsy determined the baby had likely been born deceased.

"It left me with a bunch of questions about what sort of blame should be attached to the various actors," she told me.[27]

---

* This happened often enough in the 1990s—or at least, received enough media coverage—to merit *Family Guy* doing an infamous cutaway joke, a musical number called "Prom Night Dumpster Baby." ["Family Guy Song: Prom Night Dumpster Baby," posted June 6, 2018, by RaphaelOfTheInternet, YouTube, https://www.youtube.com/watch?v=50kQJyiLMZM.] This was based on the 1997 case of teenager Melissa Drexler giving birth at her high school prom, then allegedly killing and disposing of the infant in a trash bin before going back to the dance floor. She pled guilty to aggravated manslaughter and was sentenced to fifteen years in prison before being freed on parole in 2001. [Karen DeMasters, "Briefing: The Law: 'Prom Mom' Released," *New York Times*, December 2, 2001, https://www.nytimes.com/2001/12/02/nyregion/briefing-the-law-prom-mom-released.html.]

Two years later, Oberman received a call from a different defense attorney about a nearly identical case involving a sixteen-year-old. Staggered by the similarities, she did some research and discovered that nearly all the fifty or so cases of neonaticide in the United States that year involved unmarried teenage girls who had received no prenatal care and often had no idea they were pregnant in the first place. Another study found that a significant number of mothers who committed filicide—39 percent—were victims of physical or sexual abuse.

"I was trying to make sense of these patterns," she said. "Because if there is going to be prevention of any sort, it's going to come from the media telling a different story other than 'she's a monster.'"[28]

Oberman's experience researching teenage neonaticide led her to start researching maternal filicide in general: what women commit such acts, the reasons why, and if there were any patterns that could help determine which children were at risk. As part of her research, she interviewed forty women who were incarcerated for murdering their own children in the state of Ohio. She had two significant takeaways. The first was that these mothers were usually parenting alone without any support systems, and had a history of physical or sexual abuse.[29] "The chaos in their lives was a constant drumbeat," she said. "It was at a level I could not begin to wrap my head around—partner abuse, substance abuse, sex crimes, trafficking. And it was there from long before they got their first periods."[30]

The second was the one that surprised Oberman the most. "I went into it, on some level, thinking these women were really ambivalent about being moms and they're kind of monstrous," she said. "I thought they'd just tell me some sob story about how they didn't do it, or their lawyer let them down or whatever." But that wasn't how Oberman's conversations with these women started. Almost uniformly, she said, it started with them using the phrase: "Being a mother was the most important thing in my life."

"They'd tell you, 'OK, here's how I made it work with paying for the diapers, and here's when I would leave him without a diaper, because I knew he'd get a rash,'" she said. "They were concerned about mothering on that level. I think the binary between good moms and bad moms is a truth we cling to, because we want to believe we'll fall on the right side. And the truth is way more complicated."[31]

At the time Oberman conducted her interviews, she was the mother of two young children. Understandably, she was deeply traumatized by the interviewing experience, and suffered from nightmares. But it also made her incredibly grateful for her own relatively privileged circumstances, as well as empathetic toward the women she interviewed. "I remember feeling this keen sense of, 'there but for the grace of God go I,'" she says. "I learned about all of the things that were in place that kept me from the edge, and all of the things that had to go right in my life so I got to raise my kids the way I did, so I could give them all the support they needed."[32]

Oberman's perspective runs counter to the dominant narrative driving coverage of mothers who kill their children: that they are aberrant, that they are monstrous, that they are something other than women, their actions constituting a betrayal of their own biological nature. Every mother who has been accused of murder has been subject to this treatment: Lori Vallow Daybell, the so-called doomsday mom who in 2023 was found guilty of murdering her sixteen-year-old daughter and seven-year-old son;[33] Andrea Yates, the mother who in 2001 confessed to systemically drowning her five children in the bathtub;[34] or Susan Smith, who in 1995 was found guilty of murdering her two small sons by locking them in a car while it rolled into a lake, which she initially attributed to a carjacking.[35]

Despite the horrific nature of these stories, true crime consumers find them fascinating. They are particularly popular among women, according to Lauren Matthias, cohost of the forensic psychology podcast *Hidden True Crime*. On the podcast, Matthias and her cohost, husband and forensic psychologist John Matthias, apply forensic psychology to try to understand the backgrounds and motivations of killers. Lauren Matthias says that episodes about mothers who kill their own children draw a disproportionate number of female listeners, particularly compared to their interest in male killers like Jeffrey Dahmer.[36]

Surprisingly, however, female consumers of these types of narratives are not more likely to display empathy toward women who commit filicide—in fact, according to Matthias, they may feel significantly less. Matthias says when she covered Daybell, for instance, she mentioned Daybell was possibly a survivor of alleged childhood sexual abuse,[37] prompting a barrage of emails from mostly female listeners expressing outrage that she would attempt to provide an excuse for Daybell's actions. But this was not Matthias's point: She says she was not trying to exonerate her but to provide further context.

"When we give empathy or try to give understanding to someone like that, we have people write and say, 'No, they're just evil,'" she says. "I think that's what we want to do as human beings, just label someone evil and move on. It's a lot simpler and it helps us make sense of the world. If we can just say a person is evil, we don't have to worry about why [they did what they did]."[38]

To me, this prompts a seemingly obvious question: Why would women be *more* drawn to stories about mothers who kill, while simultaneously reserving even less understanding for them than they would for someone like Dahmer (a man who quite literally kept his victims' genitals in his cupboard)[39]? Vicary hypothesizes that there is an aspect of the true crime genre that serves as a way for mothers of small children to feel less bad about themselves and their own parenting abilities; or for true crime to serve as an instruction manual for what *not* to do as a parent.

"We all feel like bad moms sometimes, because society makes us feel that way," she said. "But then if you sit and watch the news about one of these women, you're thinking, 'Hey, I'm not doing so bad. I didn't play LEGOs with my kid because I had to work, but I also didn't drown him in the back seat of my car.'"[40]

Matthias has a slightly different theory: She believes that some women who enjoy listening to true crime stories about mothers who kill were raised by abusive mothers themselves, and that placing themselves in the position of the victims is a means of understanding their own trauma. "I often hear from survivors of abusive parents, and they [use these stories] to try to process why that happened to them," she said.[41]

I think there is some truth to Vicary's hypothesis. Certainly, looking at photos of little Caylee Anthony with her mother, her eyes wide and radiating pure adoration and trust, makes me think about my own kids and how much adoration and trust they put into me; thinking about betraying that makes my heart feel like it's been flattened by a steamroller. And certainly, learning about police finding the remains of Lori Vallow Daybell's seven-year-old son on her lover's property makes me feel less guilty about the current whereabouts of my own son, who is parked in front of the television watching *Mary Poppins* so I could get this chapter done. Sure, my child could be doing something more constructive with his time; sure, there's a possibility that this specific moment where I am not actively parenting could lead to him developing trauma in adulthood, such as a fear of abandonment or a psychosexual obsession with Dick Van Dyke or dancing penguins.* But hey, at least I didn't kill him and bury him on my weird Mormon boyfriend's farm.[42]

But truth be told, I don't think Matthias is quite right here. I don't think women enjoy listening to stories about mothers who kill because they relate to the victims. So often in crime coverage, these innocent victims are sketched out within such fuzzy parameters: a little boy who just lost a tooth, a little girl who loved chocolate milk and SpongeBob, a baby who had just started smiling. Those details serve their intended purpose, which is to invoke the simplicity and innocence of childhood and make our hearts break. But they don't really evoke a complex portrait of a victim, particularly if the victim in question is an infant. That's simply too young to be a fully realized person, and our horror stems not from the frisson of identification, but from the realization that the child was deprived of the opportunity to become one.

Nor can adult true crime consumers take away anything potentially instructive from the stories of children murdered by their parents, as someone could from a story of, say, a survivor of an attempted rape or abduction. An eighteen-month-old drowned in a bathtub by her mother cannot be on the lookout for red flags; cannot use any survival strategies she's learned on a podcast with the slogan, "Stay sexy, don't get murdered"; cannot fight back in any material way. There is nothing to be gleaned from her final moments,

---

* Not that I would know anything about that.

other than the sheer terror and confusion of being betrayed by the person who kissed your toes and diapered you and sang you songs and told you everything was going to be OK. What is there to possibly take away from that, other than horror at a world that enables such things to happen?

Which leaves us with one terrible, uncomfortable truth: If we can't identify with the victim, there is only one person left for us to identify with. It's the mother, the monster, the woman who is rendered something other than woman. We hear these stories and we're left with one dreadful thought languidly drifting into our brains like soap bubbles waiting to be popped: "Jesus. That is awful. I wonder how bad it had to get to feel like killing was the only option."

Somewhere in our minds, we know the answer to that question. We remember the exact night we learned: the husband on a business trip, the baby who won't stop vomiting and whose fever climbs higher and higher, the four-year-old who won't stop whining for juice or Bluey or Daddy, the phone that won't stop ringing, the dishes that won't stop piling up, the dog that won't stop barking and nipping at our feet, the emails that won't stop accumulating in our inbox. That feeling that none of it will ever stop: the exhaustion, the frustration, the crying, the screaming, the hopelessness, the loneliness, the self-pity. We know how much we love our children, and the lengths we would go to protect them. But we also know, to some extent, how bad it could have gotten for some of these women. Because we know that in some parallel dimension, if he had never come home, if the sitter hadn't arrived, if the baby hadn't stopped crying, if we'd had less money or less access to psychiatric medications or less of any resource at all, really, we could've been monsters, too.

* * *

While researching this subject—which was, again, something I *really* did not want to do—I came across a paper in the *Indian Journal of Psychiatry*, noting the common factors in filicide cases. The paper was about nine pages long, and at one point, it noted, almost as an aside, that there are more cases of parents murdering their own children in the United States than in any other industrialized nation in the world.[43]

I was shocked by this statistic. I had assumed that filicide was, if not rare, a somewhat universal phenomenon, one that spanned across countries and ethnicities and time, as far back to the story of Medea. But that wasn't the case. The paper noted that neonaticide rates in the United States, for instance, are almost three times as high as they are in Canada, which would seemingly indicate that there is something specific about the state of parenthood in the United States that makes parents more likely to hurt their children.

I suffered through the whole paper, my eyes scanning number after number, waiting for the authors to discuss prospective explanations for this discrepancy: the absence of universalized childcare in the US, for instance, or the lack of mandated paid family leave, or the paucity of home nurse visits after a mother gives birth, as is the case in most other industrialized countries. I kept waiting for them to point out various socioeconomic or demographic factors that would put mothers more at risk. But aside from a reference to potential prevention efforts, such as recommending that clinicians ask parents if they have "thoughts and fears of harming their children"—a question that I imagine few mothers, when asked, would answer in the affirmative—there was very little.

The paper did make note of the role mental illness likely plays in most filicides, something that is reflected in both the legal system and in media representations of the phenomenon. Mothers who kill their children are more likely to have juries accept insanity defenses, for instance, than fathers who kill their children, presumably because the role of mother as nurturer is so deeply engrained in our psyches that a woman betraying this biological impulse must be the product of madness.[44]

Media coverage is also more likely to be sympathetic toward mothers who are suspected of killing their children due to mental illnesses such as postpartum mood disorders. This was the case with Lindsay Clancy, a Massachusetts woman who strangled her three children with exercise bands in 2023 before jumping off her roof in an apparent (and failed) suicide attempt, paralyzing her from the waist down.[45] In the months prior to killing her children, there were warning signs aplenty: Clancy had cycled through a dozen different psychiatric medications, checking herself into a mental hospital, and telling her husband she had thoughts of harming herself and her children.[46]

Still, in many ways Clancy was not one of the obviously at-risk mothers Oberman interviewed in the Ohio prison. She was a middle-class woman with a supportive partner and had access to high-quality childcare[47] and mental health care. She had taken every possible opportunity to seek help. And yet, none of it had seemingly been enough.

After Clancy was arrested, her defense attorneys argued she was suffering from undiagnosed postpartum psychosis, a rare postpartum mood disorder characterized by hallucinations, paranoia, mania, and depression.[48] Her story sparked an outpouring of empathy and support from mothers on TikTok and Instagram, who shared their own struggles with the disorder with the hashtag #postpartumpsychosis.[49] Matthias, who also covered Clancy's story on her podcast, said she saw a marked difference between the reaction to the episode about Clancy and that to episodes covering other mother murderers. She also noted, perhaps unsurprisingly, that the public response to Clancy's story would probably have been significantly less empathetic had she not been a middle-class suburban white woman.[50] The fact that women saw themselves in her and her story made it impossible to declare her a monster and shove her in the closet, the way we've done with countless others.

The reaction to Clancy's story is also complicated by the fact that as I write this, it's unclear whether Clancy *did* actually suffer from postpartum psychosis. She is currently being held at a psychiatric hospital rather than a prison, with a judge ruling she is at "serious risk of imminent self-harm."[51] Yet prosecutors have argued that on the fateful evening, she was in full control of her faculties, pointing to the fact that she had the clarity of mind to order a Mediterranean power bowl prior to the murders[52] as evidence of her mental state.

Clancy also allegedly conducted Google searches for the term "ways to kill" and "can you treat a sociopath" sometime before the murders.[53] When the case goes to trial in February 2026, it's going to be pretty hard for the defense to paint her browser history in her favor.[54] And it is entirely possible that for Clancy, the postpartum psychosis narrative is just that: an easy and convenient way for people to project their own experiences onto someone who looks like them, a story that renders the inexplicable explicable, a way to blame the system instead of creating a monster to shoulder the burden.

Which brings us back to Casey Anthony, a woman whose (alleged) behavior does not benefit from a simple explanation, whose (alleged) actions are not rendered legible by any of the available context; a woman who wore a skintight bodycon purple dress and enrolled in a hot-body contest while her two-year-old daughter was supposedly missing.[55] In interviews she has given since her trial, Anthony has alleged both that she is innocent of murdering Caylee and that she was molested by her father, a defense for a supposedly nonexistent crime that is therefore functionally useless on its face.[56] Almost no one thinks she isn't lying; almost no one thinks she is anything but one of the worst mothers in history.[*] There is virtually nothing she could do to make anyone in America believe anything other than that she is a monster.

But let's assume, for a second, that Casey Anthony was not a monster. Let's assume she wasn't a sociopath, a ticking time bomb who spent almost three years pretending to care for her daughter until she could dispose of her at the earliest possible moment. Let's assume she was what she appears to be, which is a mother who was, at best, negligent, and at worst, deeply deranged.

We take for granted that even mothers who love their children are capable of hating them at their worst moments. So it follows that the opposite can also be true: that a mother who has hated, or even hurt, their child could be a mother who, at another moment, in another context, with another set of resources, kisses their child's toes,

---

[*] In early 2025, Casey Anthony launched a TikTok account and started branding herself as a "legal advocate." This made everyone hate her about 10.5 times more than they already did, which was a lot. [Casey Anthony, "#Casey Anthony Has a New Gig," posted March 3, 2025, by TMZ, TikTok, www.tiktok.com/@tmz/video/7477632444850556203?lang=en.]

sings a Beatles song to them, dries their tears, breathes in the smell of their floral tears-free shampoo. Such a mother may be capable of committing the worst act imaginable, but they may also be capable of love, even deep and profound love. It's just that, tragically, love was not enough.

9

The Perfect Storm

The Making of MAHA Moms, Anti-Vaxxers, and Housewife Insurrectionists

On an unseasonably warm January morning in 2025, Robert F. Kennedy Jr. walked into the Dirksen Senate Office Building in Washington, DC, to begin confirmation hearings as Trump's nominee for the head of the Department of Health and Human Services.[1] The nomination was, to put it lightly, a controversial one. Kennedy had spent the past two decades promoting conspiracy theories about childhood vaccines, such as the debunked belief that the MMR shot causes autism;* he also dabbled in AIDS denialism and the theory that chemicals in water[2] were turning children transgender.

---

* The belief that vaccines caused autism started circulating in the late 1990s, when a British physician named Andrew Wakefield published a paper in the medical journal *The Lancet* linking the MMR vaccine to autism. The paper was widely discredited, with *The Lancet* eventually retracting it after finding its results were fraudulent. But that didn't stop it from gaining purchase in certain vaccine-skeptical circles on the internet, where it is still received as gospel twenty-five years later. [Laura Eggertsen, "*Lancet* Retracts 12-Year-Old Article Linking Autism to MMR Vaccines," *Canadian Medical Association Journal* 182, no. 4 (February 4, 2010): E199–200. https://pmc.ncbi.nlm.nih.gov/articles/PMC2831678/.]

But when Kennedy strode into the Dirksen building that January morning, the gallery erupted in cheers, as if the star quarterback had strutted into the pep rally after winning the homecoming game.[3] Many were women—some holding babies, some shouting, "We love you, Bobby!" and "MAHA!"[4]—short for Make America Healthy Again, Kennedy's unofficial campaign slogan when he'd first endorsed Trump[5] the year prior.[6] They included Jessica Reed Kraus, a former mom blogger and influencer who'd spent the past year slavering after Kennedy on the campaign trail;[7] Vani Hari, an Instagram influencer with millions of followers known as the Food Babe, who was accompanied by her eight-year-old daughter;[8] and Megyn Kelly, the former Fox News host.[9]

These women were part of a group known as the MAHA moms, the media's terminology for female RFK supporters. This was not their first public event: they'd all gathered to celebrate Trump's win a week prior at the MAHA Ball, a lavish event at the Waldorf Astoria featuring seed oil–free hors d'oeuvres like lobster, steak, and gluten-free butternut squash.[10,11] Photos from the event had appeared on my Instagram feed, featuring gorgeous women in jewel-toned dresses, ombré-haired and tawny-limbed and pillow-lipped.

They were yoga teachers, natural herbalists, integrative medicine specialists, special ed teachers. They were "content creators" with hundreds of thousands of followers, hawking aluminum-free deodorant or detox smoothies or hair growth supplements or chemical-free skin care regimens* on Instagram; or exhausted single moms, desper-

---

* Press images from celebratory RFK events, such as the 2025 MAHA Ball, appear to bely this somewhat. Most of the female supporters in attendance appeared to have gotten an extensive amount of filler in preparation for the event, their foreheads injected with enough botulinum to kill a D-I lacrosse team.

ate to speak on behalf of those who could not speak for themselves. They were rich and poor,* white and Black,† stay-at-home moms and high-powered career women.

Above all else, the MAHA moms were apolitical—or at least, they had been prior to RFK's presidential run the year before. The MAHA movement was "a call to arms," as Jacqueline Capriotti, the former communications director for Kennedy's New Jersey campaign, later put it. The mother of a twenty-nine-year-old son with cystic fibrosis, Capriotti had never been involved in politics until she saw Kennedy announce his candidacy in a 2023 speech.

"Women and mothers are starting to wake up," she told me.[12]

They saw themselves as fierce advocates for their children, many of whom had autism or diabetes or debilitating allergies—chronic conditions that Kennedy claimed could have been prevented, had they not been brainwashed by Big Food and Big Pharma to eat unhealthy food and take unnecessary medications.[13] For years, these women said, they'd fought to make their concerns about their children's health heard, and in return had been dismissed by Democrats and Republicans alike as crackpots, zealots, conspiracy theorists. But not Bobby, as many of the women volunteering on his campaign referred to Kennedy. Bobby listened. Bobby cared. Bobby heard.

On the Senate floor, the MAHA moms—or "mama bears," as some of them proudly called themselves—filled the floor, taking selfies and shouting, "We love you, Bobby!" and "Confirm him!" They viewed Kennedy as nothing less than a savior for American children—a totally nonpartisan cause, as they saw it, and they couldn't believe anyone would view it otherwise. After years of being

---

* But mostly rich.

† But mostly white.

"mocked, gaslit, silenced, and bullied" by the medical establishment, as one woman told me,[14] the MAHA moms had finally come to Washington to prove, once and for all, that hell hath no fury like a mama bear scorned.

* * *

The media first started seriously covering the rise of MAHA moms in early 2025, a few months after Trump's reelection. They breathlessly quoted soccer moms and yoga influencers singing Kennedy's praises, framing them as guardians of gentle domesticity who "post videos explaining their politics while cooking dinner or resting a swaddled baby in their arms," as a *Guardian* trend piece put it.[15] People seemed shocked that Kennedy would resonate with crunchy moms and babywearers, particularly in light of several public scandals, including one extremely weird story involving a bear carcass in Central Park.[16] But Kennedy's popularity among the MAHA mom contingent did not surprise me. I'd seen it all before, albeit in a slightly different context.

In March 2020, when Covid hit, I was a writer at *Rolling Stone*, focusing on internet culture and trends. A month or two into quarantine, I started seeing momfluencers—women who had previously only posted lactation cookie recipes and how to turn your baby's nursery the perfect shade of beige—posting about QAnon, the pro-Trump conspiracy theory positing that Democratic establishment figures like Hillary Clinton were involved in a secret child trafficking ring.[17]

Prior to the pandemic, QAnon followers tended to be white male MAGA heads who'd flock to semi-obscure internet communities like 4chan to decipher Trump's tweets using numerology and "secret codes"—sort of like Swifties, except more anti-Semitic and into posting fly-fishing memes on Facebook. But it was largely viewed as a fringe theory until 2020, when the world shut down and people started plummeting down internet rabbit holes about Democrats kidnapping children from Walmart.

Mothers seemed particularly vulnerable to this messaging. Because schools were closed, mothers assumed most of the domestic and childcare labor and struggled more than ever to keep their heads above water. Many were also concerned about how things like school closures and mask mandates would impact their children's development. All of a sudden, the movement became flooded with what Will Sommer, author of *Trust the Plan: The Rise of QAnon and the Conspiracy That Unhinged America*,[18] describes as "mama bears": "[T]he idea of a mandatory vaccine to go to school set off a lot of moms who were already steeped in anti-vaccine stuff or were just getting into it," he says. "So it was kind of a perfect storm for a lot of moms to get into conspiracy theories."

After Trump lost the 2020 election, interest in the QAnon conspiracy theory seemingly ebbed. For a short period of time, it seemed the QAMom—a term I coined in a 2020 *Rolling Stone* article on the subject[19]—was just a blip on the radar. But this turned out to be overly optimistic. Following the 2020 election, right-wing "mama bear" organizations like the lobbying group Moms for Liberty started popping up to campaign against life-saving gender-affirming health care for trans youth, referring to LGBTQ+ adults as "pedophiles"[20] and "groomers,"[21] and spewing transphobic hate at school board meetings. The anti-trans, anti-LGBTQ+ rhetoric spearheaded by Moms for Liberty ushered in a slew of legislation aimed at curbing transgender people's rights, as well as people calling in anonymous bomb threats to hospitals treating queer kids.*[22]

Mothers were also instrumental in the events leading up to the January 6 attack on the Capitol, such as mother/daughter duo Amy and Kylie Jane Kremer, who, with their group Women for America First, helped organize the "Stop the Steal" rally that preceded the riot.[23] (They later distanced themselves from the violence, claiming it was perpetuated by "bad actors."[24]) Jean Lavin and her daughter, Carla Krzywicki, also pled guilty to parading, demonstrating, or picketing in a Capitol building after posting a Facebook photo from inside.[25] One Pennsylvania mother of eight was caught on camera directing protesters via a bullhorn and using a battering ram to smash in the building windows.[26] Overall, more than one hundred

---

* For all its talk about promoting family values, Moms for Liberty has been implicated in its fair share of salacious scandals. In 2024, cofounder Bridget Ziegler, who was active in promoting Florida governor Ron DeSantis's anti-LGBTQ+ "Don't Say Gay" legislation, was implicated in a Florida criminal investigation after a woman accused Ziegler's husband of sexually assaulting her and recording her without consent. (He said the relationship was consensual.) According to the police report, the Zieglers had previously engaged in group sex with the woman, and Bridget regularly instructed her husband to pick up women for threesomes at local bars, saying, "Don't come home until your dick is wet." The police did not pursue charges against the couple. [Samantha Riedel, "New Report Reveals a Florida GOP Power Couple's Possibly Criminal Threesome Sex Tape Scheme," Them, May 17, 2024, www.them.us/story/christian-ziegler-briget-threesome-sex-tape-police-report-investigation; Bon Norman, "Sex, Barflies, and Videotape: Report Details How GOP Power Couple Prowled Pubs for Threesome Partners," Florida Trident, May 16, 2024, https://floridatrident.org/sex-barflies-and-videotape-report-details-how-gop-power-couple-prowled-pubs-for-threesome-partners/.]

women were charged in connection to the Capitol riots, with one report finding that women played a "front-facing role" and put a "friendly face" on the attacks.[27] By the time white women went for Trump in the 2024 election,[28] it was clear they were being underestimated by the mainstream media at its own peril.

All of this was fascinating to watch, for a few reasons. As a reporter at *Rolling Stone*, I'd spent the first half of my career watching extremism take root on encrypted messaging apps like Telegram and anonymous forums like 4chan, where mostly male posters spewed hatred about Jews and Black people and queer people. Now all of a sudden, I was watching the same types of messages going viral on mainstream social media platforms like Instagram, Tik-Tok, and Facebook. They were making TikToks claiming the Trolls franchise promoted pedophilia,[29] or posting about how they were boycotting Disney because the corporation endorsed grooming. Except the people sharing these messages weren't angry young white men with greasy hair and acne-scarred faces but moms just like me, except with veneers and more expensive haircuts.

Not only was I watching the face of American extremism change seemingly overnight—I was watching the definition of what it meant to be a "good" or "bad" mother change as well.

For years, the consensus in this country has been that a mother's job is, ostensibly, to protect her children at all costs. There are other factors, but they are largely cosmetic; ultimately, the distinction between "good" and "bad" comes down to the ability to shield one's offspring from the abject horrors of the world.

But as the political climate becomes more fractured and the world more terrifying to navigate, this has become increasingly difficult to do. And as mothers on the right lead the charge in attempting to "protect" their children from an unseen enemy—from so-called groomers, or Democrat traffickers, or the government, or vaccines—they ultimately, and ironically, end up making their children far less safe.

We've seen this happen countless times: in the heartbreaking tales of Daisy and Kayley, an eight-year-old and a six-year-old who died of measles in early 2025 after their parents refused to have them vaccinated.[30] We see it in the story of Rebecca Vance, the Colorado mom who became so deeply invested in "Great Reset" conspiracy theories, or the belief that elites were plotting to take over the world, that she moved her thirteen-year-old son, Talon, to the wilderness, the two of them ultimately dying of malnutrition and hypothermia in early 2023.[31] Or the tragic story of Danielle Johnson, the astrology influencer who became obsessed with QAnon conspiracy theories and tossed her eight-month-old infant out of a moving car on the freeway, fatally crashing into a tree minutes later.[32]

Over the past few years, there have been countless examples of these types of narratives in the media, of mothers who have been so radicalized by right-wing conspiracy theories that they ultimately end up harming their children. But this radicalization occurs in less extreme ways as well—and often, it happens for extremely understandable, even sympathetic, reasons.

I think it's very hard for people to admit this to themselves, especially in such a polarized political climate. As mothers, they are so invested in instilling positive moral values in their children that it's easy to demonize those on the other side of the aisle who are attempting to do the exact same thing, even if they fervently disagree with those values. But I've seen this trajectory unfold enough in real time to know how easy it is for bad actors to prey on women's anxieties about being good mothers, and how rapidly people can fall down rabbit holes. It's easy to dismiss the MAHA moms and QAnon Karens of the world as horrible people. It's a lot harder to acknowledge the reality: that when women become so consumed by the desire to be good mothers, so unilaterally focused on protecting their children from both the real and imagined horrors of the world, that they may find themselves becoming the worst kind of all.

* * *

Moms have played an important role in the far-right extremism space since well before the ascendance of the QAMoms and MAHA mama bears. During the early twentieth century, for instance, women and children were heavily involved in the Ku Klux Klan's activities, with the organization enlisting children to pass out pamphlets at cross burnings[33] and ride on parade floats beneath a "Ku Klux Kiddies" banner; one 1927 photo shows a group of Klansmen baptizing a seven-month-old infant, who is wearing a miniature Klan hood.[34] The women's chapter WKKK (Women's Ku Klux Klan) routinely planned weddings, funerals, and fundraising events for the KKK, as well as food drives to foster trust with the greater community.[35]

This has, weirdly, resulted in far-right communities being one of the few spaces where maternal labor is explicitly celebrated, rather than dismissed or ignored.[36] And this sense of validation can be extremely powerful for women. In Seyward Darby's book *Sisters in Hate: American Women on the Front Lines of White Nationalism*, which profiles three women in the white supremacist space, Darby speaks with a woman named Ayla Stewart, a trad wife influencer who goes by the handle @wifewithapurpose. Prior to becoming an anti-feminist influencer, Stewart self-identified as a crunchy granola type, posting raw food recipes and pursuing a master's degree in women's spirituality.[37] But she quickly realized there was no place in mainstream feminism for a stay-at-home mom like herself. "It didn't support me as a traditional mother [and] didn't consider my needs valuable," she said.[38] Stewart found a home and a sense of purpose in the white nationalist movement, where mothers are viewed as the "teachers, keepers, and defenders" of so-called traditional white American values.[39]

Though women enjoy a special role in white supremacist spaces, these communities are still inherently misogynistic, which means they rarely assume leadership roles or wield any power. The anti-vaccine movement, however, is an exception to this rule. A 2017 study looking at data from anti-vaccine content on Facebook found that the vast majority of those posting anti-vaccine messaging were women.[40] Another 2022 study found that most anti-vaccine influencers use maternal imagery in their marketing to target anxious mothers, employing such tropes as the "protective" and "doting" mother to encourage women to adopt a "feminine, intuitive, holistic approach" to their children's care.[41]

It's hard to draw a straight line between far-right extremism or white supremacy and anti-vaccine views; in my experience, it's more like two overlapping circles in a Venn diagram, with people tending to gravitate toward the center the longer they spend in the community. Not every mom who chooses not to vaccinate is affluent, conservative, and/or white; and not every mom who is pro-vaccine *isn't* those things. But it is true that the widespread cultural perception of anti-vaccine mothers is that they are upper-middle-class suburban women, whose affluence, selfishness, and helicopter parenting tendencies drives them to put the health of others at risk.* They're often referred to in the same breath as the "Karen" archetype, a meme referring to a white woman in her thirties or forties who "is a pseudoscientist/anti-vaxxer/flat-earther, an MLM participant, [and] an avid user of Facebook to post shitty motivational posts/'Live Laugh Love' [memes]," as one Redditor put it in a 2020 *Vox* article.[42]

To be fair . . . there *is* some truth to this. Some studies have shown that anti-vaccine parents tend to be white, college-educated, and wealthy, which certainly encompasses the Karen archetype as well as many of the MAHA moms who attended Kennedy's confirmation hearings. This demographic has also been referred to as "Whole Foods moms,"[43] suburban women who can afford to spend $15 on organic strawberries but whose aversion to chemicals and pesticides does not extend to, say, getting fillers or an upper-eye blepharoplasty. There is also, indubitably, a certain degree of self-absorption required to make medical choices that put the health of other community members, including medically compromised children and newborns too young to be vaccinated, at risk.

---

* This perception is so widespread that there's even an academic study about it: a 2022 paper titled "Good Karen, Bad Karen: Visual Culture and the Anti-Vaxx Mom on Reddit." It found that most memes mocking anti-vaxxers depict them as "white cisgender heterosexual" women; notably, the study's coauthors write, "[W]hile one might expect the presence of two or more parents in a discourse so heavily tied to children's health, fathers are comparatively absent." [Miranda J. Brady et al, "Good Karen, Bad Karen: Visual Culture and the Anti-Vaxx Mom on Reddit," *Journal of Gender Studies* 32, no. 6 (2023): 616–31. https://www.tandfonline.com /doi/full/10.1080/09589236.2022.2069088.]

But it's also true that as the movement has evolved, the picture of the anti-vax "Whole Foods mom" has become a lot more complex. For instance, though most research focusing on the anti-vaccine community has promoted the idea that the majority of women in it are white, this is not entirely true. As early as 2017, a Pew Research study found that Black parents were less likely than white parents to see the health benefits of the MMR vaccine and more likely to consider the risks of potential side effects. In a 2022 *Gender and Society* paper analyzing anti-vaccine sentiment among Black women on social media, coauthors Jennifer A. Reich and Courtney Thornton detailed some of these concerns, writing that Black mothers' decisions about whether to vaccinate their kids were highly informed by "experiences with structural gendered racism in interactions with healthcare and education systems," viewing childhood vaccines as "extensions of state power that are alienating and disempowering."[44]

Honestly, it's hard to argue these concerns aren't valid. From the Tuskegee experiments of the mid-twentieth century to the fact that maternal mortality rates are three times higher for Black mothers than they are for women of other races,[45] it is easy to understand why a Black mother would feel unsafe navigating the US health care system in virtually any capacity, and would be vulnerable to misinformation.*

---

* Kennedy in particular has played a huge role in targeting the Black community with anti-vaccine messaging. In 2021, his organization Children's Health Defense released a fifty-seven-minute anti-vaccine documentary targeted at the Black community, *Medical Racism: The New Apartheid*, which (falsely) suggests that Black children are at increased risk of autism due to vaccination. [Will Stone, "An Anti-Vaccine Film Targeted to Black Americans Spreads False Information," NPR, June 8, 2021, https://www.npr.org/sections/health-shots/2021/06/08/1004214189/anti-vaccine-film-targeted-to-black-americans-spreads-false-information.]

"The structural racism that shows up in hospitals and health care institutions has been an under-examined contributor to how people die," the reproductive justice scholar Monica McLemore explained when I spoke to her a few years ago. "If Black people are less likely to be believed, either in recognizing their own symptoms or in explaining to their health care [providers] what their symptoms are, and they don't receive the care they need, what are they supposed to do?"[46]

Additionally, though it is not as endemic as it is in the Black community, the phenomenon of women's pain being dismissed or ignored by medical providers is well-documented: multiple studies have shown that women on average receive less treatment for chronic pain conditions than men, as well as less intensive and effective pain relief care.[47] This is particularly true for soon-to-be mothers, with 20 percent of women and 30 percent of Black women reporting mistreatment by their doctors during labor and delivery.[48]

With so many women having negative experiences with the health care system, it's far from surprising that many of them develop skepticism or outright hostility toward medical providers. This can manifest itself in various ways, but one of the most frequent outcomes is vaccine hesitancy, according to a 2023 study from the University of Maine, which interviewed anti-vaccine mothers between the ages of twenty-five and sixty. The study found that the majority of women who were vaccine-hesitant had experienced some form of "ongoing and repeated instances of medical harm they experienced from childhood through childbirth," ranging from being threatened with institutionalization to forced Pitocin administration during labor. One antivaccine mom reported having a rectal exam performed on her without her consent when she was just twelve.[49]

Often, however, it's not one single experience with the health care system that results in radicalization. Usually, it's an aggregate of different encounters with the medical field. I spoke with one MAHA mom, Ceara Foley, who served as a southeastern field director for Kennedy's ill-fated presidential campaign. She said she started questioning vaccines relatively early, believing she developed rheumatoid arthritis in part as a reaction to a childhood inoculation. When her daughter was four months old, Foley noticed she was having trouble breathing, so she rushed her to her pediatrician's office. The doctor diagnosed Foley's daughter with asthma and suggested medication. Foley took her daughter home and "tried some natural things," but she didn't seem to get better, so she took her back a week later. This time, another doctor at the practice said her daughter was fine, characterizing Foley as "just a nervous new mother."

"[The doctor] just completely shamed me," Foley recalled. "They were like, 'You're a nervous new mother.' [My] experience was I had to figure out everything on my own."

Foley later discovered there was mold in their home that was causing her child to have trouble breathing; once it was removed, her daughter seemed to get better.[50]

Foley had always been skeptical about mainstream medicine and interested in alternative treatment methods. But the experience with her daughter's breathing problems deepened her distrust. So, like many MAHA moms, she did her own research, leading her to decide not to vaccinate her daughter. Through her research, she became friends with dozens of other moms of kids with autism, with childhood cancer, with type 2 diabetes, many of whom attributed their children's health issues to vaccines.

"These women have watched their children get ill," she explained. "They've been through a lot of fear. They've watched their children die, and they've been silenced and shamed and mocked and gaslit for a very long time by the medical industry."[51] When Kennedy announced he was running for office in 2023, she says, she and the other MAHA moms instantly supported him: "He was a champion for those women who saw that something was wrong with their child, and nobody else was listening to them."[52]

Over the course of the past ten years or so, I can't tell you how many of these stories I've heard: a mother with an ill or disabled child desperately searching for answers, finding them in places far outside the mainstream medical establishment. Often, they were driven by desperation, a need to believe any explanation, no matter how outlandish, to explain their children's pain.

In early 2025, for instance, *New York* magazine covered a group of moms featured in *The Telepathy Tapes*, a popular podcast premised on the belief that nonverbal autistic children who cannot communicate via any other means can do so via telepathy. Though there is no evidence that this is true, the mothers quoted in the piece are desperate to hold on to any form of hope that they can communicate with their children, no matter how outlandish, that they are virtually forced to believe it. (It is no surprise that some of the moms quoted in the piece also harbor the belief that vaccines caused their children's autism.)

In one heartbreaking moment, writer Liz Weil visits a woman named Manisha, whose twenty-three-year-old son is minimally verbal, to test whether her son is truly telepathic. When he fails to demonstrate his abilities, Manisha is devastated. "'This has opened up my child to me. This is working,'" Weil quotes Manisha as saying, describing her belief in telepathy as "the necessary terms of her universe, one in which she is profoundly and inalienably bonded to her son."

"'If you are telling me this is not working, what else do you have that works? Give me that. I tried everything. I have tried *everything*.'"[53]

Another such example is the story of a woman I'll call Becca, a mom of two boys who were diagnosed with autism when they were quite small. According to Becca, both of her kids had developed normally, hitting their milestones and learning how to walk and talk. But after they received the MMR vaccine when they were eighteen months old, she says, they "regressed," developing rashes and losing the ability to walk and talk.*

"Mainstream doctors had no answers for me," she told me. "I was desperate. Then I found other moms on the internet who were going through other things I was going through." After poring through journals and studies of varying degrees of legitimacy and connecting with other moms of "vaccine-injured"† children on Facebook, she became convinced that the MMR vaccine had caused

---

* Many anti-vaccine parents have similar stories like this, reporting their children started showing signs of autism after they got their first dose of the MMR vaccine at twelve to fifteen months old. The consensus among medical experts, however, is that this has less to do with the side effects of the vaccine itself and more to do with the fact that children with autism tend to start exhibiting symptoms around that same age.

† "Vaccine-injured" is a popular term within the anti-vaccine community, as is "vaccine-critical" or "vaccine-skeptical" as opposed to simply "anti-vaccine," which most of those within the community consider extremely pejorative. "I do think anti-vaxxer is used in the same way as words that were used for people who have different sexual preferences or different races," Becca told me when I interviewed her. Because this is, in my opinion, an insane thing to say, and because there is little substantive difference between the language and arguments used by "vaccine-skeptical" individuals and anti-vaxxers, I have opted to use the latter term.

her sons' autism, and she became a prominent lobbyist for the anti-vaccine movement.

In listening to the stories of women like Becca and Manisha, I'm always struck by two things. The first is that they are hyper-cognizant of the fact that most people view them with skepticism at best, and outright contempt at worst. "I don't know any other issue where we have more women screaming for people to listen and we are constantly ignored," Becca told me.

They usually attribute this skepticism to one factor: sexism. "If we had a movement of dads that was worried about the health of our children, it would be an entirely different scenario," Ceara Foley told me.[54]

The second thing I am struck by, though, is how clear and cogent these women sound when they describe how they arrived at their beliefs, and how deeply they felt betrayed by the medical establishment. And though I think it's disingenuous to attribute people's resistance to their messaging entirely to sexism, I have to be honest: I also don't think they're entirely wrong. I believe they are taken less seriously because they are mothers because I'm a mother, too, and I know what it's like to feel utterly isolated and failed by a system you have naively always believed would protect you.

To be clear, I think what these women are doing is horrifying. Not only are they peddling nonevidence-based propaganda that puts the lives of vulnerable children at risk, but they are also, consciously or not, preying on other mothers clinging to literally any explanation to make sense of the inexplicable. (And, to top it all off, they're using misogyny as a shield against criticism.) I do not think these women are unfairly stigmatized by society. They deserve every amount of the pushback they get for promoting their dangerous views.

But when they say the system has failed them and their children, I believe them. When they say people are less likely to listen to them because they are mothers, I believe them. I believe them because I'm also a mother who has shouted into a void, imploring people to believe me when I said my child needed help—and I know how frustrating it is not to be listened to, how isolating it is to struggle alone, and how tempting it can be to think that you've finally found some answers. I believe women like Becca and the MAHA moms are predators, plain and simple—but I also believe that they are victims.

*   *   *

A few years before I watched the MAHA moms congregating around RFK Jr. during his confirmation hearing, listening to him spout misinformation about vaccines and antidepressants and Lyme disease* and wondering how his parasitic brain worm had somehow managed to self-replicate and slither its way into millions of other people's heads, I was a mom trying to find my own answers.

When Harry was almost three years old, his teacher mentioned on the first day of preschool that he struggled with transitions be-

---

* One of the most unintentionally (and darkly) hilarious moments of the confirmation hearings was when Colorado senator Michael Bennet asked Kennedy about a past comment he had made, that it is "highly likely" that Lyme disease is a bioengineered "military weapon." Rather than walk back his comments or deny that he had made this absolutely batshit assertion based on zero evidence, Kennedy conceded that it did, indeed, sound like something he might say. ["Colorado Senator Asks RFK Jr. If He Said Pesticides Make Kids Trans," posted January 29, 2025, by WFAA, YouTube, https://www.youtube.com/watch?v=_guKswjrI1I.]

tween activities, as well as alternating his feet to climb the stairs, and she also found it concerning that he wasn't speaking in full sentences yet. When I brought it up to our pediatrician, she gave us a reference for an early intervention evaluation. The first time he got an evaluation, he didn't qualify, but something in my gut told me to demand another one a few months later. This time, he did. He was assigned an OT, a speech therapist, and a special education teaching assistant.

Various prospective diagnoses were thrown around, each more obscure and terrifying than the last: Did he have SPD? PDD? OCD? ADHD? ASD? ODD? My life as a parent, which had previously been relatively unmarked by medical intervention, became a whirlwind of specialists and doctor's appointments and neuro-psychological assessments and uncomfortable, euphemism-filled conversations with teachers. I'd sit there, taking notes and holding back tears, and then I'd come home and report back what I'd learned to my husband and family members, who told me I was being overly anxious and Harry's teachers didn't know what they were talking about.

For years, it felt like I occupied two different realities: one where I was constantly being told I wasn't doing enough to help my child and another where I was told that I was doing far too much. It felt a little bit like that GIF from *Curb Your Enthusiasm* where Larry David is standing between a group of angry Jews and a group of equally enraged Muslims in the parking lot of his favorite Palestinian chicken restaurant, and he's trying to decide which side to go to.[55] It's possibly the clearest visual representation of what it feels like to be a mother in the United States: No matter how hard you do or don't try, everyone is always mad at you.

At the same time, I was also trying to sift through various therapeutic options for Harry, weighing which ones were legitimate and which ones were snake oil. I realized there was an entire industry built on the wallets of parents like me, who knew their kid needed extra support and would pay any amount of money to try to help them. There were vision therapists, executive functioning coaches, parent-child-interaction therapy providers who watched me and Harry play with his Paw Patrol toys on Zoom and gave me instructions via earpiece for how to talk to and play with him, like Cyrano de Bergerac for stressed-out moms.

It was all so exhausting and terrifying that I tried to tell myself what everyone else in my life seemed to be saying: That it was nothing; that Harry was just "quirky"; that he didn't need a ton of extra support or a diagnosis. One of his therapists, apparently sensing my anxiety, told me that I should think of the services as a temporary stopgap measure, so Harry could be more "normal" when he got older. He talked about Harry not as if he were my child, my world, my everything—a beautiful, silly boy with chestnut curls who shook all over when he was excited and loved chasing our cat and giving people hugs and kisses—but as if he were a broken toy that needed to be fixed. Still, I am ashamed to admit that I thanked him for saying this. I am even more ashamed to admit that I believed him.

A few months after Harry started receiving services, Covid-19 hit. My first and only thought after the offices and schools closed, and people started hoarding toilet paper and wiping down their groceries and leaning out their windows to cheer on health care workers, was: *What is going to happen to Harry? What is this going to do to him? Is he only going to get worse? How did this happen? How had I failed him, and what could I do to ensure I not fail him now?*

I fell into an internet rabbit hole, searching every single thing he did or said to find an answer to this question. I quickly realized that for every snake-oil salesman out there looking to profit off parental anxiety, there were about four hundred people on the internet eager to do the same thing. There was no shortage of explanations for kids' developmental delays, from vaccines to environmental toxins to the Tylenol I took for a headache once during my pregnancy. And there was no shortage of very expensive solutions, from supplements to heavy metal detoxes to gluten-free diets to raw camel milk. It was probably when I started seeing moms in Instagram comments recommend bleach enemas that I vowed never to use Google as a health care resource again.

I stopped eating and I stopped sleeping and I stopped talking about anything other than my concerns for my child's development, trying to find reassurance that Harry would be OK, though I had no idea what that actually meant, or what that actually looked like. For other mothers, hitting rock bottom may look like posting about sex trafficking conspiracy theories or how "toxins" in artificial food dyes turn children gay. For me, it looked like losing ten pounds and having daily panic attacks before my therapist diagnosed me with OCD and put me on a shit-ton of medication. Worst of all, my relationship with Harry suffered. There was nothing he could do, no interaction we could have, that I would not see through the lens of his developmental issues. I loved him more than life itself, but it was impossible not to view everything he was as a clue, a puzzle piece, a lead to a solution to a problem that was, of course, not a problem at all.

There is a lot that happened between the pandemic and my writing this right now, years later, listening to Harry read *Pete the Cat and His Magic Sunglasses* to his little brother after a bath. But for the sake of both brevity and respecting Harry's privacy, I only feel it necessary to recount the following: Neither those who told me I had nothing to worry about, nor my OCD-addled brain, were right. Harry continues to have struggles, some of which are shared by every other kid on the planet, and some of which are beautifully, wonderfully unique to him. His various therapies were not a stop-gap, a Band-Aid to slap over my own parental anxieties en route to him becoming "normal." He is so much fucking better than normal. He is funny and observant and kindhearted and loving and pro-digiously talented and cool and passionate and obsessive and, very often, a huge pain in the ass. He drives me crazy, and he is also the most remarkable person I have ever known. And I swear to God, this is probably the most earnest sentence I will ever write, but it's 1,000 percent true: I wake up every morning and I go to bed every night thanking God that he is happy, healthy, and that I have the privilege to know him and, even better, to love and be loved by him.

This book largely explores the external factors that make moth-erhood in the United States as incredibly beautiful and incredibly difficult as it is. But there is one factor inherent to motherhood that can't be attributed to any nefarious outside forces, and that is fear. Fear is the control variable that unites us all, the fixed value in every equation. The fear of something bad happening to our children is what gets us out of bed in the morning, drives us to work and back home every day, motivates every decision we make, both good and bad. Fear is what drove Ceara Foley, the MAHA mom, to take her then-newborn daughter home from the hospital and vow never to subject her to medical interventions like vaccinations. "I immedi-ately started crying, because I realized I was going to be worried for the rest of my life," she told me. "I realized there was so much to worry about."[56] And it's what drove me to lose my mind a few years ago, because I believed people who told me my son was a problem to be solved, instead of the sweet, charming, beautiful, explosively gifted, occasionally infuriating little weirdo that he is.

I say all of this not to excuse my behavior or that of other mothers, but just to prove how terrifyingly easy it is to let that fear grip us and refuse to let go. And that's especially true if there are other people out there with a vested interest in keeping us afraid, in keeping us searching for explanations for the inexplicable.

Over the past few years as a reporter, I've watched with horror as this fear raises its ugly head. I've watched as the mothers responsible for the moral development of future generations have ushered in nothing but hate and dissent. I've watched so-called mama bears storm the capitol, shouting that they wanted to stop the steal and save the children while simultaneously putting them directly in harm's way. I've watched the "joyful warriors" in Moms for Liberty claim to protect their kids while quoting Hitler on Facebook.[57] I've gotten into countless rifts with momfluencers who, in disagreeing with my political views or my reporting, have attacked my own mothering, even my own children: the white supremacist who posted Instagram photos of Marco,[58] the anti-Semitic far-right podcast host who baselessly suggested to her millions of followers I was a pedophile;[59] the extremists who showed up to my office with picket signs calling me a demon, prompting my family to have to relocate to a hotel for the night.*[60]

I've seen fear morph into hate, and hate morph into fear, and pain and panic morph into real harm, over and over and over again. And with the Trump administration wielding unlimited power and

---

* They didn't like a movie review I'd written. Which is fair! I'm sure Gene Siskel got death threats for panning *Patch Adams*.

the MAHA moms gaining prominence on a national stage, it's only going to get worse before it gets better. My hope is that we are brave enough to hold people accountable for the harm they are doing, while simultaneously trying to understand what drives them to do it. We can hate them. We can judge them. We can think of them as stupid or even evil. But how can we blame them for being afraid? We all are.

10

Lighter, Easier,
and More Joyful

The Eternal Appeal of Trad Wives and Momfluencers

This is what a typical morning is like for Hannah Neeleman, better known as the influencer behind the handle @ballerinafarm. She wakes up early and heads over to her farm with her adorable, towheaded children, where she squeezes a fresh, frothy batch of milk and collects eggs from her hens. She then puts the eggs in a pristine ceramic bowl before kneading and scoring a loaf of sourdough. As her adorable baby naps in her high chair, Neeleman boils the eggs and saws off a slice of bread before making herself a pristinely composed slice of egg-and-sprouts toast, all set to the soundtrack of a jaunty swing tune by Benny Goodman. (Also, it's worth noting that she looks fucking amazing while doing all of this.[1])

Neeleman posted this video on Instagram in May 2023; as of this writing, it has almost a million likes and thousands of comments, many of which struck me on first glance as inexplicably irate. I scrolled through a few times, trying to figure out what her followers could potentially perceive as objectionable. Was it the shot of her baby napping in her high chair while she cooked? The way she boiled the eggs? Or was it the music? Had Benny Goodman been canceled postmortem without me realizing it?

I was wrong. A substantial chunk of the nearly four thousand comments on the post were from users complaining that Neeleman drank the milk without boiling it. At first, this surprised me—mostly because, as a born-and-bred urbanite, I would never have guessed that you had to boil milk fresh from a cow's (or in this case, sheep's) udder prior to consuming it. If you asked me anything about the details of the pasteurization process, I would not in a million years have been able to tell you. Frankly, if someone told me that the only way to safely drink cow's milk was to give the cow a little kiss on its cheek beforehand, I probably would have believed you.*

---

* Since Neeleman's 2023 post, the general public has learned more about the pasteurization process, whether they consented to or not, thanks to the rise of the raw-milk movement. Advocates of raw milk believe, without any real evidence, that drinking unpasteurized milk is healthier from a nutritional perspective than drinking pasteurized milk, and that state regulations requiring milk be pasteurized prior to consumption should be eliminated. This has become an extremely popular talking point among Trump supporters, even though the risks of drinking raw milk—including diarrhea, stomach cramps, vomiting, and in extreme cases, even kidney failure and death—are well documented. [Centers for Disease Control Food Safety, "Raw Milk," January 31, 2025, https://www.cdc.gov/food-safety/foods/raw-milk.html.] Neeleman has capitalized on this trend by selling jars of raw milk for $6 at a local farm stand, though they are unavailable for purchase online, likely due to federal law preventing the transportation of raw milk across state lines. [Lizzy Gulino, "Ballerina Farm's Raw-Milk Stand Is Open for Business," *The Cut*, April 9, 2025, https://www.thecut.com/article/ballerina-farm-selling-raw-milk.html.]

But on the other hand, the rage was not surprising at all. Neeleman is one of the most divisive figures on the internet, a willowy blond Juilliard-trained ballerina and pageant queen with the sun-kissed waves of a Malibu mermaid and the abs of a nineteen-year-old gymnast. She lives on a bucolic 328-acre Utah ranch with her eight children* and her husband, Daniel,[2] where she posts videos in her sun-drenched kitchen making stunning floral arrangements[3] or grilled cheese sandwiches with a homemade sourdough starter.[4] She has more than ten million Instagram followers,[5] enough to partner with brands like FedEx[6] and sell $74 Ballerina Farm–branded cookware on her website.[7] Her husband is rich† and gorgeous,‡ [8] her children flaxen-haired and well-behaved, her Kamas, Utah, farmstead well-appointed. As I write this, she just came back from attending cookery school in Ireland, where she learned to make something called "rose blossom meringue roulade."[9] Also, she has a lovingly hand-restored thirty-year-old Swedish AGA stove. It costs thousands of dollars, and its name is Agnes.[10]

More than perhaps anyone else on the planet, Neeleman is the ultimate demonstration of American motherhood: a beautiful blond stay-at-home mom who derives immense satisfaction from

---

* She delivered her eighth, Flora Jo, in her bathtub in front of her children. Two weeks after her delivery, she competed in Mrs. World, a beauty pageant competition for married women, donning a swimsuit and performing a dance routine to "Viva Las Vegas." She made it to the top 10. [Madison Malone Kircher, "She Gave Birth Two Weeks Ago. Now She's in a Beauty Pageant," *New York Times*, January 30, 2024, https://www.nytimes.com/2024/01/30/style/ballerina-farm-mrs-world-hannah-neeleman.html.]

† Daniel Neeleman is the son of JetBlue cofounder David Neeleman.

‡ Well, kind of. He looks like a beefier version of the comedian Michael Ian Black.

cooking, cleaning, child-rearing, and wearing an interminable selection of prairie dresses. She is also something of an unlikely political lightning rod. Her critics refer to her as a "trad wife,"[11] a term for a woman who embodies the ideals of conventional femininity and stay-at-home motherhood. Most trad wives on social media are, like Neeleman, thin, white, conventionally attractive young mothers in 1950s-style dresses, who film themselves making home-cooked meals from scratch while bouncing an infant on their hip.[12]

Reactions to trad wives on social media typically fall in one of two camps: people either find them genuinely aspirational, or creepy and problematic. This aligns pretty closely with how people feel about Neeleman. Some of her followers find her beautiful and inspiring; others are obsessed with tearing her apart. Her comments are replete with people castigating her for doing physical labor while pregnant or feeding her kids too many carbs or eating a hamburger while standing up.[13]

Many, if not most, of the critiques against Neeleman are legitimate. Is she promoting an overly idealized and restrictive version of motherhood for mass consumption? Absolutely. Should she be selling unpasteurized milk—essentially, bloody diarrhea in a mason jar—to her millions of followers? Probably not. Nonetheless, the critiques of Neeleman's brand are more often than not characterized by something akin to desperation. She inspires the kind of anguish more commonly associated with a Meghan Markle, or a Blake Lively—this sense that any woman who appears to check so many of the Good Mother boxes must actually secretly be a bad one.

The skepticism about Neeleman reached its apex in the summer of 2024, when the *Sunday Times* published an extensive interview with her and her husband, Daniel. Writer Megan Agnew visited Neeleman and her family at their Utah farm and came away with the impression that Neeleman was constantly "being corrected, interrupted or answered for by either her husband or a child," as she wrote in the piece. Agnew was particularly scathing toward Daniel, portraying him as misogynistic and controlling, a man who worked Neeleman to the bone and insisted she give up her ambitions to raise his children. Neeleman herself came off not as a beatifically happy pioneer woman but as an exhausted, overworked hausfrau.[14] (Neeleman denied this, calling the article "an attack on our family and my marriage.")

When the *Times* piece came out, many of Neeleman's fans defended her, accusing Agnew of projecting a feminist agenda onto the interview (Neeleman herself echoed this view in an Instagram Reel responding to Agnew's piece, expressing her belief that "the angle taken was predetermined."[15]) Neeleman's haters, however, responded by, essentially, gloating. They didn't seem overly concerned about Neeleman's mental health or that of her children, nor did they find it alarming that, as Agnew wrote in the piece, Neeleman was so exhausted by caretaking that she had to stay in bed a week at a time, or that she seemingly felt so pressured to give birth without pain medication that she kept it a secret from her husband.[16] They viewed it as nothing less than a vindication. "Oh my I'm eating up [this] Ballerina Farm article . . . it was only a matter of time," one X user wrote, including a GIF of a woman saying "Boom!"[17] Another TikToker posted a viral video mocking "white feminis[ts]" who felt sorry for the wealthy and privileged Neeleman, but had limited empathy for "brown women using tent scraps for their periods."[18]

To some extent, I understood this reaction. Before the *Times* piece came out, I, too, had spent many late nights scrolling through Neeleman's feed, vacillating between being furious at her for promoting a lifestyle I found unrealistic and anti-feminist, and secretly wondering whether I would be happier if I made choices similar to hers. I, too, had harbored fantasies about quitting my job and moving to the country and buying an extremely expensive stove and wearing corn-colored prairie dresses, wondering if my life could be as light, easy, and joyful as hers. True, these fantasies were relatively short-lived, and I immediately realized that the second I had spotty Wi-Fi or couldn't find a decent everything bagel, I'd run kicking and screaming back to New York, J.C. Wiatt–style. Still, I was no more impervious than anyone else to the narrative she was selling.

But I also knew that buying into Neeleman's narrative required a certain amount of suspension of disbelief. Enjoying Ballerina Farm's content means accepting the premise that everything she shows on Instagram is reflective of her reality, *and* that she chose that reality of her own volition. You have to believe that she *wants* to wake up at 4:00 a.m. and traipse through hen shit to collect raw eggs. To believe that this lifestyle can make you happy, you have to believe that it makes *her* happy.

The *Times* piece cast serious doubt on that premise. It implied that Neeleman had not willingly chosen her lifestyle at all; that she was nothing less than a hostage to her husband's desires. Of course, the primary reaction was schadenfreude. Agnew's piece lifted a previously impenetrable veil; the woman who had for years made mothers feel deficient had been exposed as deficient herself. And if that were the case for the Queen of the Trad Wives, then it had to be true for other momfluencers as well. It wasn't just Hannah Neeleman who had been dealt a blow. It was the entire online industry of performing good motherhood in itself.

* * *

The momfluencer industry is one of the largest and most misunderstood sectors of the social media ecosystem. It is also remarkably lucrative. Moms make up a huge swath of the consumer market, controlling about 80 percent of all household purchases, as reported by Taylor Lorenz, author of *Extremely Online: The Untold Story of Fame, Power, and Influence on the Internet*.[19] Over the past few decades, brands have taken advantage of this captive audience by partnering with momfluencers to target millennial and Gen Z women, resulting in billions of dollars of sales.

Momfluencing has always attracted women like Neeleman, stay-at-home moms who "had achieved successful careers before becoming mothers and held aspirations beyond homemaking," Lorenz writes in *Extremely Online*.[20] But in the early days, momfluencer content was a lot less polished and aspirational than it is today. Most started out as bloggers, like Heather Armstrong, the ex-Mormon housewife turned founder of the confessional, highly profane blog *Dooce*. Armstrong started *Dooce* a few years before she had her daughter.[21] When I spoke to her in 2018, she told me she pivoted to blogging about motherhood as a way to deal with her postpartum depression. "I felt alone and [I felt] very bad about being home by myself with her and I wanted to work," she said.

When *Dooce* took off, it gave Armstrong a way to profit off of the stereotypical roles that she felt constrained her. "I've made a business out of the thing that Mormonism taught me to do," she told me, "which is to love being a mother."[22]

Armstrong was, in many ways, perfectly equipped to dominate the momfluencing space. Willowy, blond, and classically gorgeous,

226 One Bad Mother

she fit the mold of what we expect momfluencers to be. But she was also an excellent writer, with a deeply wry voice that offered readers "solace, entertainment, and camaraderie during a period of life that was often isolating and overwhelming," Lorenz writes.*[23] Her early posts were unvarnished accounts of diaper blowouts and breastfeeding woes and postpartum sex mishaps, a warts-and-all depiction of motherhood that was totally absent from mainstream media at the time. Brands also took note, and in 2004, Armstrong became one of the first mom bloggers to make money from banner

---

* Aesthetically, and in terms of their respective voices, Armstrong and Neeleman could not be more different: One can hardly imagine Neeleman, in her Instagram captions, comparing breastfeeding to a man "lay[ing] out his naked penis on a chopping block, plac[ing] a manual stapler on the sacred helmut head, and bang[ing] in a couple hundred staples," as Armstrong did on her blog. [Heather Armstrong, "A Heartbreaking Work of Super Pooping Genius," *Dooce* (blog), February 9, 2004, https://dooce.com/2004/02/09/a-heartbreaking-work-of-super-pooping-genius/.] But they do share one major thing in common: They both grew up in the LDS church (though Neeleman continues to practice, and Armstrong had left before she started her blog).

Historically, Mormon women have long been attracted to mom blogging and momfluencing. This is likely because they tend to be highly educated but are encouraged to stay inside the home after getting married and having kids; therefore, social media has enabled them to carve out careers while simultaneously making space for their domestic obligations. LDS scripture also encourages church members to keep diligent records as a sacred practice [Terrence L. Szink, "Writing the Things of God," BYU, accessed July 22, 2025, https://rsc.byu.edu/living-book-mormon-abiding-its-precepts/writing-things-god)], an ethos that lends itself quite well to a job that requires professional oversharing.

ads, earning her hundreds of thousands of dollars in advertising revenue.[24]

Armstrong quit blogging in 2015, citing her mental health issues and the increasing toxicity of the internet. In 2023, after years of battling depression and alcoholism, she died by suicide at the age of forty-seven.[25] She played a huge role in inventing the modern-day creator economy. By proving to brands that forging intimate relationships with internet audiences can be profitable, and that authenticity can provide a pathway toward monetization, women like Armstrong were "among the first people to commodify themselves online," Lorenz writes.[26] And millions upon millions of people, mothers and non-mothers alike, have followed suit: The creator economy, as it is now called, was worth an estimated $250 billion in 2023.[27]

Since the early years of mommy blogging, creators have largely pivoted to image-based platforms like Instagram, where there is more of an emphasis on pristine aesthetics than an unvarnished view of motherhood. But a few things about the momfluencer industry have, for better or worse, stayed relatively consistent. Though the space has gotten more diverse in recent years, the most popular momfluencers are still women like Neeleman: white, thin, conventionally attractive stay-at-home mothers who hew to more traditional ideals of motherhood, says Sara Petersen, the author of *Momfluenced: Inside the Maddening, Picture-Perfect World of Mommy Influencer Culture.*

"There's this construction of the ideal American mother and in order to get into that club, you have to be not only white, but you have to be a certain social class, and you shouldn't be working outside of the home," says Petersen. "These racist ideologies are still deeply embedded in how we conceive of a good mother and a bad mother [online]."[28]

Many Black and brown momfluencers can attest to this, reporting getting less engagement and making less money—35 percent, according to one study—than their white counterparts.[29]

I spoke to a woman named Donnya Negera, a content creator with three kids and tens of thousands of followers across platforms, who is a stay-at-home mom with a successful diaper bag brand; a hot, doting husband; and brand deals with high-profile companies. She struck me as the platonic ideal of a brand-friendly momfluencer, yet even she said she struggled to make a living based solely on her influencer income. "Every brand has a budget cap, and they will literally disperse the majority of their money to white creators," said Negera. "People gravitate and engage more with white creators. So the brands are giving the money to where the audiences are."[30]

Shanicia Boswell, an entrepreneur and founder of the *Black Moms Blog*, agrees. She says that when she first started monetizing the website in 2016, she was offered $500 by a major baby carrier brand to do a series of Instagram and blog posts to promote the product. When she excitedly told her momfluencer friends about the deal, they were horrified by how much she had been lowballed. "They were like, 'With your following, with your engagement, this should have been a $10,000 deal,'" she told me. "But most influencers weren't talking about this back then, out of fear of shortening their check."[31]

* * *

There's another element of the online parenting space that has also, unfortunately, stayed consistent since the days of *Dooce* and "mommy blogging": A lot of people harbor contempt for momflu-encers.* Despite the enormous amount of money generated by the industry, as well as the labor required to build and maintain a social media brand,† momfluencers are often met with derision for fail-ing to do "real" jobs, feeding into age-old misogynistic stereotypes about women and work.‡[32] Mary-Katherine Fleming, a Georgetown and Wharton business school graduate who pivoted to influencing while working for the fitness-based multimedia platform Another Mother Runner, says that when she told her former business school colleagues she was a content creator, "They were like, 'That's really

---

* As arguably evidenced by the fact that the phrase "mommy blogging" exists. Malcolm Gladwell writes about parenting all the time, but no one ever calls him a "dad blogger" because he's a man who has written for the *New Yorker* and the most boring person you know quotes him on LinkedIn.

† A common misconception about the influencer space in general is that creators make tons of money off very little work. This is patently un-true, to the degree that Petersen says only about 9 percent of influencers make enough money to be able to support their families. Those who are fortunate enough to earn a living often have to put in incredibly gruel-ing hours. "For work that's so psychologically exhausting, like having to constantly figure out what parts of your authentic self you want to re-package and what you want to share with the rest of the world and what you want to keep private—those are shitty numbers," she said. [Petersen author interview, April 5, 2023.]

‡ I am using the phrase "momfluencer" not because I particularly love it but because it's much easier than writing "mothers who are also con-tent creators" or "moms on social media" over and over again. "Momflu-encer" is also a fairly broad term that encompasses all types of labor on the internet, from YouTube family vloggers to TikTokers to Instagram content creators to podcast hosts. So . . . get off my ass, please.

cute. You have a little hobby,'" she said. "I'm like, 'No, this is a business.'" When she started telling people she was an entrepreneur rather than a content creator, "They'd be like, 'Oh, you sell Avon?' No, I don't sell fucking Avon."[33]

Momfluencers are also subject to extreme levels of criticism for their parenting, from the food they serve their children to the clothes they wear to whether there are dirty dishes visible in the background. Blogs like *GOMIBLOG* (Get Off My Internets) and so-called snark subreddits focused on individual influencers have made mom-shaming a competitive sport. Some members of these subreddits have even resorted to extreme means such as contacting the police or CPS,[34] while drama YouTubers have built massive brands off criticizing the parenting of the same creators, over and over and over again.[35] There are countless stories of parenting influencers like Hannah Hiatt, a Utah-based nurse who went viral for a video showing dirty diapers strewn about her house. That video and another post, which appeared to show her son flinching when his father handed him a package at the grocery store, led many of her followers to call local police, prompting an investigation. (Hannah denied the allegations of abuse.*[36])

To an extent, this reaction is unsurprising: Most high-profile women on the internet face trolling and harassment, and mothers are no exception. Still, the level of cultural scrutiny reserved for momfluencers is extreme and somewhat disproportionate. True crime programs maintain an obsessive focus on criminals like Ruby Franke, the vlogger behind the now-defunct *8 Passengers*,

---

* As of this writing, no charges have been filed against Hiatt.

who was sentenced to more than four years in prison for child abuse after her son was found severely malnourished having been tied up in her home;[37] or Machelle Hobson, the mother of seven adopted children who, before her death in 2019, was accused of physically abusing them and forcing them to participate in her YouTube channel.[38] Movies like *A Simple Favor* depict momfluencers like Anna Kendrick's character Stephanie as conniving yet pathetic strivers, constantly mocked by other school parents and trying to hide her loneliness and desperation by pushing her zucchini chocolate chip cookies in front of a camera.[39] In an interview with Seth Meyers promoting the film, Kendrick herself professed to being perturbed by some momfluencers, calling them "creepy" and "dead-eyed."[40]

Petersen attributes the cultural hatred toward momfluencers as "anger that's misplaced—hatred for the ideal itself and hatred for the position that so many of us are in in this country. The influencer is just an easy target for us to level that rage and that resentment at."[41] And there's truth to that. After all, it's easy enough to feel like a failure as a parent without throwing Hannah Neeleman's rock-hard abs and flawlessly composed floral arrangements into the mix.

Over the past decade or so, however, this discourse has somewhat shifted. The question is no longer whether women like Neeleman are perpetuating oppressive and unachievable standards of motherhood; it's whether they should be posting at all. Specifically, there's debate around mom creators whose content relies on the participation of their children, who cannot provide active and informed consent to do so.

Sarah Adams, a.k.a. the TikTok creator mom.uncharted, is one of the primary figures behind this discourse. After the birth of her first child in 2017, she casually followed a handful of momfluencers, mostly for child-rearing tips. But during the pandemic, she noticed many of them were sharing content that made her uncomfortable, such as videos about their kids' medical diagnoses or showing them getting out of the bath. She was further horrified when she learned that the momfluencer industry is not subject to federal child labor laws, nor are children guaranteed compensation for their labor. While California law, for instance, dictates that guardians of child actors in Hollywood must put at least 15 percent of their income in a trust, it's only been until very recently that states have considered such legislation for the children of influencers.*

"I was like, 'I think we need to be having more conversations about this,'" she told me. "Because we all don't know how to raise kids in the digital world."[42]

Adams has more than 300,000 followers on her page, where she posts critiques of various momfluencers.[43] She usually doesn't refer to them by name for fear of indirectly encouraging her followers

---

* In September 2024, Governor Gavin Newsom signed a bill into law requiring channels that feature children in at least 30 percent of monetized content to set aside a percentage of the channel's earnings in a trust [California Legislative Information, Senate Bill No. 764, "SB-764 Minors: Online Platforms," September 27, 2024, https://leginfo.legislature.ca.gov/faces/billTextClient.xhtml?bill_id=202320240SB764]. The year before, Illinois had also passed a similar law [Samantha Murphy Kelly, "Illinois Passes a Law That Requires Parents to Compensate Child Influencers," CNN, August 16, 2023, https://www.cnn.com/2023/08/16/tech/kid-influencer-law/index.html], and numerous states are considering their own version of the legislation.

to harass them, nor does she think she is actively participating in mom-shaming by calling them out.

"I don't believe that the moms who are doing this are necessarily bad moms," she said of the women she critiques on her page. "I think maybe they're making a bad parenting decision. I try my best to really be mindful of my words, because women, specifically mothers, already get shit on enough on the internet."[44]

But Adams also believes that in an ideal world, all parents would take their children off the internet, full stop. There would be no family vlogs, no adorable infant TikTok accounts, no special-needs mom blogs—nothing. "With all of this, it comes down to, where's the line between what is beneficial to the parent, finding support or finding community, and being mindful of a child's right to privacy and informed consent and safety?" she said.[45]

What the anti-momfluencer argument boils down to is this: whether, by virtue of putting their children on the internet, momfluencers are prioritizing their own interests ahead of those of their families. And as we all know, that's not what a good mom is supposed to do—ever. This is the main reason why even women who closely hew to white heteronormative images of motherhood, such as Hannah Neeleman, get so much hate. Many of the comments on her Instagram account appear to be asking the same question: How can this woman possibly devote enough time and attention to her children while also making so much social media content and building a lifestyle brand? And why are these kids being monetized for the benefit of their parents when they can't provide consent to do so?

The first part of this question is easy to answer: Hannah Neeleman is rich. She has to be, in order to afford the lifestyle she maintains. And although we rarely see nannies or babysitters or caretakers of any kind in Neeleman's content, it's a relative certainty that they are getting a substantial amount of help offscreen. How else does a woman with eight children find the time to hit the gym, do her makeup, set up her shots, and film and edit hours of content? I have two children, and I usually don't have the time to take a shower without one of them pounding on the door and demanding I charge their Nintendo Switch, or remove a barely perceptible seed from an apple slice.

The second question, however, is more difficult. It's true that Neeleman has a financial incentive to incorporate her kids into her brand; after all, her adorable brood is one of the main reasons why people come to her page to begin with. And it's also true that her kids are probably too young to fully understand the implications of performing on camera for more than ten million people every day. Through this lens, the skepticism around momfluencing is justifiable: If good mothers are expected to sacrifice everything for the welfare of their children, why would they potentially embarrass them or exploit them or place them in harm's way for monetary gain—especially when it's related to something as frivolous as we perceive influencing to be? How dare mothers like Hannah Neeleman do absolutely everything we as a society tell wives and mothers they must do—cook like Ina Garten, look like Margot Robbie, parent like June Cleaver, dress like an American Girl doll, and fuck like a porn star*—and ask for compensation for the enormous labor that entails? How dare any mother demand compensation for anything?

We hate momfluencers for the same reason we hate stage mothers, or any mother who has the audacity to view parenting as

---

* (I'm assuming, given the eight kids.)

remotely transactional. Culturally, we view motherhood as a one-sided proposition; our reward for raising our kids is the joy we get from raising them. It's sort of like going into your boss's office and asking for a raise, and getting your workload doubled along with a pay cut. As much as people like to sympathetically cluck that motherhood is the hardest job there is, it's still the only one where the only reward for labor is more labor. And we are all supposed to not only be OK with that, but perform our gratitude every single day. If we fail to do so, or if we let the veil slip for even a moment, the consequences can be dire.

By monetizing the one job that is not supposed to be monetizable, momfluencers expose the fallacy that motherhood should be a reward unto itself. They sell a promise that keeps women scrolling and liking and buying branded crockpots, that motherhood can be inherently light, easy, and joyful if you embrace the labors that come with it without expecting anything in return. But their very existence proves that to be a lie. We don't hate Hannah Neeleman because she makes us feel bad about our cooking skills or our lack of taut abdominal muscles. We hate her because she forces us to reveal the truth: that we are all performing the light and easy joys of motherhood, every second of the day. But unlike her, we're doing it for free—and what's worse, we're not even doing it particularly well.

* * *

I'm a millennial mom, so I'm a member of the demographic targeted by brands that partner with Hannah Neeleman. I'm sure accounts like hers are the reason why I get served Instagram ads for weight loss drugs and organic food brands and $45 wooden beige baby rattles every day, even though I am not interested in any of those things. But I don't think I'm the target audience for her content. I don't find her aesthetic cozy or enticing. I find it exhausting. There are very few things I would rather do less than make lilac jelly or go on a transatlantic flight with seven children to learn about French dairy agricultural operations, as she documented in April 2023.*[46] Her posts remind me of precisely the domestic drudgery that I log onto Instagram and TikTok to avoid: the picking up, the putting away, the chopping, the stirring, the cutting, the pouring, the stooping, and the scurrying that constitute the physical act of mothering, the things I do every day that I, unlike her, do not get paid for.

It also disturbs me that there is an appetite for her specific brand of content—and as the cultural climate skews more conservative, that appetite is only growing. It is perhaps no coincidence that, in the year leading up to Trump's reelection, trad wife content exploded, funneling followers into an algorithmically driven, far-right content pipeline, according to a 2024 investigation by Media Matters.[47] Trad wives like Nara Smith, a model known for making Cheetos from scratch[48] while wearing brands like Rodarte and Chanel,[49] have exploded in popularity, accumulating millions of followers. Meanwhile, publications like *Evie* magazine—a right-wing *Cosmo* for

---

* I do, however, love that trips like this give Neeleman an opportunity to flex her creative writing muscles, as she demonstrated in an April 16, 2023, caption on a photo dump of the trip: "stomping through lush green pastures silhouetted against ancient castles, we peeked briefly into the agricultural engine that has propelled France's ambitions for hundreds of years." Does briefly peeking into the agricultural engine that has propelled France's ambitions for hundreds of years sound like a diverting family vacation to me? Absolutely not. Do I respect anyone attempting to start a sentence with a gerund? Sure do.

Gen Z that has published such headlines as "Why Getting Married Young Was My Best Decision Yet"[50] and "The Trad Wife Aesthetic Is Popular Because Women Are Tired of Ugliness"—have become increasingly popular, with its Instagram almost doubling its following[51] in the last year.*[52,53]

The glamorization of the young, beautiful, traditional housewife has neatly coincided with the rise of pro-natalism, a movement that promotes people having as many children as possible to boost flagging US birth rates.† Pro-natalism adherents, including Elon Musk and Vice President J. D. Vance, have repeatedly argued that women should have more children, with the implication being that marriage and motherhood take priority over work or individual self-fulfillment.[54] It's not surprising that trad wife content, which is predicated on making domesticity look as glamorous as possible, would be popular, and it's not surprising that Neeleman, a woman who is in many ways the embodiment of inherently racist and classist ideals of motherhood, would be popular as well.

But I also find it difficult to directly fault Neeleman for contributing to this climate. Her content is only implicitly, not explicitly,

---

* Coincidentally—or perhaps not so coincidentally—*Evie* magazine featured Neeleman as the cover star of a 2024 print issue, photographing her with her husband on her farm in a massive full-color spread. ["Ballerina Farm and the New American Dream," *Evie*, November 25, 2024, https://www.eviemagazine.com/post/ballerina-farm-and-the-new-american-dream.]

† Declining birth rates *are* a thing in the United States—for years, data has suggested that people are increasingly delaying having kids or opting out of parenthood altogether. But there's significant debate as to whether this is a problem, which typically breaks down alongside partisan lines. (Conservatives think it is; liberals, not so much.)

political; unlike many other influencers of her ilk, she doesn't quote Bible verses or advocate for delayed vaccination schedules or blame antidepressants for school shootings. She has given her audience no obvious reason to suspect that she is a harmful person; even if there are aspects of her content that do harm, it doesn't have any reflection on her character or her fitness as a mother. She is a symptom of a larger problem, not the problem itself.

My issue with momfluencers is more along the lines of a question that MK Fleming, the Wharton School grad, posed when I spoke with her. We were discussing how there were many things she loved about momfluencing—the money, the flexible hours, and finding a sense of community with other mothers. But over time, she said, she started to become uncomfortable with the expectation that she was supposed to share details with her audience about her children's lives. Once, she said, she mentioned offhand on a podcast she hosted that her daughter had unsuccessfully auditioned for a role in the school play; a few days later, Fleming was at the airport and was approached by a listener who asked how her daughter was coping with the rejection.

Fleming was floored. Up until that point, it hadn't quite occurred to her that finding communion with other mothers and profiting off it could potentially come at the cost of her children's privacy. "I thought, 'Is that something I really want? What am I putting out here?'" she recalls. She ultimately stepped away from the platform, rebranding as a fitness coach. Her audience is much smaller now, but she's OK with it. "You have to ask yourself: At what point does your story stop and someone else's start?"[55]

It's a complicated question, and it's one that, as the children of the OG momfluencers come of age, has been at the forefront of many of their minds. Cam, a twenty-six-year-old who uses she/they pronouns and goes by softscorpio on TikTok, grew up with their mother sharing images of them on MySpace and Facebook. They later testified on behalf of HB 1627, a Washington bill that, if passed, would give children of influencers the right to permanently delete their images from the internet once they reach adulthood. (The bill died in committee in 2023 but was reintroduced the following year.[56]) "I know firsthand what it's like to not have a choice in which a digital footprint you didn't create follows you around for the rest of your life," Cam said in their testimony.[57]

Even Heather Armstrong's daughter Leta, who is now in her early twenties, has spoken about the impact that her mother blogging about her had on her. "I was a little frustrated because, like, I have all this content being put of me online and sometimes it's not even accurate," she told NPR in 2023. "It's just embarrassing."[58]

As the cultural conversation about children's privacy and momfluencers evolves, some creators are drawing their own lines in the sand about where their stories end, and where those of their children begin. Amber Fillerup Clark, an outrageously photogenic mom of four* whose Instagram has more than one million followers, announced in 2021 that after years of posting her kids, she'd had an "epiphany" and decided to stop sharing images of them.[59] And Maia Knight, a single mother of twin girls who has amassed millions of followers on TikTok, announced in late 2022 that she had decided to stop showing her daughters' faces in her videos.[60]

Both of these decisions were, somewhat predictably, met with immense backlash. According to Clark, she lost around 100,000

---

* Who was also raised Mormon.

followers as a result of her decision to stop posting her kids,[61] while Knight was deluged with messages from fans. In a follow-up TikTok video, Knight framed her decision as "a choice for my daughters, to protect them."

"I'm not taking a big stance about showing your kids or not online," she said. "I'm just doing what's best for me and my daughters."[62] Nonetheless, mom-shamers continue to flock to Knight's page to criticize her for, among other things, letting her dogs play outside while she makes her kids breakfast,[63] painting squiggles on her children's playroom walls,[64] and tapping on an egg with a spoon before using it to make egg salad sandwiches.[65]

Many creators have addressed privacy issues and coping with the pressures of their platforms by stepping away from them altogether, in some cases leaving hundreds of thousands of dollars on the table in the process. This was, ultimately, what Heather Armstrong did when she stepped away from her own platform in 2015. When I spoke to her a few years prior to her death, she seemed uncomfortable with the industry she helped to build, referring to the shift toward pristine aesthetics as "the Pinterestification" of the parenting space. "I grew up and became successful in an age where we were seeking a community of people who were having a hard time," she told me. "Now it's all aspirational and put together. No one shows the side of the dirty room anymore."[66]

I don't think Armstrong would've loved creators like Hannah Neeleman making bank off only showing the clean side of the room. But I like to think that if the two ever met for coffee over Neeleman's heirloom hardwood table, if Neeleman asked her JetBlue Michael Ian Black husband to shove the kids in a room for a few minutes for some much-needed *Bluey* time, they would've had a lot to talk about: about being hot and growing up LDS, sure, but also about feeling judged, misunderstood, shamed, underappreciated. About thinking that you can have it all, and the crushing realization that you can't, not any of it, not even a very little bit, without being accused of taking too much for yourself.

11

The Rise of the Huns

In Defense of MLM Mommies

I t all started about six or seven years ago, when my mom started posting on Facebook about selling children's clothing.[1] The business wasn't her own, exactly—she was working as a representative for a company I'll call Totville,* buying clothes wholesale and selling them on social media. The posts showed cherubic children posing in various adorable outfits: ringleted girls wearing tie-dyed matching sets,[2] newborn babies in tie-dyed gowns and caps, looking like wizened mini-Dumbledores.[3]

When I first heard about my mom's involvement with Totville, I thought it could potentially be a great opportunity for her. Though she'd worked in corporate communications her entire adult life, she'd recently retired and didn't have a ton of outlets for her boundless amount of energy (to this day, I am not convinced that she is

---

* One may wonder why I chose the pseudonym "Totville" to refer to this particular company. The reason is actually quite stupid. I have a group chat with a bunch of my friends, and we've been referring to breasts as "tots" for the past decade, due to a spelling error one of us made in 2014. So think of "Totville" as an Easter egg, intended specifically for the purposes of eliciting a polite chuckle of recognition from six thirtysomething borderline alcoholics you will never meet.

biologically capable of REM sleep). Though she ping-ponged back and forth between volunteer positions at nonprofits and freelance gigs, she still seemed a bit adrift. Starting a side hustle seemed like a great way for her to harness her energy into pursuing what she had always told me was her dream of starting a children's clothing line. Also, she always had Totville clothes for Harry and Marco whenever she came over. Not having to go on Amazon and give Jeff Bezos $30 every time the boys grew out of a pair of Carter's sweatpants was a huge plus.

But as my mom started to get more and more involved with Totville, my sister and I got more and more concerned. It didn't seem like she was actually turning a profit: Though she was presumably spending hundreds, if not thousands, of dollars buying up inventory, every time I came over, I'd see piles of toddler-size sweatpants and hoodies lined up in her closet. "It's wholesale," she'd say when I asked her exactly how much she was spending on Totville clothes. "And I think it's a great product. And anyway, gotta spend money to make money!"

She also tried to rope me into helping her sell, posting fliers for Totville in the lobby of our apartment building and texting my friends with kids Harry's age. When I bristled at the prospect of inundating someone I barely knew with messages about a 20-percent-off deal on leggings or dresses, she'd get defensive. "This is my business," she'd say. "Why wouldn't you want to support me?"

Frankly, I didn't have a good answer for that. Yes, my mother's involvement with Totville had started to encroach on my life in increasingly irritating ways; and yes, I would have preferred for her to channel her passion and talent into starting her own business, rather than wasting her money and time promoting someone else's. But I also knew my mother had set aside her own ambitions in the process of raising us, and after decades of slaving away in the workforce, she was looking for something—anything—to give her a sense of purpose. She had given me everything—and now, she was also giving me free and/or heavily discounted clothes (even if the matching robin's-egg-blue tie-dyed sweatpants and hoodie sets were a little Susie Greene–esque for my taste). Who was I to piss on her parade?

One day, a few years into my mom's involvement with Totville, my sister, Sami, texted me. She'd been watching a documentary exposing LuLaRoe, a clothing brand valued at a billion dollars that's known for its "buttery soft" leggings.[4] LuLaRoe leggings were hugely popular but not available in any brick-and-mortar stores or directly for sale online: The company relied on direct-to-consumer marketing, meaning it recruited "consultants" to sell its products, and many critics were coming out of the woodwork to accuse its business practices of being predatory.[5]

Sami wanted to know the answer to a question we probably should've asked much sooner: "Is Totville an MLM?"

* * *

"MLM" stands for "multilevel marketing," a term used to describe a company that relies on tiers of vendors to sell their products, and recruit others to do so. Unlike a traditional, commission-based sales model, people involved in MLMs make money both on their own sales and the commissions they make off the new distributors they recruit.[6] Your recruits, as well as the distributors *they* recruit, are part of your "downline." LuLaRoe is an MLM, as was skin-care and cosmetics brand Rodan + Fields before it revised its business model in 2024;[7] so is doTERRA, which sells essential oils,[8] and Herbalife, the dietary supplement company.[9]

"The MLM model is built on the premise of rewarding people who recruit others who seek to be rewarded to pursue a business opportunity," William Keep, a professor of marketing emeritus at the College of New Jersey who studied MLMs, told me.[10]

MLMs have often been compared to "pyramid schemes," a business model that relies on a few people at the top recruiting an increasingly large number of members (hence, the "pyramid" structure). Per the Federal Trade Commission (FTC), there is a distinction, albeit a hazy one: "legitimate" MLMs can generate income based on sales of a specific product, while illegal "pyramid schemes" generate income primarily by offering promises of wealth based on how many members or investors you recruit. "If the MLM is not a pyramid scheme, it will pay you based on your sales to retail customers, without having to recruit new distributors," the FTC notes[11] (though sales across the MLM industry are usually self-reported, raising questions about the accuracy of most companies' figures[12]).

Whether MLMs are ethical, however, is an entirely different question. Though MLMs lure people in by promising they can make hundreds of thousands of dollars, most research indicates that only a very small percentage of people at the top actually do— in fact, the vast majority of those who get drawn into MLMs lose money.[13] "When you pursue a business opportunity in an MLM you yourself must maintain purchasing behavior," Keep explains. "You have to keep buying or you have to generate purchase volume from the people you recruit."[14] One of the primary slogans used by people in MLMs is that you have to "spend money to make money"—exactly how my mother justified buying up so much inventory from Totville.

Over the past few years, there's been more public awareness about the dangers of MLMs thanks to documentaries like *LuLaRich* and podcasts like *The Dream*. This media attention has ushered in a stereotype that women who fall for MLMs are largely dumb, white Midwestern ladies with Kate Gosselin haircuts, former high school mean girls who reemerge from the woodwork to prey on unsuspecting relatives and Facebook friends. Most of these women are either stay-at-home moms or women who have opted out of the workforce after having kids.

"Overall, the corporate workplace is incredibly toxic and not really viable for the majority of mothers," says Jo Piazza, the host of the podcast *Under the Influence*. "MLMs have become very attractive to women who still want to earn money to support their family, but need those more flexible hours."[15]

On online forums like Reddit's r/antimlm, which has more than 840,000 members,[16] moms who fall for MLMs are widely referred to as "huns," inspired by the faux-earnest "Hey, hun!" that opens a typical MLM recruitment Facebook message.[17] The subreddit is replete with horror stories from people whose friends or relatives or mothers have become deeply involved in MLMs like Herbalife or LuLaRoe, painting them as manipulative bullies who become involved at their children's expense. "My mom started working with Herbalife about 2 years ago, shes gotten so attached to it that she neglected me," reads the headline to a typical Reddit thread;[18] others are full of horror stories of women pushing essential oils or supplements on their families in lieu of seeking medical treatment.[19]

For years, I viewed women who fell for MLMs through this lens. When I saw former high school classmates pop up on Facebook hawking "a unique opportunity to make money at home," my first thought was that these women must be ridiculously bored to get snookered into such an obvious scam. As insecure and anxious as I am, there is no universe, I thought, in which I would be dumb enough to believe that all my problems could be solved by selling organic cleaning products on Instagram. While I wouldn't go so far as to say that I thought the women involved with MLMs were "bad" moms, I certainly didn't think it spoke well of them that they would fall prey to such a scam.

The more I started looking into MLMs, however, the more I realized how uniquely positioned they are to take advantage of mothers' insecurities. This is apparent in their marketing materials, which expertly adapt the "Angel in the House" trope for a twenty-first-century audience. A promotional video for LuLaRoe, "We Are LuLaRoe," is the perfect example of this, incorporating shots of sleek-haired young mothers playing with their kids before cutting to an image of a woman receiving a standing ovation at a corporate event, the messages "We strengthen families" and "We nurture growth" flashing on the screen.[20] MLMs Frankenstein the contemporary language of boss-babe entrepreneurship and work/life balance with more traditional images of domestic stay-at-home motherhood. *We know you're looking to "have it all,"* they seem to be saying. *Well, spend $1,500 on this luxury skin-care starter kit, and you can have it.*

The brand ambassadors themselves also become expert at such messaging, adopting it in their own marketing materials and social media posts. In one such post, later shared on an anti-MLM Reddit, someone claiming to be a representative for Monat, the skin-care and makeup MLM, posted an Instagram photo of herself in a hospital bed, nursing her newborn baby and flanked by two small children while texting. The image of a newly postpartum mother working instead of bonding with her newborn is deeply depressing—but that is not how this representative framed it in the caption, in which she boasts about growing "an organization of thousands," earning a "consistent income," and "qualify[ing] for a car bonus program." "I haven't had to think about going back to work in an office since!" the post concludes.[21]

The glorification of "hustle culture" and "girlboss" culture in the 2010s has only exacerbated this pressure. The cultural messaging that a modern, independent woman's value lies in her work, when presented alongside more traditional ideology that a woman's place is in the home, makes the image of the badass bitch being her own boss while taking her kids to and from soccer practice all the more attractive. But MLMs profit off the lie that women can "have it all," while simultaneously having a vested interest in keeping mothers tied to the home. It's the same ideology that guided MLM founder Mary Kay Ash in the early 1960s: "God first, family second, career third."[22]

This financial interest is not just because women make up the bulk of the MLM workforce. It's also because right-wing politicians have deep ties to MLMs, most notably via the Direct Selling Association, a lobbying group supporting multilevel marketing, which regularly donates to conservative candidates to curry favor and promote MLM-friendly legislation.[23] That's to say nothing of traditional family values Republicans who directly profit off MLMs, such as Betsy DeVos, the former Trump education secretary who made $75 million from Amway's parent company during the first Trump administration alone. (DeVos's father-in-law was one of the company's founders.[24])

It's no coincidence that MLMs are particularly popular in evangelical communities, in which women are largely encouraged to withdraw from the workforce and stay at home to raise children. Many of these communities also promote the prosperity gospel, or the idea that faith in God is inextricably connected to wealth.[25] Many MLMs such as LuLaRoe have their roots in the

LDS Church[26]—an organization that has historically discouraged women from entering the workforce and demanded they prioritize their roles as homemakers and mothers. The Church has spent years honing its social media marketing skills and partnering with mothers in the community to disseminate this ideology, and MLMs, with their emphasis on idealized portrayals of stay-at-home motherhood combined with boss-babe materialism, mark the apotheosis of this trend.

This association has led to the perception that women involved with MLMs are largely religious, white, middle-class mothers who can afford to stay at home and take care of the kids, and are simply selling eyelash cream door-to-door so they can have some disposable income. But this is not an accurate portrait of the women who traditionally participate in MLMs. Over the past decade or so, for instance, Latinos have been overrepresented in the MLM space, with one study showing they make up more than 20 percent of MLM participants. That same study also concluded that MLMs are more likely to be popular in low-income areas where women traditionally find it difficult to find work,[27] complicating the perception of "huns" as pert-nosed, blond-bobbed Karens.

Piazza says that one of the most frustrating misconceptions about women involved with MLMs is that they tend to all come from the same educational or socioeconomic backgrounds. She notes that many of the people who "look down their nose" at women in MLMs are working mothers with traditional nine-to-five jobs who fail to recognize that many, if not most, of the mothers who become involved do so out of a place of desperation, feeling they have no other options to support their families.[28]

Even my own mother apparently shared this perception. When I texted her to ask whether Totville was an MLM, she was extremely defensive. "It is not an MLM really truly not in any way," she told me.

I wasn't sure if I believed her. As a recent retiree who was not super savvy to the ways of the internet, my mother would be an ideal target for an MLM, I figured—she wouldn't ask too many questions, and she'd be more likely to swallow the narrative of achieving financial freedom via $40 machine-washable smiley-face leggings. So I started looking into Totville, reading various reviews and Reddit threads.

At first, I was relieved to learn that my mother was right: Totville was not an MLM. Its business model is not based on recruiting new members, and its income is based entirely on sales. But I was troubled by some of the language Totville used on its website to attract its "consultants." The company touted itself as a "business [for] moms, by moms," and it used virtually all the verbiage I had seen on the websites for other MLMs: terms like "work/life balance" and "empowerment," addressed to an audience of "entrepreneurs who want it all."[29] Clearly, this was a business that, like a traditional MLM, seemed to be exploiting the frustrations of mothers who had left the workforce to get them to spend hundreds of dollars on tie-dyed racerback ruffle skorts.

What really made me angry, though, was not that Totville seemed to be preying on the insecurities of moms—it was that it seemed to be preying on *my* mom. Granted, she was in a different situation than most women who join MLMs, who are stuck at home raising small children, but I could see how she found Totville attractive for similar reasons as they did. She wanted financial empowerment and a sense of purpose; she wanted to use her retirement as an opportunity to fulfill her entrepreneurial dreams. And if my mom—a brilliant, driven, highly educated woman, a woman who had been the first in her family to get an MBA, a woman who had risen to the top of the ranks of not one but two major US corporations, a woman whose drive and intensity and search for justice at all costs had resulted in our family getting banned from at least one prominent Manhattan dining establishment*—had fallen prey to this, then that meant anyone could.

* * *

I wanted to dive a little deeper into what, exactly, drives mothers in particular to join MLMs, and how the companies benefit from their labor. I also wanted to know if the cultural vilification of such women was merited. In some ways, they seemed similar to the anti-vaccine MAHA moms I spoke to in the previous chapter—true, they were preying on the financial insecurities of other women in their downline, but they also had irrefutably fallen victim to exploitation the moment they themselves had been recruited. So I emailed Emily Lynn Paulson, the author of *Hey, Hun: Sales, Sisterhood, Supremacy, and the Other Lies Behind Multilevel Marketing.*

For nearly a decade, Paulson was a top-earning sales rep for an unnamed multilevel marketing company that sells skin-care products. She knows firsthand just how MLMs prey on the insecurities of middle-class moms, because she spent years doing exactly that and made hundreds of thousands of dollars in the process, making her one of a very small percentage of individuals who actually make money off MLMs.

---

* Pastrami Queen, if by any chance you are reading this, please let us order from you on Seamless again. I don't know what my mom did to you guys, but whatever it was it surely wasn't worth depriving an entire family of mini latkes and brisket sandwiches for the rest of our natural lives.

When I first meet Paulson on Zoom, it is immediately apparent to me why she was so successful. She looks like the type of hot white suburban mom an early-2000s pop-punk band would write a song about: Her hair hangs in sleek curtains around her face, her eyebrows expertly plucked, her nails perfectly manicured. She instantly strikes me as someone who has their shit together, and if she told me to buy a specific brand of moisturizer or anti-wrinkle serum, I would probably consider it. (Actually, I'll be perfectly honest: Considering I bought a $40 Garfield-themed eyeshadow palette off Tik-Tok literally the day before my Zoom call with Paulson, I almost certainly would.)

Paulson is the mother of five children. Like many moms who join MLMs, she told me, she had quit her full-time job in order to raise her children and discovered MLMs at a time in her life when she was bored, frustrated, and highly vulnerable. "I was very much looking for something," she told me. "But getting back into the workforce would have been next to impossible with all the kids and day care and my husband's schedule. . . . I had sort of cornered myself into thinking I was making a choice and realizing that I really didn't have any."[30]

In 2014,[31] a former high school acquaintance messaged Paulson out of the blue to say she was in town for business and asked if she wanted to meet for drinks. When Paulson arrived, she was ambushed by a group of other MLM representatives, who wanted to give her "the momboss version of a timeshare presentation," as she writes in the book.[32] She was skeptical but intrigued. "I was craving community, and feeling kind of lonely," she says. "I wanted to do something and contribute in some way."[33]

Paulson was an extremely successful brand representative for the company, entering the top 3 percent of sellers within her first year.[34] At first, she says, her stint with MLM offered her exactly what she needed, both financially and emotionally: She was lavished with praise and gifts from execs and high-earning members[35] (a process that she characterizes in her book as "love bombing"),[36] and she had a community of like-minded mom friends who encouraged and supported each other. But there were still red flags.

The scripts provided by the company to pitch new recruits were entirely tailored to women. "Targeting men wasn't a thing," she says. "I think it's because women don't have as many opportunities and women make good targets because they are in a more vulnerable position. If you have fewer choices, bad choices are going to seem better."[37] However, Paulson couldn't help but notice that despite the language of female "empowerment" touted by the company's marketing materials, it was the people at the top—the male executives— who were making most of the money.

Paulson also noticed that the women she recruited in her "downline" were working much harder than she was and earning far less. In fact, she says, they were hemorrhaging money and constantly had to pay for inventory, travel, or corporate training sessions. When they complained about how little they were making, they were told by leadership that it was their fault for not working hard enough.

"You're like rah-rah, I want women to succeed, but then you're telling them they suck if they're not making sales," she said. "And you're recruiting these women into a system that has a 99 percent loss rate. There's just nothing empowering about it."[38]

Still, Paulson says that for years, she was a true believer. Whenever she met another mother, she would figure out a way to pitch them on the concept that becoming a consultant—the company's term for a sales rep—could solve any problem they had. Want to stay home with your kids, but still be able to afford piano lessons? Become a consultant. Want to treat postpartum acne? Here's a discount on this serum. Most important, it gave her a sense of purpose and belonging after being isolated at home caring for her children.

"You're doing all these power hours, you're getting on all these Zoom calls, you have all these meetings," she said. "It's all this busy work, and your wheels are spinning, and you feel like you're being productive. And that feels powerful when you're wiping butts at home."[39]

When she said this, I was taken aback. Because the feeling she was describing, this ersatz sense of purpose, wasn't just what she was experiencing while she was peddling overpriced skin-care products. It felt like she was articulating thoughts I've had about my own traditional office job—or even how I feel now, sitting here on my third cup of Starbucks cold brew, typing these words out.

I had always thought I worked not just because we needed the health care and my husband and I didn't make nearly enough money for one of us to stay home, but also because I loved it, and because it made me happy. But truly, there was very little distinction between the feeling Paulson was describing and the feeling I got when I sat down at my laptop to do my own work or take my own calls: that vague surge of empowerment that comes from productivity, that frisson from the sense that you are doing something more important than wiping asses or folding laundry or building towers out of Magna-Tiles all day. So, at the end of the day, what was the difference between my Zoom calls, my office happy hours, my meetings . . . and the busywork that filled the days of these MLM huns?

I of course recognize that there are many, many substantive distinctions between the traditional capitalist workforce and the multilevel marketing model. For starters, unlike MLMs, my income is not contingent on vaguely defined and constantly variable metrics; I receive a fixed salary and pretty good benefits, and I don't have to pay out of pocket to attend weird little boondoggles to teach me how to sell leggings. Additionally, because I am a professional writer and not a salesperson, I am significantly less charming and attractive than the average beauty and skin-care company representative. Were they ever to specifically recruit weird, hollow-eyed little laptop gremlins with terrible posture and an encyclopedic knowledge of memes, I may be a better fit.

But there are also, admittedly, a lot of parallels. I, too, had decided to have children after having been sold the lie that I could have it all, only to learn it was much harder than it looked; I, too, had been indoctrinated with the belief that if I worked harder than anyone else I would succeed, and if I didn't I only had myself to blame; and I, too, was a woman putting in countless hours of labor for the benefit of executives who made ten times my salary and did a fraction of the work. When I took the time to think about it, it was hard for me not to agree with the writer Meg Conley, who wrote in 2020 that motherhood in America is "a multilevel marketing scheme" and a "scam": "We're told if we work hard enough, raise our children well, and faithfully support the American dream, then we'll end up on top," she wrote. "No one ever mentions how the hierarchy of success is shaped like a pyramid. A few mothers get to the top. They give TED Talks and write self-help books. But mostly, we're the cracking base of a condemned structure."[40]

Did I really think I was any better, or any smarter, than these ladies? Weren't we all just sitting at our laptops, spinning our wheels, killing time, trying to convince ourselves we had a purpose? Was the only difference between me and a hun really that I was slightly less annoying on Instagram?

* * *

MLMs have often been compared to "cults," a parallel that Paulson describes at length in her book. According to Paulson, MLMs adhere to what cult expert Steven Hassan has termed the BITE Model, which stands for the four tactics cultlike organizations use to establish their influence: behavior control, such as dictating what a person eats or wears; information control, such as restricting access to information from the outside world; thought control, such as using buzzwords or group-specific jargon to cultivate a sense of insularity and belonging; and emotional control, such as rewarding those who embrace the cult's ideology with praise and compliments, and punishing those who don't by instilling in them a sense of guilt and shame.[41]

I am not Hassan,* nor am I an expert on cults, so I can't say definitively whether MLMs, or even MLM-adjacent organizations like Totville, fall into this category. But generally speaking, joining cults is a way for people to feel like they are regaining a sense of power and control, at a time when they have none—and there is perhaps no situation more guaranteed to make you feel powerless than raising very small children, than having the lens through which you see yourself and other people see you become narrower and narrower and narrower overnight, until there's nothing but a microscopic speck of someone who once, a long time ago, sort of looked and acted like you. And when someone messages you on Facebook and

---

* Though I've interviewed him a few times, and he's very pleasant. He looks a bit like Michael Gross from *Family Ties*.

says not only that they see you but they see *all* of you—and they think you could be so much more, if only you check out this 20-percent-off family and friends code!—it's understandable why someone would click. It's the exact same impulse as the one that prompts mothers of severely disabled children to fall down a disinformation rabbit hole and lobby Congress for dangerous legislation, or frustrated housewives to assign themselves the roles of the protectors of children and rant on Facebook about imaginary organ harvesters. MLMs allow women who feel unappreciated and invisible to feel appreciated and seen.

This is why Paulson believes the vilification of women in MLMs is somewhat unfair. She believes they should be held accountable for the harm they do by preying on vulnerable individuals, and she sees her book as a mea culpa of sorts for perpetuating the cycle: "I'll be the first to say, I did all these things, and I take full responsibility for what I did," she said. But she also characterizes women in MLMs as "victims and predators, simultaneously, whether they want to see it that way or not."[42]

"Everybody who joins really thinks they're doing a good thing," she said. "Nobody joins a cult, like, 'Hey, do you want to scam people and have everyone think you're brainwashed?' Nobody wants to do that. Everyone who joined wanted to improve their family or improve their health or improve something about their lives, and I was the same way. But at some point, you have to realize the intention and the impact are not the same."[43]

Paulson left after learning that a number of MLMs were allegedly training representatives how to take advantage of the Payroll Protection Program (PPP), a loan system organized by the US government to help small business owners during the pandemic. "The level of harm that I felt like I was doing to other people was high enough that I couldn't be involved anymore," she said.[44]

She feels lucky she got out when she did. After briefly peaking during the pandemic, MLMs have been on the downturn, with the Federal Trade Commission cracking down on their business practices,[45] platforms like TikTok issuing blanket bans of MLM advertising,[46] and companies like doTERRA conducting massive layoffs.[47]

"Consumers are becoming more aware that maybe these aren't the greatest things. And I think women who are being targeted are more aware of them," she said. "There's so much legally and politically wrapped up in them, I don't think they'd ever become illegal. But I think if people just stopped joining them, or buying their products, they would just crumble."[48]

At the very end of our call, I remembered: There was one more thing I wanted to ask her. Though my mother has thankfully refrained from directly texting or calling my parent friends or posting fliers in the lobby of my building, she never really stopped selling for Totville. In fact, if I looked in my kids' closet, I'd probably see about three-quarters of the brand's current boys' clothes inventory in there. We hadn't really talked about it at length; mostly, she'd just shove a giant bag full of clothes in my hand and ask me to Venmo her. Regardless of how I felt about her involvement, I gladly accepted the clothes. Some of them are cute. And besides, unless you are a maximum-security corrections officer, my mother is not someone you can easily say no to.

But after speaking to Paulson, I felt a pang of guilt—both for mocking my mom's involvement while taking advantage of the spoils, and for looking the other way while she spent years on what I knew to be an at best fruitless and at worst exploitative endeavor. So

I asked Paulson directly: What should I do? How could I continue to support someone I loved and admired very much who was involved in something like this?

"I think you have to weigh the good against the bad," she told me. "And it also depends on the level of harm that's being done there. For me, I couldn't reconcile the level of harm I was doing, but you have to think about what your mom is getting out of this, and what kind of support she needs. And maybe, support for your mom is watching her do something that she feels good about, even if it isn't really moving the needle."[49]

The next time I saw my mom, I decided to sit her down and talk to her about Totville.* I told her I was working on this chapter, and I wanted to know what drew her to it and what she got out of it. I told her that I knew it wasn't an MLM, but I was concerned about it using MLM-type messaging, and I wanted to better understand what exactly she found valuable about it. She was skeptical, but she agreed.

During this conversation, my mom told me things about Totville that I had never known before. She hadn't gone in blindly, as I'd assumed. She'd had a specific sales strategy, hoping to sell to other women her age who had recently become grandparents. I thought this sounded pretty smart, but she told me it had been less successful than she anticipated: "Most of the grandparents have to consult with their daughters or daughters-in-law about the clothes they pick out," she said. "And sometimes they don't like them. Most mothers care a lot more about the clothes they put on their children than you do."[50] Fair enough.

---

* It was sort of like an interview, because I was recording it, but with more screaming.

I also learned that my assumption that my mom had lost a great deal of money on Totville was incorrect. She told me she'd basically broken even, and that though she would've quit if she'd lost more money, the amount required to buy in was negligible enough to not significantly impact her. I was most surprised to hear, however, that my mom now had extremely mixed feelings about Totville.

"It's very hard to make enough money to write home about," she said, "and it's extremely time-consuming. You have to put in a lot of time."

She also took issue with the fact that it was targeted exclusively at affluent people. "Only privileged people can sell it because you're not making a lot of money, and only privileged people can buy it because it's expensive," she said.[51]

Overall, my mother felt misled by some of the claims made by Totville—but she also acknowledged that there were things about the company she enjoyed. "What I really liked was just talking to people," she said. "I wasn't working full-time. I liked having the interaction."[52] Hearing that I had mocked my mother for reaching out for a connection at a time when she really needed it made my heart sink.

There were things my mother said about Totville that made me think she had, to some extent, internalized toxic aspects of its messaging. She said she blamed herself for not making as many sales as she otherwise could have, attributing it to her not having worked hard enough. (This is not true: I personally witnessed her working extremely and annoyingly hard on behalf of the company for years.) But overall, I was surprised by how clear-eyed her perspective was. I still would have preferred for her to channel her energy in other ways, and I could see how someone with fewer resources than her could have had a much worse experience. But I also felt that by talking to her about what she had gotten out of it, I was seeing more of her than I had in a long time.

I still think MLMs, and even MLM-adjacent companies that prey on the fragmented sense of self that invariably occurs when you become a mother, are gross and predatory. And I'm still repulsed when I see an Instagram momfluencer sell their followers on exclusive opportunities to sell hair growth supplements or essential oils or bioresonance devices that heal eczema. But now, when I see a high school friend or relative or lifestyle influencer falling prey to what is obviously a pyramid scheme, I find it hard to display the type of opprobrium toward them that I would have in the past. These women aren't necessarily Karens or grifters or any other type of social media super-predator. They are people trying to carve out meaning in a world that very much denies them the opportunity to do so. And letting go of my own hun hate—it felt good. It felt—dare I say?—empowering.

Conclusion

Ramsay Bolton Was Right

If You Think This Has a Happy Ending, You Haven't Been Paying Attention

I've spent basically the entirety of this book defending, or at least trying to understand, "bad" mothers. So it's somewhat ironic that, around the time I started working on it, I became deeply obsessed with the idea of becoming a good one.

At that time, my husband and I had been trying for well over a year to get pregnant, a process that involved a lot of joyless sex and peeing on sticks and using apps with names like OvaFlow and LunaCycle and MoonGlow to track my bodily secretions. So, when I finally learned I was pregnant in January 2022, I was jubilant—but I was also terrified. And I became obsessed with ensuring that every aspect of my pregnancy went absolutely perfectly.

This wasn't just a question of avoiding deli meats. I gave up things that my doctor had assured me were totally OK in moderation: caffeine, antidepressants, Tylenol, red meat, penetrative sex, going through the TSA scanner. I was committed to doing everything "right" this time. I promised myself I'd have a vaginal birth instead of a C-section; that I'd exclusively breastfeed instead of formula-feeding. I even called a lactation consultant five months into my pregnancy, and when I showed up for our Zoom consultation without a baby, she was highly weirded out. I think she thought I was one of those women Lacey Chabert would play in a Lifetime Original Movie about pregnancy fakers.

At the time, I reasoned that I was being "cautious": Because my first pregnancy had been marked by chaos and unpredictability, I felt I owed it to my second child to ensure that he wouldn't enter the world the same way. I'd spent so long yearning for Harry to have a little brother and/or sister and/or gender-neutral play companion that there was absolutely no way I was going to do anything other than be the best possible mother I could be. In retrospect, I realize that the lengths I went to to ensure this would happen were insane. However, to (begrudgingly) give credit where it's due, it was ultimately thanks to my OCD-addled, serotonin-deprived brain that Marco, my youngest, is alive today.

When I was about twenty-three weeks pregnant, I went to the hospital for a checkup. Because Harry had been a month premature, I was technically a preterm labor risk, but so far everything had been fine. I figured the ultrasound technician would do her thing and say everything was OK and I'd get to stop at the place on Second Avenue with the good vegan BLTs and fries afterwards.

That is not, however, what ended up happening. The woman performing my scan kept asking me to repeat how many weeks I was, then looking over to the screen with an unmistakable expression of concern. I'd spent a year in college volunteering at the sexual health center, and it was exactly the same expression I tried to avoid having when I gave people their STI panel results.

Afterward, a clean-cut young doctor asked me to come into his office to discuss the results, which had never happened before. "Your cervix has basically whittled away to nothing since your last checkup," he told me. "It's too late for surgical intervention, so you have to go on bed rest immediately, because your baby isn't viable yet."

At this point, exactly two things were going through my mind: (1) Is this doctor Mormon? Because he has a degree from the University of Utah, and I don't know anyone who isn't Mormon from Utah, especially someone who looks as Mormon and from Utah as this guy does; and (2) is he telling me that the baby that I've yearned for, prayed for, cried on the bathroom floor for, given up cheeseburgers for, might die?

I called my gynecologist, who confirmed what the possibly-Mormon doctor told me: Because I was at risk for preterm delivery, and because my baby was not yet viable, I had to completely stay off my feet to keep him "cooking." This is the term she used, "cooking," as if he were a buffalo chicken sandwich and my uterus was an oven at Domino's.

"Does that mean I can't walk the dog?" I asked her, in between sobs.

"No, you can't walk the dog," she said.

"What about make lunches for Harry?"

"No, you can't make lunches for Harry."

"Can I pee?"

"Yes, you can pee. But no leaving the house, and no sex."

"What about blow jobs? Or hand jobs?"

"Just try not to move around or do things," she said before hanging up.

For the next few weeks, I was a wreck. I'd uncontrollably sob for hours at a time between playing *Oregon Trail* on my phone and watching MTV dating reality shows. Desperate to speak to other women who had gone through similarly difficult pregnancies, I hired a "bed rest coach" I found online, to the chagrin of my husband, who thought it was a waste of money.* My family and friends had no idea what to say to me, and my husband was totally overwhelmed having to take care of the household on his own. The only person who was happy was Harry, who, with Mommy in bed all day, had free rein to sit around and watch Sonic the Hedgehog video game playthroughs on YouTube.

The hardest part was coming to terms with the fact that I had absolutely no semblance of control over anything: my body, my pregnancy, the health of my baby. It was impossible to accept that even though I had done everything "right" this time, there was nothing I could do to keep my baby safe. The same thought kept running through my head:

Dear God, please keep my baby safe. I promise I will do everything right. I'll be the best mom I can be. I will give him all of myself. I won't make the same mistakes as last time. I'll have a vaginal delivery. I'll breastfeed. I'll teach him sign language. I'll sleep-train. I'll make organic baby food. I won't ever let him watch TV or look at my phone. I won't be a selfish bitch anymore. I'll quit my job if I have to. I'll be nicer to my husband, who is taking good care of me and Harry, even though that will be hard because he keeps leaving his socks and Popsicle sticks and wrappers next to the bed and it's starting to feel like I'm living with a mouse hoarding small objects in preparation for winter. I'll even stop caring about how I look, and about all the weight I'm gaining on bed rest. I know I've gained like fifty pounds because

---

* He was right. The woman was very nice, but beyond listening to me cry and recap *Real Housewives of Salt Lake City*, she was unqualified to offer any type of therapeutic service.

I can't stop ordering vegan BLTs on DoorDash but I promise you, I don't care. I'll be happy at whatever weight I am at for the rest of my adult life if only you please, please, please keep my baby safe.

In retrospect, the unraveling started almost immediately. It started with the vaginal birth: at thirty-nine weeks, my gynecologist told me the baby's head had gotten too big, and I was no longer a good candidate for a VBAC (vaginal birth after Caesarean). Then came the breastfeeding. Marco wouldn't latch; to make matters worse, when he was six days old, we found blood in his diaper, prompting us to rush him to the ER at 2:00 a.m. He was diagnosed with a milk/soy protein allergy and prescribed a special formula.

The doctor advised against my breastfeeding, saying I wouldn't be able to get enough nutrients if I eliminated dairy and soy from my diet as well as protein. I ignored her and kept trying, hiring at least three lactation consultants in the process. One of them, a very nice older woman, diagnosed Marco with a tongue tie and referred me to an ENT, who clipped it. When that didn't help, the lactation consultant told me he had a lip tie, and referred me to another ENT, who told me my previous lactation consultant didn't know what she was talking about. The second lactation consultant referred me to a third, who told me that I should take Marco to a baby chiropractor. That's what finally convinced me to quit breastfeeding. The suggestion that I pay $400 to a guy in Park Slope with an Ithaca College ethnomusicology degree to give my newborn a massage was simply too dumb to accept.

Ultimately, none of my plans ever came to fruition. I did not do any of the things I'd set out to do, or keep any of the promises I'd made to myself. I was just as "bad" a mother as I had been before; in fact, given how exhausted and distracted I was from work and shuttling him around to consultants and specialists and doctors, I was probably worse.

But I also realized something else: I didn't care. It all just seemed so silly, so pointless, to worry about anything other than my children being reasonably happy and OK. Raising Harry had taught me that parenting was invariably accompanied by a million potential outcomes and variables that couldn't be controlled. I slowly started to come out of my hyper-anxious fugue state, wondering how I could possibly have been naïve enough to think I would be able to beat the odds where every other mother in human history had failed. I was reminded of what Ramsay Bolton tells poor Theon Greyjoy in *Game of Thrones,* right before he castrates him: If you think this has a happy ending, then you haven't been paying attention.[1]

So I gave up. I gave Marco a bottle. I started putting on Ms. Rachel during breakfast. I threw out the sign language book.* I stopped striving for something that I realized was simply never going to happen. Emily Lynn Paulson, the former MLM hun I spoke to, perhaps put it best: Having children is the quickest way to discover not only that the universe isn't centered around you, but that the things you do that you think are really, really important just don't matter. "I realized not everything about my kids is a product of me," she says. "They need to be loved, they need to be fed, they need to be driven around. But really, they need very little to survive. So I've stopped trying to be

---

* He actually ended up learning a bunch of signs anyway, mostly due to his constant exposure to that angel of a woman. Ms. Rachel, if you are reading this, thank you for speaking out on behalf of the children of Gaza, and for all children everywhere. Thank you for giving me five minutes to cook or make calls or clean up after dinner. Thank you for all you do for the parents and babies of the world. And I am sincerely very sorry that I made a joke about you possibly having a nipple ring 250 pages ago.

any kind of mom, because no matter what you do, someone thinks it's wrong. So you might as well, you know . . . do what you want."[2]

* * *

In an earlier chapter, I briefly alluded to the panopticon, the architectural penitentiary design by eighteenth-century British philosopher Jeremy Bentham that consists of a circular building with rows of cells situated around a guard tower at the center, so everybody can feel that they are being watched at all times.[*] I learned about the panopticon in college, when I was assigned a chapter of the book *Discipline and Punish* by Michel Foucault. A French philosopher who died in 1984, Foucault is widely considered to be one of the greatest postmodernists of the twentieth century.[3] But when I was in college, I loathed him. I found his prose incredibly dense, and every time I Google Image searched him, I got a little scared. He looked a lot like Judge Doom, the villain played by Christopher Lloyd in *Who Framed Roger Rabbit.*[†][4]

Had you asked my twenty-one-year-old self, in my Adderall-and-Genesee-Cream-Ale-addled state, to summarize Foucault's *Discipline and Punish* argument, I probably would have said something like, "Society is like a panopticon. Because we think everyone is always policing us, we are always policing ourselves." Which I don't think was . . . wrong, exactly.[‡] But I have to say, it took

---

[*] This design continues to be used in prisons, hospitals, and schools to this day; also, the Hyatt Regency Hotel at the Orlando International Airport.

[†] He also looked a lot like the author Michael Pollan, as evidenced by the existence of the remarkably smart Tumblr, "Michael Pollan or Michel Foucault?"

[‡] Though, frankly, I can't say for sure, because you'd have to pay me an entire year's salary to convince me to read that shit again.

becoming a mother for me to realize just how spot-on that little French weirdo was.

As I get older and watch my kids grow up and become wise and wonderful little people, I have become convinced that the most revolutionary act a mother can do is to try to live outside the panopticon, to the best of their ability, within their own set of individual circumstances. To refuse to be judged, to refuse to judge others, and to refuse to judge themselves; to stop leaning in and start lying down; to find comfort and grace in the knowledge that our presence is enough, that we are enough. To serve the chicken fingers and turn on the TV and disassociate on your phone for a few minutes, without caring about the other imaginary people peering between their fingers from the other cells. We should try as best as we can to live like no one else is watching, because a lot of the time, we're all just in our little cells, doing the best we can, making the most of our time with the families we've been blessed to build.

And I have to say: I am so grateful for that July afternoon, when a hot doctor who may or may not have been Mormon told me that my cervix was paper-thin, and that I needed to lie down and play *Oregon Trail* all day or my baby would die. I'm grateful for the hours and hours and hours I spent on the phone and on Zoom calls and in the offices of doctors and teachers and therapists and city employees who worked with Harry: the ones who made me feel stupid, the ones who made me feel crazy, the ones who took my money selling weird little interventions they knew wouldn't work, the ones who made me sob for days on end, and the ones who truly opened their hearts to help him, who are some of the most beautiful and insightful and special people I have ever known. And I'm grateful for the manager who sat me in her office when I was four months pregnant and told me my position was being eliminated and my health insurance cut off. She was a fucking bitch. But I'm grateful to her.

Whenever bad or scary things have happened on my parenting journey*—and trust that if you are blessed enough to become a parent in whatever form, bad and scary things *will* happen—I find that I am not plagued with feelings of guilt or anger or grief over the loss of the mother I had wanted to be. The only thing I feel is an almost overwhelming sense of gratitude that I have been lucky enough to be a mother at all.

I am not the type of person to try to retroactively assign meaning or reason to bad things that happen; that's for people who have a level of unearned optimism that is totally foreign to me, like evangelicals or Jets fans. But I am truly grateful to have been liberated from the tyranny of caring about dumb shit. I feel that way whenever I hear Marco laugh, or watch Harry roughhouse with his dad during a Knicks game, or see the boys run shrieking down the hallway of our apartment building together in their pajamas, plotting some misadventure, our three-legged epileptic border collie running after them. During those moments, I don't think about the mistakes I've made or the right or wrong way to do things. All I can think is: *I am so blessed to know these children, and to have made this beautiful, weird little family with my husband, a man who is both incomparably brave and gentle and smart and also happens to be among the top .01 percent of the sexiest people I have ever known.* And I hope, one day, that my kids will read this book and not only be extremely uncomfortable when they read that last sentence, but also know in their bones how deeply, how ardently, they were loved.

---

* And I have to say, I am extremely proud of myself that I wrote almost an entire book without using this absolutely horrible phrase.

In writing this book, I have basically come to one conclusion: That even under the best of circumstances, there is nothing harder than becoming a parent, in whatever form that may take. Bringing a child into the world, knowing all the suffering they may encounter upon entering it, is equal parts staggeringly brave and incredibly reckless. For mothers in particular, who have been tasked with giving all of themselves in exchange for indifference at best and widespread condemnation at worst, suffering is not a possibility, but a guarantee. There is no task more thankless, no job less tangibly rewarding—except maybe freelance journalism.

It's under these brutal conditions that many of the mothers in this book manage, somehow, by the grace of some divine spirit or selective serotonin reuptake inhibitors or some combination thereof, to survive. They make mistakes, sometimes terrible ones; they cause wounds, sometimes deep ones. But they keep going. They raise their children—smart, beautiful, inquisitive, generous, pain-in-the-ass children—and love them without reservation. However loathsome we may find some of these women, however far outside the template of "good" motherhood they may be, they are all united by that single act of bravery, or recklessness, depending on how you look at it—whatever it takes to sign up for something that you know will bring you joy, yes, but also fear and heartbreak and pain beyond what you can even imagine. Some people may be more naturally equipped for motherhood than others, or at least have access to the tools needed to be better at it. But there is not a single mother on the planet who I don't think is courageous as hell simply for taking the job.

I'm not a very good mother. I'm distractible, short-tempered, impatient, mercurial, narcissistic, neurotic, and obsessive. I don't cook. I don't clean. I don't use my indoor voice when I'm mad or tell my kids it's OK for them to have big feelings or whatever the hell Dr. Becky suggests nice progressive moms do when they're throwing a tantrum over not being allowed to swallow a battery or stick their finger in a socket. I don't read most of the emails from Harry's school, and audibly groan when they pop up in my inbox.* Had Coventry Patmore met me while he was penning *The Angel in the House*, he would have been, for starters, extremely confused to see a woman wearing pants. But he would also probably have been horrified that someone so clearly unfit to mother had been given the opportunity to do so.

And yet, as unqualified and shitty as I am, or as any of the other mothers in this book are—and I don't deny that some are not deserving, that some cannot and do not live up to the task—the fact remains: We have all been given this opportunity. We have been granted this joy, this pain, this blessing, this misery, to love our children as fiercely and as messily as we can, to fight for them, to live for them, to die for them, to bravely venture forth and shepherd them

---

* In my defense: They send way too many of them, and for virtually no reason that I can think of other than a compulsive need for attention. In theory, I would respect that, but in practice, the endless onslaught is insufferable. What the fuck do I care that the fifth graders are doing New York state standardized testing? My child isn't in the fifth grade. What material impact does that information have on my life, or on my family? Is there any reason why I need to be privy to this information? Are you going to send me an email every time my child goes to the bathroom on school grounds as well? And why are you inviting me to coffee commons with school parents and the administrative staff? I have a full-time job. Do you really think I have nothing better to do at one thirty on a Friday than drink Dunkin' coffee with a balding stay-at-home dad who only wants to talk about the public school admissions process? Please. We are working parents of small children. Have we not been punished enough?

through the vagaries of this cruel planet. And we're here. We're showing up, in a world where showing up is far from guaranteed.

So to answer a question that absolutely no one has asked, yes: I'm a bad mom. But I'm also here. I'll always be here, no matter how hard it gets, or how badly I might mess up in the process. And honestly, I think that's more than half the battle.

Besides: My kids are *alive*, aren't they? So get off my dick.

Acknowledgments

People always say it takes a village to raise a child, and it takes a village to write a 278-page book with dumb jokes about RFK Jr. and horses. This is going to be a very long section.

Thank you to my agent, Carly Watters, for taking a chance on me when I sent her a very different version of this book proposal five years ago and very calmly walking me through rejection after rejection with her characteristic Canadian mien. Thank you to my editor Ronnie Alvarado for her brilliant notes, including letting me keep in a line about dead rats and dead rat photos. Thank you to my fact-checker and good friend Andrea Marks, who did not tell me until long after the fact-checking process that she herself was twenty-one weeks pregnant by posing the now-infamous question: "Do you have any questions for me about my life?" Your baby will be a very good dancer. She will also have amazing grammar.

Thank you to Jenny Kutner for reading an early version of the momfluencer essay and being nice about it (also thanks for leaving an amazing birthday message this year including a very graphic description of your shingles). Thank you to Matt Asman for reading an early version of the MILF essay and being nice about it. Thank you to Jordyn Taylor for being like, "You should write a book!" and guiding me through the proposal process so many years ago. I owe you a beverage of some sort. Thank you to Mirella Brussani, for being wonderful.

Thank you to all of the teachers and therapists and SEITs and counselors in our little "village," but perhaps none more so than Rasha Hamid, a beautiful soul who sees the little light in everyone. You are a very special person and we are so grateful to you.

Thank you to all the brilliant editors I've learned so much from: Ellie Krupnick; Margaret Wheeler Johnson; Cooper Fleishman; Catherine Thompson; Jordan Larson, Marisa Carroll, Jen Ortiz, and Lindsay Peoples at *The Cut*; and Maria Fontoura, Noah Shactman, Lisa Tozzi, Kate Storey, and Sean Woods at *Rolling Stone*. CT Jones and Brittany Spanos, I miss you both every day; it's, like, physically painful. Liz Garber-Paul, you are one of the smartest, most hardworking bitches I know, and I am beyond honored to call you a friend.

Thank you to Dr. Nicholson from Riverdale Country School, who read an essay I wrote about Brangelina in the eleventh grade and somehow didn't throw it across the wall and quit in shame. Thank you to Professors David Walker and Wendy Hyman from Oberlin College, the only two people I would ever want to teach my kids Shakespeare. Thank you to Susie Linfield at CRC. Thank you to the Oberlin comms folks—Ben Jones, Scott Wargo, Amanda Nagy, and of course Jeff Hagan, the Jack to my Liz. And thank you to all the people who have hired me who I have somehow forgotten to name here: Thank you for taking a chance on me. I don't know why you did it, and I'm almost certain you regretted it, but thank you.

Thank you to the SATC Sluts, Dan Stein, Georgia Horn, Cathy Skulnik, Evan Morehouse, and Lizzy Rodkin, for being hot and smart. Every day I wonder, "Do I deserve to have friends as great as these?" And the answer is usually "No!" And then I wonder, "Do they secretly hate me?" And then I have to stop thinking about it because I get depressed. Thank you to Free Drankz (Marisa Kabas, Miles Klee, Kevin Collier, Gabe Bergado, Cooper Fleishman, King Cup, and Drankz Emerita Greg Seals) for making me howl with laughter every single day.

Thank you to Power Moms and informal book advisors Jessica Machado, Annie Lutz, Kim Friedlander, Adrianne Wright, Robin Fitzgerald, Nikki Matelliano, Lajhem Cambridge Sulat, Emily Gould, Tessa Stuart, Kate Storey, Julyssa Lopez, Chantal Fernandez, Briana Borenstein, Angelina Chapin, Julia Friedman Rubin, Joh Kelly, Lina Dorado, and all the other women who have slid into my texts or DMs to say, "Hey, isn't this thing about being a mom messed up?" To quote Miley Cyrus, "You make me laugh. You make me cry. I don't know which side to buy." Except I do! You inspire me every day, and I love you all. Oh, and special thanks to Rebecca Rogers for somehow making me look like an attractive person in my headshots. How did you do it? You are a witch. Thank you to Peepee: my favorite Swifties Marc Goldstein and Edward Baida, Jason Lutz, David Friedlander, Cameron Marshad, Nate Sulat, and Alex Rifkin.

Thank you to my enormous family: Grandpa Ted; Ali and Abe; Hilary and David; Barry and Katie; Sue and Mitchell; Rachele and Brad; and the billions of cousins who are far too numerous to individually name here except for Rebecca because she's been nice enough to let me rag on her about that Battleship game for all these years. If it weren't for your encouragement—for showing up at all those weird high school and college plays and improv shows and readings—I would not have had the confidence to wake up and do this every day. To paraphrase Dominic Toretto, family is everything. And thank you to Grandma Florence and Grandpa Sol. I miss you every day, and I'll never forget to stay away from Baisley Boulevard.

Forever thanks to the women who inspire me to mom better every single day: Dester Samuel, one of the strongest and most badass ladies I know; Sandy Dickson, who somehow managed to raise four boys while barely aging a day and only consuming vodka and ice cream; my mother-in-law, Ruth La Ferla, who is my journalism hero, an A+ babysitter, and the woman singlehandedly keeping Zara from filing for bankruptcy; my sister, Sami, who is my sister wife and an angel sent from heaven who fills my heart with hope for the future of humankind (and a pretty freaking incredible auntie to boot); and of course, the star of this book, Toby Axelrod Dickson, the toughest bitch in the whole entire world and as far as I'm concerned the template for the good mother as we know it. I love you all so, so, so much. Thank you to the La Ferla family, specifically my father-in-law, Sandro, for teaching my children to love art and beauty and pasta and Renato Carosone. I love you dearly.

I don't even know how to say thank you to my father, Clifford Dickson, who with his wise words, "I'd rather you become a crack whore than go to law school," is the sole reason why I went to journalism school and became a writer today. He is far funnier and more talented than I ever will be, but I am grateful that I inherited barely a tenth of his wit and curiosity. I couldn't be more grateful for your love and support. The next one is for you.

To my children, Harry and Marco: I love you both more than words can say. You are huge pains in my ass, and I can't believe how lucky I am to know you and watch you grow up. Dank oo for letting me be your mama. It's Push O'Clock, boys!

To my husband, Alex: Since the very moment I saw you in the fall of 2006 in a forest-green sweatshirt at the Cleveland-Hopkins

Airport, I knew I needed to spend every minute of my life with you, and I can't believe I was lucky enough for that to actually happen. You are the smartest, kindest, most generous, sexiest person I know, and I am forever grateful to you for building this beautiful, messy little life with me. Mouse–Mouse Doctor '08.

Notes

Introduction: This Was a Bad Idea
or, Why I Should Lie to People More

1. Vivian Kwarm, "Sophie Turner Breaks Silence on Claims She Was a Bad Mom During Jonas Split," New York *Daily News*, May 15, 2024, https://www.nydailynews.com/2024/05/15/sophie-turner-addresses -bad-mom-stories-amid-joe-jonas-split/.
2. Bindu Bansinath, "What We Know About the Mommy Vlogger Accused of Child Abuse," *The Cut*, March 25, 2024, https://www.thecut .com/article/ruby-franke-utah-mommy-vlogger-pleads-guilty-to-child -abuse.html.
3. Pilar Grace, "I Was Mom Shamed for Not Hitting My Kid When He Wet His Pants," *New York Post*, September 10, 2023, https://nypost.com /2023/09/10/i-was-mom-shamed-for-not-punishing-my-kid-when-he -wet-his-pants/.
4. Claudia Savage, "Community in 'Total Shock' After Mother and Son Are Killed in House Fire in Co Cavan Named Locally," *Irish Examiner*, September 10, 2023, https://www.irishexaminer.com/news/arid-41223 430.html.
5. Steven Mintz interview conducted by author, September 5, 2023.
6. Ashley Fetters, "The Many Faces of the 'Wine Mom,'" *The Atlantic*, May 23, 2020, https://www.theatlantic.com/family/archive/2020/05 /wine-moms-explained/612001/.
7. Totempael, "Spoiler! Bad Moms Party Scene," YouTube, October 26, 2016, https://www.youtube.com/watch?v=21dvcRp9x8E.

8. Saba Sarfraz et al., "Early Screen-Time Exposure and Its Association with Risk of Developing Autism Spectrum Disorder: A Systematic Review," *Cureus* 7, no. 15 (July 22, 2023): e42292, doi:10.7759/cureus.42292.

9. Mintz interview.

10. NPR Staff, "Child's Death Casts Light on Pedestrian Traffic Woes," *All Things Considered*, July 30, 2011, https://www.npr.org/2011/07/30/138855279/convicted-suburban-mom-has-city-planners-nervous.

11. Nicole Acosta, "'Take Care of Maya' Trial: Hospital Found Liable in Mother's Suicide After Munchausen by Proxy Accusations," *People*, November 9, 2023, https://people.com/take-care-of-maya-trial-hospital-found-liable-mothers-suicide-munchausen-by-proxy-accusations-8400157.

12. Linda Seidel interview conducted by author, August 31, 2023.

Chapter 1: The Marvelous Mrs. Mommy Paradox
Why Being a Working Mother Is Like Doing Ayahuasca

1. Ej Dickson, "Where Are the Marvelous Mrs. Maisel's Children?," *Vox*, January 18, 2019, https://www.vox.com/culture/2019/1/18/18159589/marvelous-mrs-maisel-missing-kids-children.

2. *Vox* (@Vox), "Midge Maisel tells jokes. She cooks brisket. She charms the pants off everyone. But one thing she cannot do—or, perhaps more accurately, one thing she has no interest in doing—is parent," Facebook, May 26, 2023, https://www.facebook.com/Vox/posts/pfbid023fezxZrghshfXkSUGa5s1qXsarDKfF34e8t5iz8UkedZ7HB2y3HaDTaGQz7LnVZ1l.

3. Jamie Doward, "Working Mothers 'Up to 40% More Stressed,'" *The Guardian*, January 27, 2019, https://www.theguardian.com/money/2019/jan/27/working-mothers-more-stressed-health.

4. L'Oreal Thompson Payton, "Nearly Half of Working Mothers Surveyed Have Been Diagnosed with Anxiety or Depression. Here's What Can Help," *Fortune*, March 17, 2023, https://finance.yahoo.com/news/nearly-half-working-mothers-surveyed-194731918.html#.

5. Jeff Grabmeier, "Mothers' Alcohol Use Changed During the Covid-19 Pandemic," Ohio State News, December 20, 2022, https://news.osu.edu /mothers-alcohol-use-changed-during-the-covid-19-pandemic/.

6. "Moms Multitask 10 Hours More Per Week Than Dads: Study," *Toronto Star*, December 1, 2011, https://www.thestar.com/life/moms-multitask -10-hours-more-per-week-than-dads-study/article_5e3ad1c9-d6ce -549f-8a02-375a22e49717.html.

7. Women's Bureau, "Women's Labor Force Participation Rates by Age of Youngest Child Since 1975," US Department of Labor, https://www .dol.gov/agencies/wb/data/mothers-families/Laborforceparticipation rates-women-ageyoungestchild.

8. Bureau of Labor Statistics, US Department of Labor, "Employment Characteristics of Families—Employment Characteristics of Families—2024," news release, April 23, 2025, https://www.bls.gov /news.release/pdf/famee.pdf.

9. Jason Wilson, "'Dangerous and Un-American': New Recording of JD Vance's Dark Vision of Women and Immigration," *The Guardian*, August 31, 2024, https://www.theguardian.com/us-news/article/2024/aug /31/jd-vance-podcast-feminism-immigration.

10. Emily Baker-White, "Elon Musk Wants to Raise the Birth Rate. He's Cutting Medical Care for Mothers and Babies," *Forbes*, April 14, 2025, https:// www.forbes.com/sites/emilybaker-white/2025/04/11/elon_musks_war _on_moms_and_babies/.

11. Stephanie Coontz interview conducted by author, August 29, 2023.

12. Coontz interview.

13. Sara Petersen, *Momfluenced: Inside the Maddening, Picture-Perfect World of Mommy Influencer Culture* (Beacon Press, 2023), 36–44.

14. Coventry Patmore, *The Angel in the House* (Cassell & Company, Ltd., 1891), ed. Henry Morley, https://www.gutenberg.org/files/4099/4099-h /4099-h.htm.

15. Coontz interview.

16. Janet L. Yellen, "The History of Women's Work and Wages and How It Has Created Success for Us All," Brookings, May 2020, https://www

.brookings.edu/articles/the-history-of-womens-work-and-wages-and
-how-it-has-created-success-for-us-all/.

17. "Labor Force Characteristics by Race and Ethnicity, 2023," US Bureau
of Labor Statistics, December 2024, https://www.bls.gov/opub/reports
/race-and-ethnicity/2023.

18. Coontz interview.

19. Yellen, "The History of Women's Work and Wages."

20. Evan K. Rose, "The Rise and Fall of Female Labor Force Participa-
tion During World War II in the United States," *Journal of Economic
History* 78, no. 3 (September 2018): 673–711, https://doi.org/10.1017
/S0022050718000323.

21. Rose, "The Rise and Fall of Female Labor Force Participation."

22. *Mildred Pierce*, directed by Michael Curtiz (1945, Warner Bros.).

23. Ellen Moody, "Mildred Pierce 1945: Starring Joan Crawford: A Mud-
dle," *Ellen and Jim Have a Blog, Two*, July 1, 2012, https://ellenandjim
.wordpress.com/2012/07/01/mildred-pierce-1945-starring-joan-crawford
-a-muddle/.

24. Roy Hoopes, *Cain: The Biography of James M. Cain* (Holt, Rinehart and
Winston, 1982), 349–350.

25. Hoopes, *Cain*, 349–350.

26. Joanna Pepin interview conducted by author, September 1, 2023.

27. Rebecca Plant interview conducted by author, August 31, 2023, 24:36.

28. Mitra Toosi, "A Century of Change: The US Labor Force, 1950–2050,"
Monthly Labor Review, May 2002, p. 18, https://www.bls.gov/opub/mlr
/2002/05/art2full.pdf.

29. Allyson Sherman Grossman, "Working Mothers and Their Children,"
Special Labor Force Reports—Summaries," *Monthly Labor Review*,
May 1981, p. 49, https://www.bls.gov/opub/mlr/1981/05/rpt3full.pdf.

30. Robert Pear, "Federal Cuts Forcing States to Curb Day Care Service for
Poor," *New York Times*, October 22, 1981, https://www.nytimes.com
/1981/10/22/us/federal-cuts-forcing-states-to-curb-day-care-service
-for-poor.html.

31. Susan Faludi, *Backlash: The Undeclared War Against American Women* (Crown, 1991), 125–136.

32. Faludi, *Backlash*, 276.

33. *Baby Boom*, directed by Charles Shyer (1987, United Artists).

34. Linda Seidel interview conducted by author, August 31, 2023.

35. Caitlin Gibson, "The End of Leaning In: How Sheryl Sandberg's Message of Empowerment Fully Unraveled," *Washington Post*, December 20, 2018, https://archive.is/NvXD6.

36. Chelsea Simeon, "Mom Found Not Guilty of Charges After Leaving Kids in Liberty Motel While She Worked," WKBN, May 26, 2021, https://www.wkbn.com/news/local-news/mom-found-not-guilty-of -child-endangering-charges-after-leaving-kids-alone-in-liberty-motel -while-she-worked/.

37. Donnya Negera interview conducted by author, December 28, 2023.

38. Jennifer Nash interview conducted by author, September 9, 2023.

39. Emily Peck, "There Are More Women in the Global Workforce Now Than Before Covid," Axios, March 8, 2024, https://www.axios.com /2024/03/08/women-workforce-labor.

40. *I Don't Know How She Does It*, directed by Douglas McGrath, (2011, The Weinstein Company).

41. *The Intern*, directed by Nancy Meyers (2015, Warner Bros.).

42. *Workin' Moms*, season 1, episode 1, "Bare," CBC Television, 2017.

43. Sa'iyda Shabazz, "Black-ish Is Nailing Modern Motherhood, and We're Here for It," Scary Mommy, February 12, 2018, https://www.scary mommy.com/black-ish-nailing-modern-motherhood.

44. Kayla Hawkins, "Bow's Major Life Decision on 'Black-ish' Is No One Else's Business," *Bustle*, January 3, 2018, https://www.bustle.com /p/bow-decided-to-be-a-stay-at-home-mom-on-black-ish-because -women-can-always-change-their-minds-about-whats-best-for-them -7770382. Carolyn Hinds, "Bow Is No Longer a Working Girl on 'Black-ish,'" *Black Girl Nerds*, January 9, 2018, https://blackgirlnerds.com /black-ish-4-x-10-working-girl/.

45. Stephanie Soteriou, "'And Just Like That's' Approach to Abortion Has Sparked Backlash as Fans Pointed Out Its Unplanned Pregnancy Storyline Is Less Progressive Than a 20-Year-Old Episode of 'Sex and the City,'" BuzzFeed News, August 18, 2023, https://www.buzzfeednews.com/article/stephaniesoteriou/and-just-like-that-backlash-abortion-storyline.

46. Celine Yap, "'And Just Like That': Scene-Stealing Jewelry Moments from the Series So Far," *Vogue* Singapore, December 13, 2021, https://vogue.sg/and-just-like-that-jewellery/.

47. *Hacks*, season 2, episode 5, "Retired," 3 Arts Entertainment, May 26, 2022.

48. u/astroidbabe, "Sad about Midge's future," r/TheMarvelousMrsMaisel, Reddit, 2023, https://www.reddit.com/r/TheMarvelousMrsMaisel/comments/13d2sqf/sad_about_midges_future/.

49. Nicolas DiDomizio, "A Complete Guide to Taylor Swift's Boyfriends, Arranged by What Kind of Cereal They'd Be," Mic, July 14, 2016, https://www.mic.com/articles/148663/a-complete-guide-to-taylor-swift-s-boyfriends-arranged-by-what-kind-of-cereal-they-d-be.

Chapter 2: "Hal, It's About Cats"
The (Relatively Recent) Birth of the "Bad" Mother

1. Marga Vicedo interview conducted by author, September 9, 2023.

2. *Broadway: The American Musical*, season 1, episode 6, "Putting It Together," PBS, 2004.

3. Barbara Saylor Rodgers, "Euripides' *Medea* as Historical Commentary," University of Vermont, last updated October 14, 2004, https://www.uvm.edu/~bsaylor/classics/medea.html.

4. Cait Caffrey, "Medea (mythology)," Ebsco, 2022, https://www.ebsco.com/research-starters/history/medea-mythology.

5. Euripedes, *Medea* (431 BCE), trans. E. P. Coleridge, rev. Roger Ceragioli and further rev. George Nagy, Center for Hellenic Studies, Harvard University, https://classics.mit.edu/Euripides/medea.html.

6. Euripides, *Medea*, lines 1387–1388, ed. David Kovqcs, https://www
.perseus.tufts.edu/hopper/text?doc=urn:cts:greekLit:tlg0006.tlg003
.perseus-engl:1361-1388.

7. Giacomo Presciuttini, "Agrippina the Younger," World History Encyclopedia, April 1, 2021, https://www.worldhistory.org/Agrippina_the
_Younger/.

8. Cassius Dio, "Epitome of Book LXII," 13.5, in *Roman History* (Loeb
Classical Library VIII, 1925), http://penelope.uchicago.edu/Thayer/e
/roman/texts/cassius_dio/62*.html.

9. Stephanie Coontz interview conducted by author, August 29, 2023, part
one, and email from Stephanie Coontz, May 19, 2025.

10. Coontz email.

11. Monica C. Witkowski, "Justice Without Partiality: Women and the Law
in Colonial Maryland, 1648–1715" (PhD diss., Marquette University,
2010), https://epublications.marquette.edu/cgi/viewcontent.cgi?referer
=&httpsredir=1&article=1028&context=dissertations_mu.

12. Donna Gawell, "Y Is for Ye Olde Disciplines and Punishments for
Youths," https://donnagawell.com/the-redemption-of-mehitabel-bray
brooke/abcs-of-crime-and-punishment-in-puritan-new-england/y-is
-for-ye-olde-disciplines-and-punishments-for-youths/.

13. John E. B. Myers, "A Short History of Child Protection in America," in
Child Protection in America: Past Present and Future, 2, https://us.sage
pub.com/sites/default/files/upm-binaries/35363_Chapter1.pdf.

14. Stacey Schiff, *The Witches: Salem, 1692* (Little, Brown and Company,
2015), 131.

15. Laurel Thatcher Ulrich, *Good Wives: Image and Reality in the Lives of
Women in Northern New England, 1650–1750* (Vintage Books, 1991), 19.

16. Irvine Loudon, "Deaths in Childbed from the Eighteenth Century to
1935," *Medical History* 30, no. 1 (January 1986), 1–41, https://doi.org
/10.1017/S0025727300045014.

17. Steven Mintz interview conducted by author, September 6, 2023.

18. Schiff, *The Witches*, 135.

19. Schiff, *The Witches*, 135.

20. Douglas O. Linder, "Sarah Good," Famous Trials: Accounts and Materials for 100 of History's Most Important Trials," UMKC School of Law, https://famous-trials.com/salem/2039-sal-bgoo.

21. Schiff, *The Witches*, 76.

22. Devon McMahon, "Suckling Familiars and Unnatural Protrusions: The Witch's Mark in the Salem Witchcraft Trials of 1692" (paper, Cornell University, November 28, 2012), 5–6, https://ecommons.cornell.edu /server/api/core/bitstreams/b0bbd30c-8d3b-439b-9553-26fceb42f611 /content.

23. McMahon, "Suckling Familiars," 5.

24. Schiff, *The Witches*, 63.

25. Marga Vicedo interview conducted by author, September 9, 2023.

26. Sara Petersen, *Momfluenced: Inside the Maddening, Picture-Perfect World of Mommy Influencer Culture* (Beacon Press, 2023), 36–44.

27. Email from Steven Mintz, August 11, 2023.

28. Carrie Mullins, *The Book of Mothers: How Literature Can Help Us Reinvent Modern Motherhood* (St. Martin's Press, 2024), 43–51.

29. Louisa May Alcott, *Little Women or Meg, Jo, Beth, and Amy* (Little, Brown and Company, 1868), 91.

30. Hannah Zeavin, *Mother Media: Hot and Cool Parenting in the Twentieth Century* (MIT Press, 2025), 10–11.

31. B. G. Jefferies and J. L. Nichols, *Searchlights on Health: The Science of Eugenics* (J. L. Nichols and Company, 1920), https://www.gutenberg.org /files/13444/13444-h/13444-h.htm.

32. Sara Petersen interview conducted by author, April 5, 2023.

33. Jennifer Hallam, "Slavery and the Making of America: The Family," PBS Thirteen, https://www.thirteen.org/wnet/slavery/experience/family /history2.html.

34. Sara Petersen interview conducted by author, August 24, 2023, part two.

35. Nina Banks, "Black Women's Labor Market History Reveals Deep-Seated Race and Gender Discrimination," *Working Economics Blog*, Economic Policy Institute, February 19, 2019, https://www.epi.org

/blog/black-womens-labor-market-history-reveals-deep-seated-race-and
-gender-discrimination/.

36. Marian Eide, "The First Chapter of Children's Rights," *American
Heritage*, July/August 1990, https://www.americanheritage.com/first
-chapter-childrens-rights.

37. Genevieve Carlton, "Mary Ellen Wilson and the 19th-Century Child
Abuse Case That Changed History," *All That's Interesting*, December
15, 2022, https://allthatsinteresting.com/mary-ellen-wilson.

38. Eide, "The First Chapter of Children's Rights."

39. Howard Markel, "Case Shined First Light on Abuse of Children," *New
York Times*, December 14, 2009, https://www.nytimes.com/2009/12/15
/health/15abus.html.

40. "Mary Connolly in the Tombs," *The Sun*, April 14, 1874, archived via
newspapers.com.

41. Eric A. Shelman and Stephen Lazoritz, *The Mary Ellen Wilson Child
Abuse Case and the Beginning of Children's Rights in 19th Century America* (McFarland & Company, 2005, courtesy the George Sam Johnston
Archives of the NSPCC), 95, https://archive.org/details/maryellenwilson
c0000shel/page/n9/mode/2up.

42. Steven Mintz interview conducted by author, September 5, 2023.

43. Mintz interview.

44. Peter L. Winkler, "The Man Who Hated Moms: Looking Back on Philip
Wylie's 'Generation of Vipers,'" *Los Angeles Review of Books*, August 13,
2021, https://lareviewofbooks.org/article/the-man-who-hated-moms
-looking-back-on-philip-wylies-generation-of-vipers/.

45. Rebecca Jo Plant, *Mom: The Transformation of Motherhood in Modern
America* (University of Chicago Press, 2010).

46. Mintz interview.

47. Mintz interview.

48. Zevin, *Mother Media*, 123.

49. Jessica Grogan, "The Biggest Problem with Parenting Advice," *Psychology Today*, December 13, 2014, https://www.psychologytoday

.com/us/blog/encountering-america/201412/the-biggest-problem -parenting-advice.

50. Rebecca Plant interview conducted by author, August 31, 2023.

51. Plant interview.

52. Plant Interview.

53. Patricia L. Dobkin, Richard E. Tremblay, and Catherine Sacchitelle, "Predicting Boys' Early-Onset Substance Abuse from Father's Alcoholism, Son's Disruptiveness, and Mother's Parenting Behavior," *Journal of Consulting and Clinical Psychology* 65, no. 1 (February 1997): 86–92, https://doi.org/10.1037/0022-006X.65.1.86.

54. Dobkin, et al., "Predicting Boys' Early-Onset Substance Abuse," 25–27.

55. Robert Karen, "Becoming Attached," *The Atlantic*, February 1990, https://www.theatlantic.com/magazine/archive/1990/02/becoming -attached/308966/.

56. Karen, "Becoming Attached."

57. John Bowlby, *Maternal Care and Mental Health* (World Health Organization, 1952), 11.

58. Lindsey Blake Churchill, "The Feminine Mystique," Britannica, https:// www.britannica.com/topic/The-Feminine-Mystique.

59. Evelyn S. Ringold, "Bringing Up Baby in Britain," *New York Times*, June 13, 1965.

60. Zeavin, *Mother Media*, 152–153, 160.

61. Zeavin, *Mother Media*, 113–115.

62. Marga Vicedo interview conducted by author, September 9, 2023.

63. Vicedo interview.

64. Christopher Sterwald and Jeffrey Baker, "Frosted Intellectuals: How Dr. Leo Kanner Constructed the Autistic Family," *Perspectives in Biology and Medicine* 62, no. 4 (2019): 690–709, https://dx.doi.org/10.1353 /pbm.2019.0040.

65. Zeavin, *Mother Media*, 135.

66. Brandon S. Aylward, Diana E. Gal-Szabo, and Sharief Taraman, "Racial, Ethnic, and Sociodemographic Disparities in Diagnosis of Children with Autism Spectrum Disorder," *Journal of Developmental and*

Behavioral Pediatrics 42, no. 8 (October–November 2021): 682–689, https://doi.org/10.1097/dbp.0000000000000996.

67. Zeavin, *Mother Media*, 133–134.

68. Anne Harrington, "The Fall of the Schizophrenogenic Mother," *Perspectives: The Art of Medicine* 379, no. 9823 (April 7, 2012): 1292–1293, https://doi.org/10.1016/S0140-6736(12)60546-7.

69. Mitzi M. Waltz, "Mothers and Autism: The Evolution of a Discourse of Blame," *AMA Journal of Ethics* 17, no. 4 (April 2015): 353–358, https://doi.org/10.1001/journalofethics.2015.17.4.mhst1-1504.

70. Josephine Johnston, "The Ghost of the Schizophrenogenic Mother," *AMA Journal of Ethics* 15, no. 9 (September 2013): 801–805, https://doi.org/10.1001/virtualmentor.2013.15.9.oped1-1309.

71. Mary Platts, "Doctors Demand the Removal of Anti-Vaccine Ad from Times Square," *The Guardian*, April 18, 2011, https://www.theguardian.com/science/blog/2011/apr/18/anti-vaccine-advertisement-times-square.

72. Courtney Swan, host, *Realfoodology*, podcast, "Vaccination Controversies: Measles, Autism, and Health Risks with Dr. Bob Sears," Spotify, March 13, 2025, 12:00, https://open.spotify.com/episode/6QwWvzqqw2sjgtz8SgJCwh?id=top.

73. Zeavin, *Mother Media*, 127–129.

74. DailyWire+, "Bad Parenting and 'Transgender' Children," *The Matt Walsh Show*, episode 425, February 12, 2020, https://www.youtube.com/watch?v=XXXqUulzybg.

75. Julie Gerstein, "Megan Fox Claps Back at Accusations She Forced Her Sons to Wear 'Girls Clothes' Against Their Will: 'You're a Clout Chaser,'" *Business Insider*, June 12, 2023, https://www.businessinsider.com/megan-fox-sons-forced-to-wear-girls-clothes-accusation-response-2023-6.

Chapter 3: "No More Wire Hangers Ever"
Wrestling with the Ghost of Joan Crawford

1. *Mommie Dearest*, directed by Frank Perry (1981, Paramount Pictures).

2. "AFI's 100 Years . . . 100 Movie Quotes," American Film Institute, https://www.afi.com/afis-100-years-100-movie-quotes/.

3. Jerry Parker, "Like Daughter, Like Son Chris," *Los Angeles Times*, October 29, 1978, https://www.joancrawfordbest.com/latimes78oct29.htm.

4. The Concluding Chapter of Crawford, "Joan Crawford's Children Deny 'Mommie Dearest' Accusations," YouTube, May 10, 2014, https://www.youtube.com/watch?v=Y_EjKfzuNB4 (footage sourced from interview with Cindy Jordan in Gene Feldman and Suzette Winter documentary, *Joan Crawford: Always the Star*, A&E, 1996). Closer Staff, "The Truth About Joan Crawford: Late Star's Family Denies *Mommie Dearest*'s Story of Abuse and Cruelty," *Closer*, August 14, 2021, https://www.closerweekly.com/posts/joan-crawfords-family-denies-stories-of-abuse-and-cruelty/.

5. Charlotte Chandler, "Daughter Dearest," *Vanity Fair*, February 5, 2008, https://www.vanityfair.com/news/2008/03/crawford200803.

6. Karina Longworth interview conducted by author, November 2, 2023.

7. Joanna Robinson, "*Feud*: Why the Real Fight Between Joan Crawford and Marilyn Monroe Was Even Nastier and Juicier," *Vanity Fair*, March 5, 2017, https://www.vanityfair.com/hollywood/2017/03/feud-joan-crawford-marilyn-monroe-golden-globes-photoplay-dress.

8. Jessica Bennett, "Pamela Anderson, Amber Heard, and the Limits of the Feminist Redemption Plot," *New York Times*, May 9, 2022, https://www.nytimes.com/2022/05/09/opinion/pamela-anderson-amber-heard-redemption-plot.html.

9. Stephanie Soteriou, "People Are Calling Out Paris Hilton's 'Rebrand' by Pointing Out Her Long History of Racist and Anti-Gay Comments," BuzzFeed News, January 30, 2023, https://www.buzzfeednews.com/article/stephaniesoteriou/paris-hilton-history-racism-anti-gay-problematic.

10. Office on Women's Health, "Mental Health Conditions," US Department of Health and Human Services, https://womenshealth.gov/mental -health/mental-health-conditions.

11. Kara Zivin et al., "Perinatal Mood and Anxiety Disorders Rose Among Privately Insured People, 2008–20," *Health Affairs* 43, no. 4 (April 2024): 496–503, https://doi.org/10.1377/hlthaff.2023.01437.

12. Maria Yagoda, "Stars Who've Opened Up About Their Struggles with Postpartum Depression," *People*, March 16, 2022, https://people.com /parents/stars-with-postpartum-depression/.

13. Nehaa Khadka et al., "Trends in Postpartum Depression by Race, Ethnicity, and Prepregnancy Body Mass Index," *JAMA Network Open* 7, no. 11 (November 20, 2024): e2446486, https://doi.org/10.1001/jama networkopen.2024.46486.

14. Notable Indie (@notableindie), "happy pride month from queer icon the babadook," X, June 3, 2017, https://x.com/notableindie/status/87114 4014484873217.

15. Lindsey Beyer, "From Heart Disease to IUDs: How Doctors Dismiss Women's Pain," *Washington Post*, December 13, 2022, https://www .washingtonpost.com/wellness/interactive/2022/women-pain-gender -bias-doctors/.

16. Vidya Rao, "'You Are Not Listening to Me': Black Women on Pain and Implicit Bias in Medicine," *Today*, July 27, 2020, https://www.today.com /health/implicit-bias-medicine-how-it-hurts-black-women-t187866.

17. Antoineta Contreras, "Trauma Is Not a Diagnosis," *Psychology Today*, July 11, 2024, https://www.psychologytoday.com/us/blog/traumatization -and-its-aftermath/202407/trauma-is-not-a-diagnosis.

18. Rainey Horwitz, "Medical Vibrators for Treatment of Female Hysteria," Embryo Project Encyclopedia, Arizona State University, February 29, 2020, https://embryo.asu.edu/pages/medical-vibrators -treatment-female-hysteria.

19. Cecilia Tasca et al., "Women and Hysteria in the History of Mental Health," *Clinical Practice and Epidemiology in Mental Health* 8 (2012): 110–119, https://doi.org/10.2174/1745017901208010110.

20. Samantha Franco, "Female Hysteria: The Social Epidemic," (undergraduate paper, University of Guelph), 1–3, https://journal.lib.uoguelph.ca/index.php/footnotes/article/view/5188/4959.

21. Barbara Ehrenreich and Deirdre English, *For Her Own Good: Two Centuries of the Experts' Advice to Women* (Anchor Books, 1978; rev. 2005), 147–154.

22. Charlotte Perkins Gilman, "The Yellow Wall-Paper," *New England Magazine*, January 1892, https://gutenberg.org/cache/epub/1952/pg1952-images.html.

23. Amy Gagnon, "Charlotte Perkins Gilman," ConnecticutHistory.org, March 28, 2023, https://connecticuthistory.org/charlotte-perkins-gilman/.

24. Charlotte Perkins Gilman, "Why I Wrote *The Yellow Wallpaper*," *The Forerunner*, October 1913, https://ic.media.mit.edu/people/davet/yp/whyiwrote.html.

25. Deanna Stover, "'The Yellow Wallpaper': A Critical Reflection on an Edition by Students for Students," *IDEAH* 4, no. 2 (2024), https://doi.org/10.21428/f1f23564.5ac4fb07.

26. Stover, "'The Yellow Wallpaper.'"

27. Gagnon, "Charlotte Perkins Gilman."

28. Millicent Bell, "Pioneer," *The New York Review of Books*, April 17, 1980, https://www.nybooks.com/articles/1980/04/17/pioneer/.

29. Kimberly Fanshier, "A Critical History of the Yellow Wallpaper," CoHo Productions, January 12, 2016, https://cohoproductions.org/blog-critical-history-of-the-yellow-wallpaper/.

30. Tasca et al., "Women and Hysteria in the History of Mental Health."

31. Caitlin Gallagher, "Joan Crawford Reveals a Sad Secret on *Feud*," March 17, 2017, https://www.bustle.com/p/joan-crawfords-story-about-having-sex-with-her-stepfather-on-feud-raises-serious-concerns-44813.

32. *Feud: Bette and Joan*, FX Networks, Ryan Murphy, 2017.

33. Gabrielle Stecher, "New Bio Explores What Fueled Joan Crawford's 'Ferocious Ambition,'" PopMatters, December 4, 2023, https://www.popmatters.com/joan-crawford-ferocious-ambition-robert-dance.

34. "Florence Walsh 'Thank You' Letter to Joan Crawford," *The Concluding Chapter of Crawford* (blog), July 9, 1973, http://www.theconcluding chapterofcrawford.com/letters_florencewalsh.

35. Julie Miller, "Fact-Checking *Feud*: The 5 Most Incredibly Bizarre Joan Crawford Details," *Vanity Fair*, March 5, 2017, https://www.vanityfair .com/hollywood/2017/03/feud-joan-crawford?srsltid=AfmBOoptv7S b1aG8KQnhrfr7ZFJf9cZh4u-E7Q8F-XWAL4Cd1yu1IS7u.

36. David Denby, "Escape Artist," *New Yorker*, December 26, 2010, https:// www.newyorker.com/magazine/2011/01/03/joan-crawford-escape -artist.

37. Paul Davis, "Mommie Dearest 'She's Drunk,'" YouTube, July 9, 2019, https://www.youtube.com/watch?v=exv--lX6u3E.

38. Sara Murray, "The Four Men Who Left Joan Crawford Loveless," *Movie World*, February 1971, https://www.joancrawfordbest.com/magmovie world71.htm.

39. Christina Newland, "How Joan Crawford Embraced Film Noir (and Middle Age)," British Film Institute, August 1, 2018, https://www.bfi .org.uk/features/joan-crawford-film-noir-mildred-pierce.

40. Lee Pfeiffer, "Whatever Happened to Baby Jane?," Britannica, https:// www.britannica.com/topic/What-Ever-Happened-to-Baby-Jane.

Chapter 4: Stifler's Mom Has Got It Goin' On
Battle Hymn of the MILF

1. *American Pie*, directed by Paul Weitz, Universal Pictures, 1999.

2. ChiPhiMike, "Wow! I saw the pictorial in the Feb issue and boy was I impressed," alt.mag.playboy, Fabulous After Forty, January 12, 1995, on Know Your Meme, https://knowyourmeme.com/photos/986084 -milf.

3. ChiPhiMike interview conducted by author, January 13, 2025.

4. "Pornhub's Top 10 Search Terms 2009–2015," Pornhub Insights, https:// www.pornhub.com/insights/pornhub-search-term-history.

5. "2023 Year in Review," Pornhub Insights, December 9, 2023, https://www.pornhub.com/insights/2023-year-in-review#top-searches-porn stars.

6. Stir, "MILF on the Shilf," YouTube, December 3, 2023, https://www.youtube.com/watch?v=OjSDT14fBoQ.

7. Katie Rook, "Jennifer Coolidge Once Had a Job She Couldn't Get Fired From: 'It Was Sort of 50/50 Whether I Made the Shift or Not,'" Showbiz Cheat Sheet, December 21, 2022, https://www.cheatsheet.com/entertainment/jennifer-coolidge-job-couldnt-get-fired-from-sort-50-50-whether-made-shift-not.html/.

8. Em & Lo, "Of MILF and Men," *New York*, April 19, 2007, https://nymag.com/news/features/2007/sexandlove/30915/.

9. Steve Taylor, "How Valid Is Evolutionary Psychology?," *Psychology Today*, December 9, 2014, https://www.psychologytoday.com/us/blog/out-the-darkness/201412/how-valid-is-evolutionary-psychology.

10. Travis Dixon, "Key Study: Mate Preference Across Cultures (Buss, 1989)," *IB Psychology* (Themantic Education blog), November 28, 2018, https://www.themantic-education.com/ibpsych/2018/11/28/key-study-buss-cross-cultural-study-on-mate-preference-1989/.

11. Taylor, "How Valid Is Evolutionary Psychology?"

12. Nina Miyashita, "You've Heard of the Madonna-Whore Complex, but Do You Really Know What It Means?," Refinery29, July 20, 2023, https://www.refinery29.com/en-gb/what-is-madonna-whore-complex.

13. Julia Wolkoff, "Decoding Depictions of Eve in Art and Pop Culture," CNN, July 31, 2019, https://www.cnn.com/style/article/eve-art-pop-culture-artsy.

14. Mary Siroky, "Sex in Cinema: Creative Ways Filmmakers Skirted the Hays Code," Consequence of Sound, November 14, 2023, https://consequence.net/2023/11/skirting-hays-code-sex-in-cinema/.

15. Daisy Woodward, "How to Dress Like Supreme Seductress Mrs. Robinson," *AnOther Magazine*, June 21, 2017, https://www.anothermag.com/fashion-beauty/9942/how-to-dress-like-supreme-seductress-mrs-robinson.

16. "2019 Year in Review," Pornhub Insights, https://www.pornhub.com /insights/2019-year-in-review.

17. Aurora Snow, "'Fauxcest': The Disturbing Rise of Incest-Themed Porn," *Daily Beast*, September 17, 2017, https://www.thedailybeast.com /fauxcest-the-disturbing-rise-of-incest-themed-porn.

18. Ej Dickson, "19 Questions with MILF Porn Star Brandi Love," *Men's Health*, January 18, 2018, https://www.menshealth.com/sex-women /a19546925/brandi-love-milf-porn-president-trump/.

19. Snow, "'Fauxcest.'"

20. "2015 Year in Review," Pornhub Insights, December 2015, https://www .pornhub.com/insights/pornhub-2015-year-in-review.

21. Eva Lovia interview conducted by author, November 17, 2023.

22. Adam Herz interview conducted by author, September 23, 2024.

23. Chris Murphy, "Jennifer Coolidge, the Original MILF, Has Done Very Well Thanks to *American Pie*," *Vanity Fair*, August 4, 2022, https://www .vanityfair.com/hollywood/2022/08/jennifer-coolidge-the-original -milf-has-done-very-well-thanks-to-american-pie.

24. Julia Scott, "The Valley Exposed: Porn and the Family," *Los Angeles Daily News*, June 8, 2007, https://www.dailynews.com/2007/06/08/the -valley-exposed-porn-and-the-family/.

25. Jess Machado interview conducted by author via text message, September 9, 2024.

26. Annie Lutz interview conducted by author via text message, September 9, 2024.

27. Lovia interview.

Chapter 5: "Give 'Em Love and What Does It Get Ya?"
Why We Love to Hate (and Hate to Love) Stage Moms

1. Frank Rich, "Review/Theater; 'Gypsy' Is Back on Broadway with a Vengeance," *New York Times*, November 17, 1989, https://archive.nytimes .com/www.nytimes.com/books/98/07/19/specials/sondheim-gypsy3 .html?scp=137&sq=mr.%20broadway&st=Search.

2. Elizabeth Vanmetre, "Kim Kardashian Goes Braless in Mesh Dress at Paris Fashion Week," New York *Daily News*, April 12, 2018, https://www.nydailynews.com/2015/03/06/kim-kardashian-goes-braless-in-mesh-dress-at-paris-fashion-week/.

3. Margaret Lyons, "What's Worse: *Dance Moms* or *Toddlers and Tiaras*?," *Vulture*, April 3, 2012, https://www.vulture.com/2012/04/dance-moms-toddlers-tiaras-worst.html.

4. Lynsey Eidell, "All About Drew Barrymore's Relationship with Her Mom Jaid Barrymore," *People*, March 25, 2024, https://people.com/all-about-drew-barrymore-jaid-barrymore-mother-daughter-relationship-8406047.

5. Austin Harvey, "The Story of Teri Shields, the Stage Mom and Former Manager of Brooke Shields," *All That's Interesting*, March 29, 2023, https://allthatsinteresting.com/teri-shields.

6. Stephanie Giang-Paunon, "Christina Ricci Says Child Stardom Helped Her Escape from 'Failed Cult Leader' Father," Fox News, September 20, 2024, https://www.foxnews.com/entertainment/christina-ricci-child-stardom-helped-escape-failed-cult-leader-father.

7. Keke Palmer interview conducted by author, December 16, 2024.

8. Claire Cain Miller, "The Relentlessness of Modern Parenting," *New York Times*, December 25, 2018, https://www.nytimes.com/2018/12/25/upshot/the-relentlessness-of-modern-parenting.html.

9. r/AskReddit, "Children of helicopter parents: What was the worst or most embarrassing thing they put you through?," Reddit, 2015, https://www.reddit.com/r/AskReddit/comments/3pkgdh/children_of_helicopter_parents_what_was_the_worst/.

10. Jenna (@jennaventronet), "will the kids with a helicopter parent(s) pls stand up," TikTok, October 16, 2022, https://www.tiktok.com/@jennaventronet/video/7155261758708550958.

11. Steve Honeywell, "Helicopter ~~Parent~~ Panda," *1001Plus* (blog), January 29, 2023, https:/1001plus.blogspot.com/2023/01/helicopter-parent-panda.html.

12. Kei Nomaguchi and Melissa A. Milkie, "Parenthood and Well-Being: A Decade in Review," *Journal of Marriage and Family* 82, no. 1 (January 5, 2020): 198–223, https://doi.org/10.1111/jomf.12646.

13. Amy Chua, "Why Chinese Mothers Are Superior," *Wall Street Journal*, January 8, 2011, https://www.wsj.com/articles/SB1000142405274870411 1504576059713528698754.

14. Sarah Aswell, "12 Years After Her Book Published, the 'Tiger Mom' Is Opening Up About Her Regrets," Scary Mommy, October 3, 2023, https://www.scarymommy.com/parenting/tiger-mom-amy-chua-regrets.

15. Amy Chua, "The Tiger Mother Talks Back," *Wall Street Journal*, January 15, 2011, https://www.wsj.com/articles/SB10001424052748703583340 4576080032661117462.

16. "Strict, Controversial Parenting Style Leads to Death Threats for 'Tiger Mother' Amy Chua," ABC News, January 16, 2011, https://abcnews.go.com/US/tiger-mother-amy-chua-death-threats-parenting-essay/story?id=12628830.

17. Ann Hulbert, "Hear the Tiger Mother Roar," *Slate*, January 11, 2011, https://slate.com/culture/2011/01/amy-chua-s-battle-hymn-of-the-tiger-mother-her-new-book-will-make-readers-gasp.html.

18. Alex Mitchell, "Original 'Tiger Mom' Regrets Harsh Parenting Style: 'I Made a Lot of Mistakes,'" *New York Post*, October 2, 2023, https://nypost.com/2023/10/02/original-tiger-mom-regrets-harsh-parenting-style-mistakes/.

19. Mark Kermode, "Whiplash Review—Drumming Up the Tension Nicely," *The Guardian*, January 18, 2015, https://www.theguardian.com/film/2015/jan/18/whiplash-review-drummer-miles-teller-mark-kermode.

20. Riyaaz Roy, "*Whiplash* Reviews," Google Reviews, 2018.

21. Max Weiss, "Review: *I, Tonya*," *Baltimore* magazine, January 3, 2018, https://www.baltimoremagazine.com/section/artsentertainment/review-i-tonya/.

22. Ryan Gilbey, "Margot Robbie Saves the Ice-Skating Biopic I, Tonya from Sheer Sensationalism," *New Statesman*, February 23, 2018, https://www

.newstatesman.com/culture/2018/02/margot-robbie-saves-ice-skating
-biopic-i-tonya-sheer-sensationalism.

23. Bishop Robert Barron, "What 'Whiplash' Can Teach Us About Spiritual Mentoring," Word on Fire, March 24, 2015, https://www.wordonfire
.org/articles/barron/what-whiplash-can-teach-us-about-spiritual
-mentoring/.

24. Associated Press, "Agassi Says Dad Likely Gave Him 'Speed,'" CBC, November 1, 2009, https://www.cbc.ca/sports/agassi-says-dad-likely-gave
-him-speed-1.833447.

25. Andrew Austin, "Tennis: Agassi's Open Tale Meets High Standard," *New Zealand Herald*, November 27, 2009, https://www.nzherald.co.nz
/sport/tennis/tennis-agassis-open-tale-meets-high-standard/ONHM
N2U3SPPL7UV6CIUUTDZSAI/.

26. Andy Bull, "Comeback King Tiger Woods Delivers Vindication of Father's Tough Love," *The Guardian*, September 24, 2018, https://www
.theguardian.com/sport/blog/2018/sep/24/tiger-woods-earl-pga-tour.

27. Carolyn Twersky, "Kenzie Ziegler, Nia Sioux, and More *Dance Mom* Alums Are Calling Their 'Traumatizing' Experience on the Show," *Seventeen*, August 12, 2020, https://www.seventeen.com/celebrity/a33584679
/dance-mom-alums-calling-out-abby-lee-miller-tiktok-meme/.

28. Sabba Rahbar, "Why *Dance Moms*' Abby Lee Miller Says She Wasn't Invited to Reunion," E! News, May 10, 2024, https://www.eonline
.com/news/1401390/why-dance-moms-abby-lee-miller-says-she-wasnt
-invited-to-reunion.

29. Gretty Garcia, "Maddie Ziegler Feels 'at Peace' Not Having a Relationship with Abby Lee Miller," *Cosmopolitan*, June 14, 2022, https://www
.cosmopolitan.com/entertainment/celebs/a40289580/maddie-ziegler
-abby-lee-miller-dance-moms/.

30. Lina Das, "She Was the Original Tiger Mum Whose Bestseller Promoted Impossibly Strict Parenting. Now, a Decade on, Amy Chua Reveals . . . 'How I Realised if I Didn't Change, My Daughter Would Hate Me for Ever,'" *Daily Mail*, October 1, 2023, https://www.dailymail
.co.uk/femail/article-12581663/She-original-Tiger-Mum-bestseller

-promoted-impossibly-strict-parenting-decade-Amy-Chua-reveals
-realised-didnt-change-daughter-hate-ever.html.

Chapter 6: Peg, It Will Come Back to You
At Home with the Bundys

1. Diamond Rodrigue, "We'd Like to Remind Those Criticizing *Friends* of a Show Called *Married . . . with Children*," *Dallas Observer*, November 29, 2019, https://www.dallasobserver.com/arts/forget-friends-married-with -children-was-the-absolute-worst-11804386.

2. Wesley Stenzel, "Christina Applegate and Ed O'Neill Reflect on Crazy *Married . . . with Children* Cancellation: 'They Never Called Us,'" *Entertainment Weekly*, August 31, 2024, https://ew.com/christina-applegate -ed-o-neill-recall-married-with-children-cancellation-8704925.

3. Nicki Gostin, "'Married with Children' Star Admits It Was a 'Very Misogynist Show,'" Page Six, October 1, 2022, https://pagesix.com/2022/10 /01/married-with-children-star-admits-it-was-a-very-misogynist-show/.

4. Jackie Lam, "Katey Sagal Opens Up About the 'Exploitation of Women' in 'Married with Children,'" Aol.com, June 16, 2017, https://www.aol .com/entertainment/2017-04-03-katey-sagal-opens-up-about-the -exploitation-of-women-in-marri-22020608.html.

5. *Married . . . with Children*, "Al Wants Peg to Cook" (from season 4, episode 4, "Tooth or Consequences"), YouTube, May 26, 2021, https://www .youtube.com/watch?v=6Iq1_hJa6t8.

6. *Married . . . with Children*, "Peggy Hates Work" (from season 1, episode 9, "Peggy Sue Got Work"), YouTube, February 13, 2023, https://www .youtube.com/watch?v=H_3-ddk3B4o.

7. *Married . . . with Children*, "Peggy Speaks at Women's Career Day" (from season 3, episode 12, "My Mom, the Mom"), YouTube, 4:20, February 12, 2022, https://www.youtube.com/watch?v=bJeQGXwQc5k.

8. Ali Wong—Topic, "Leaning In" (from *Baby Cobra*, Netflix, 2016), YouTube, 1:20, February 9, 2017, https://www.youtube.com/watch?v= JI0vP8tsJec&t=65s.

9. *Married . . . with Children*, "Peggy Tries to Have Sex with Al" (from season 3, episode 22, "Here's Looking at You, Kid"), YouTube, 4:00, January 24, 2022," https://www.youtube.com/watch?v=6sCrlezyGG0.

10. *Married . . . with Children*, "Peggy Gets Amnesia" and "Marcy Tries to Tell Peggy the Truth" (both from season 11, episode 10, "The Stepford Peg"), YouTube, https://www.youtube.com/watch?v=mmLzyFRxvxo and https://www.youtube.com/watch?v=S40p8yZq1S0.

11. Tortuga del Mundo, "Married with Children—Hi Honey! Classic Al Bundy Wife Insult" (from season 5, episode 1, "We'll Follow the Sun"), YouTube, March 23, 2019, https://www.youtube.com/watch?v=sNC4y bmF3p0.

12. *Married . . . with Children*, "Marcy Tries to Tell Peg the Truth" (from season 11, episode 10, "The Stepford Peg"), Facebook, February 7, 2022, https://www.facebook.com/watch/?v=3220850551535720.

13. "Nuking the Nuclear Family," *Newsweek*, April 28, 1996, updated March 13, 2010, https://www.newsweek.com/nuking-nuclear-family-176690.

14. Tad Friend, "White Trash Nation," *New York*, August 22, 1994, https://nymag.com/news/features/46608/.

15. "Bubba Blows Town," *Time*, August 26, 1994, https://time.com/archive /6921935/bubba-blows-town/.

16. A. J. Jacobs, "*Married . . . with Children*'s Legacy," *Entertainment Weekly*, November 25, 1994, https://ew.com/article/1994/11/25/married-childrens -legacy/.

17. Philip Martin, "White Trash Chic Wearing the Badge of the Crude, the Tasteless," *Arkansas Democrat-Gazette*, February 10, 1995.

18. Brian VanHooker, "Inside the McDonald's Sketch That Defined Bill Clinton's Presidency on 'Saturday Night Live,'" *Cracked*, October 22, 2024, https://www.cracked.com/article_44068_inside-the-mcdonalds-sketch -that-defined-bill-clintons-presidency-on-saturday-night-live.html.

19. Paige Reddinger, "Guess Jeans U.S.A. Pays Tribute to Anna Nicole Smith in New Capsule Collection," *The Daily* Front Row, January 10, 2018, https://fashionweekdaily.com/guess-anna-nicole-smith-capsule -collection/.

20. Nancy Isenberg, *White Trash: The 400-Year Untold History of Class in America* (Penguin Books, 2016), 3.

21. Isenberg, *White Trash*, 37.

22. Philip Martin, "White Trash Chic Wearing the Badge of the Crude, the Tasteless."

23. Lisa Pruitt interview conducted by author, March 1, 2024.

24. Nancy Isenberg interview conducted by author, February 26, 2024.

25. "Single Parents and Their Children," United States Census Bureau, November 1989, https://www2.census.gov/library/publications/1989 /demographics/sb-03-89.pdf.

26. "Single Parents and Their Children," United States Census Bureau.

27. Amanda Marcotte, "Surprise! Single Moms Aren't to Blame for Violent Crime," *Slate*, November 28, 2012, https://slate.com/human-interest /2012/11/single-motherhood-and-violent-crime-one-does-not-lead-to -the-other.html.

28. Sara McLanahan, "The Consequences of Single Motherhood," *American Prospect*, July 1, 1994, https://prospect.org/health/consequences -single-motherhood/.

29. James Danforth Quayle, "Murphy Brown Speech," May 19, 1992, Voices of Democracy, https://voicesofdemocracy.umd.edu/quayle-murphy-brown -speech-text-2/.

30. William Raspberry, "That Disturbing Charles Murray," *Washington Post*, November 30, 1993, https://www.washingtonpost.com/archive /opinions/1993/12/01/that-disturbing-charles-murray/36604165-252f -4596-98db-5bb58710c3b9/.

31. Zack Beauchamp, "The Forgotten Book That Foretold Trump's Power Grab," *Vox*, May 21, 2025, https://www.vox.com/on-the-right-newsletter /413693/trump-musk-doge-charles-murray-by-the-people.

32. Matthew Yglesias, "The Bell Curve Is About Policy. And It's Wrong," *Vox*, April 10, 2018, https://www.vox.com/2018/4/10/17182692/bell-curve -charles-murray-policy-wrong.

33. Charles Murray and Karlyn Bowman, "The Decline of the White Working Class: A Conversation with J. D. Vance and Charles Murray,"

American Enterprise Institute, October 11, 2016, https://www.aei.org
/events/the-decline-of-the-white-working-class-a-conversation-with-j
-d-vance-and-charles-murray/.

34. Molly Fischer, "The Real Backlash Never Ended," *New Yorker*, July 21,
2022, https://www.newyorker.com/books/second-read/the-real-backlash
-never-ended.

35. William J. Eaton, "Shalala Revives 'Murphy Brown' Pregnancy Issue,"
Los Angeles Times, July 15, 1994, https://www.latimes.com/archives
/la-xpm-1994-07-15-mn-15838-story.html.

36. BBC Newsnight, "When Paxman Met Springer—'The show is stupid
but I was more ashamed of being a journalist,'" YouTube, February 26,
2014, https://www.youtube.com/watch?v=_-dHmu4AXnA.

37. "*Married . . . with Children*," IMDB, https://www.imdb.com/title
/tt0092400/.

38. John J. O'Connor, "TV View: By Any Name, Roseanne Is Roseanne,"
New York Times, August 18, 1991, https://www.nytimes.com/1991
/08/18/arts/tv-view-by-any-name-roseanne-is-roseanne-is-roseanne
.html.

39. Jeff Jarvis, "In Defense of 'Roseanne,'" *Entertainment Weekly*, March 9,
1990, https://ew.com/article/1990/03/09/defense-roseanne/.

40. Geoff Edgers, "Roseanne Barr Just Can't Shut Up," *Washington Post*,
March 21, 2019, https://www.washingtonpost.com/news/style/wp/2019
/03/21/feature/inside-roseanne-barrs-explosive-tweet/.

41. Tanner Stransky, "A Roseanne Family Reunion," *Entertainment Weekly*,
October 24, 2008, https://ew.com/article/2008/10/24/roseanne-family
-reunion/.

42. Joy Press, "The Trouble with *Roseanne* Was Always Going to Be Roseanne Barr," *Vanity Fair*, May 29, 2018, https://www.vanityfair.com
/hollywood/2018/05/roseanne-barr-was-the-biggest-problem-with
-roseanne-tv-series-reboot.

43. Lynn Hirschberg, "Don't Hate Me Because I'm Beautiful," *Vanity Fair*,
December 1990, https://archive.vanityfair.com/article/1990/12/dont-hate
-me-because-im-beautiful.

44. Dave McNary, "President Bush, Roseanne Trade Barbs in Anthem Flap," UPI, July 27, 1991, https://www.upi.com/Archives/1990/07/27/President-Bush-Roseanne-trade-barbs-in-anthem-flap/7426649051200/.

45. Daniel Jeffreys, "Roseanne Barr the Lottery Loser of All Time," *The Independent*, February 16, 1997, https://www.the-independent.com/life-style/roseanne-barr-the-lottery-loser-of-all-time-1279163.html.

46. Lynn Hirschberg, "The Ballad of Roseanne and Tom," *Vanity Fair*, December 1990, https://www.vanityfair.com/hollywood/1990/12/the-ballad-of-roseanne-and-tom.

47. Hirschberg, "The Ballad of Roseanne and Tom."

48. Gustaf Kilander, "Roseanne Barr Shrieks Conspiracy Theories into Mic as Tucker Carlson Giggles at Wild MAGA Event," *The Independent*, September 26, 2024, https://www.the-independent.com/news/world/americas/us-politics/roseanne-barr-tucker-carlson-donald-trump-b2619526.html.

49. Devan Cole, "Roseanne Tweets Support of Trump Conspiracy Theory, Confuses Twitter," CNN, March 31, 2018, https://www.cnn.com/2018/03/31/politics/roseanne-barr-conspiracy-tweets/index.html.

50. Luke Tress, "Jewish Comedian Roseanne Barr Draws Fire for Remarks on Holocaust, Jews in Hollywood," *Times of Israel*, June 28, 2023, https://www.timesofisrael.com/jewish-comedian-roseanne-barr-draws-fire-for-remarks-on-holocaust-jews-in-hollywood/.

51. Roseanne Barr (@therealroseanne), "It's almost like the deep state and democrats are in cahoots! Who would have ever believed this?," X, February 4, 2025, https://x.com/therealroseanne/status/1886935920529825974.

52. Corey Seymour, "Nine Questions for Jenny Pentland About Her Harrowing (and Hilarious) New Memoir," *Vogue*, January 27, 2022, https://www.vogue.com/article/jenny-pentland-this-will-be-funny-later-memoir-interview.

53. *Married . . . with Children*, "Al Plays Football for Polk High Again" (from season 9, episode 20, "Dud Bowl"), YouTube, October 23, 2022, https://www.youtube.com/watch?v=EJCVH4uNofI.

54. "Peggy Bundy," *Married . . . with Children* Wiki, https://marriedwith children.fandom.com/wiki/Peggy_Bundy.

55. *Married . . . with Children*, "Best of the Wankers," YouTube, June 9, 2023, https://www.youtube.com/watch?v=0NYPZXL2pc8.

56. Giulia Carbonaro, "America's Middle Class Is Shrinking," *Newsweek*, June 20, 2024, https://www.newsweek.com/america-middle-class-shrink ing-1913772.

57. Nader Elhefnawy, "The Declining Economic Viability of the Single-Income Household: A Note on the Fortunes of the Middle Class," SSRN, April 20, 2022, https://papers.ssrn.com/sol3/papers.cfm?abstract _id=4088459.

Chapter 7: One Very Bad Day
Linda Taylor, the Welfare Queen, and the Monster of Our Making

1. Sara Petersen, "Jessamine Chan Takes Aim at 'Good Mom' Worship in Her New Book," Refinery29, January 18, 2022, https://www.refinery 29.com/en-us/2022/01/10833916/school-for-good-mothers-author -interview.

2. Diane Cook, "Who Decides What Makes a Good Mother?," Electric Literature, January 12, 2022, https://electricliterature.com/jessamine -chan-novel-the-school-for-good-mothers/.

3. Miwa Messer, "Poured Over: Jessamine Chan on The School for Good Mothers," B&N Reads, January 26, 2022, https://www.barnesandnoble .com/blog/poured-over-jessamine-chan-on-the-school-for-good-mothers/.

4. "Jessamine Chan Recommends 6 Books About Motherhood," *The Week*, January 31, 2022, https://theweek.com/culture/books/1009498 /jessamine-chan-recommends-6-books-about-motherhood.

5. Viviane Eng, "The PEN 10: An Interview with Jessamine Chan," PEN America, January 27, 2022, https://pen.org/the-pen-ten-jessamine-chan/.

6. Cook, "Who Decides What Makes a Good Mother?"

7. Rachel Aviv, "Where Is Your Mother?," *New Yorker*, November 24, 2013, https://www.newyorker.com/magazine/2013/12/02/where-is-your-mother.

8. "Courts Charge Mother of 555-Pound Boy," *ABC News*, June 26, 2009, https://abcnews.go.com/Health/WellnessNews/story?id=7941609.

9. Ann Cammett, "Welfare Queens Redux: Criminalizing Black Mothers in the Age of Neoliberalism," *Southern California Interdisciplinary Law Journal* 25 (April 8, 2016): 363–394, https://gould.usc.edu/why/students/orgs/ilj/assets/docs/25-2-Cammett.pdf.

10. Laura Ziegler, "What the Adoption of One Kansas City Mother's Child Says About Race in the Child Welfare System," KCUR, NPR, April 1, 2021, https://www.kcur.org/news/2021-03-31/what-the-adoption-of-one-kansas-city-mothers-child-says-about-race-in-the-child-welfare-system.

11. Margaret M. C. Thomas, Jane Waldfogel, and Ovita F. Williams, "Inequities in CPS Contact Between Black and White Children," *Child Maltreatment* 28, no. 1 (February 2, 2022): 42–54, https://doi.org/10.1177/10775595211070248.

12. Children's Bureau, *Child Maltreatment 2014* (U.S. Department of Health and Human Services, Administration for Children and Families, Administration on Children, Youth, and Families), ii, https://www.cwla.org/wp-content/uploads/2016/01/2014-Maltreatment-Report.pdf.

13. Children's Bureau, *Child Maltreatment 2014*.

14. NYC Administration for Children's Services, "What Is Child Abuse/Neglect?," NYC Children, https://www.nyc.gov/site/acs/child-welfare/what-is-child-abuse-neglect.page.

15. Dorothy Roberts interview conducted by author, April 2, 2024.

16. Roberts interview.

17. Dorothy Roberts, "Introduction: A Benevolent Terror," in *Torn Apart: How the Child Welfare System Destroys Black Families—and How Abolition Can Build a Safer World* (Basic Books, 2022), 13–21.

18. Vanessa Peoples, "Help Vanessa Get Back on Her Feet," GoFundMe, December 9, 2022, https://www.gofundme.com/f/nb2wut-help-vanessa-get-back-on-her-feet.

19. "Ethics Explainer: The Panopticon," The Ethics Centre, July 18, 2017, https://ethics.org.au/ethics-explainer-panopticon-what-is-the-panopticon-effect/

20. Jennifer Nash interview conducted by author, September 9, 2023.

21. Jennifer C. Nash, "Introduction: The Afterlives of Malaysia Goodson, or Black Mothering in Crisis," in *Birthing Black Mothers* (Duke University Press, 2021), loc. 398 of 7755, EPUB.

22. Josie Pickens, "No Coincidence: Black Family Separations Then and Now," upEND Movement, February 16, 2023, https://upendmovement .org/2023/02/16/no-coincidence/.

23. Laura Santhanam, "Racial Disparities Persist for Breastfeeding Moms. Here's Why," PBS News, August 29, 2019, https://www.pbs.org/newshour /health/racial-disparities-persist-for-breastfeeding-moms-heres-why.

24. Rilley McKenna, "'A Mother and Fully Human at Once': Depictions of Black Motherhood in Life and Literature," *AWE (A Woman's Experience)* 6, article 3, p. 14, https://scholarsarchive.byu.edu/cgi/viewcontent .cgi?article=1104&context=awe.

25. Emily West, "Mothers' Milk: Slavery, Wet-Nursing, and Black and White Women in the Antebellum South," *Journal of Southern History* 83, no. 1 (February 2017): 37–68, http://dx.doi.org/10.1353/soh.2017.0001.

26. David Pilgrim, "The Jezebel Stereotype," Jim Crow Museum, Ferris State University, July 2002, https://jimcrowmuseum.ferris.edu/jezebel /index.htm.

27. Patricia A. Turner, *Ceramic Uncles and Celluloid Mammies: Black Images and Their Influence on Culture* (Anchor Books, 1994), 43.

28. Sarah Damaske, Jenifer L. Bratter, and Adrianne Frech, "Single Mother Families and Employment, Race, and Poverty in Changing Economic Times," *Social Science Research* 62 (February 2017): 120–133, https:// doi.org/10.1016/j.ssresearch.2016.08.008.

29. Nina Feldman and Aneri Pattani, "Black Mothers Get Less Treatment for Their Postpartum Depression," *Morning Edition*, NPR, November 29, 2019, https://www.npr.org/sections/health-shots/2019/11/29/760231688 /black-mothers-get-less-treatment-for-their-postpartum-depression.

30. "Working Together to Reduce Black Maternal Mortality," CDC.gov, https://www.cdc.gov/womens-health/features/maternal-mortality.html.

31. Nash interview.

32. Lisa R. Pruitt, "Welfare Queens and White Trash," *Southern California Interdisciplinary Law Journal* 25, no. 2 (Spring 2016): 289–312, https://gould.usc.edu/why/students/orgs/ilj/assets/docs/25-2-Pruitt.pdf.

33. Daniel Moynihan, "The Negro American Family," chap. 2 in *The Negro Family: The Case for National Action* (Office of Policy Planning and Research, United States Department of Labor, March 1965).

34. Jacqui Germain, "The National Welfare Rights Organization Wanted Economic Justice for Black Americans," *Teen Vogue*, December 24, 2021, https://www.teenvogue.com/story/national-welfare-rights-organization-black-women.

35. Moynihan, "The Negro American Family," chap. 2 in *The Negro Family*, 12.

36. Moynihan, "The Tangle of Pathology," chap. 4 in *The Negro Family*, 29.

37. Moynihan, "The Negro American Family."

38. Daniel Geary, "The Moynihan Report: An Annotated Edition," *The Atlantic*, September 14, 2015, https://archive.is/uzR6f/again?url=https://www.theatlantic.com/politics/archive/2015/09/the-moynihan-report-an-annotated-edition/404632/.

39. William H. Chafe, "The Moynihan Report: Then and Now," in *Moynihan+50: Family Structure Still Not the Problem*, ed. Stephanie Coontz (Council on Contemporary Families, March 5, 2015), 19, https://sites.utexas.edu/contemporaryfamilies/files/2015/03/2015_Symposium_Family_Structure.pdf.

40. Daniel Geary, "Beyond Civil Rights: The Moynihan Report and Its Legacy," Policy Talks @ the Ford School, University of Michigan, April 6, 2015, https://fordschool.umich.edu/video/2015/beyond-civil-rights-moynihan-report-and-its-legacy.

41. Nash interview.

42. George Will, "The Prescience of Daniel Patrick Moynihan," *Topeka Capital-Journal*, March 7, 2015, https://www.cjonline.com/story/opinion/columns/2015/03/17/george-will-prescience-daniel-patrick-moynihan/16635350007/.

43. Chafe, "The Moynihan Report: Then and Now."

44. Sam Klug, "The Moynihan Report Resurrected," *Dissent*, Winter 2016, https://www.dissentmagazine.org/article/moynihan-report-resurrected -daniel-geary-black-power/.

45. Hari Sreenivisan, "The True Story Behind the 'Welfare Queen' Stereotype," PBS News, June 1, 2019, https://www.pbs.org/newshour/show/ the-true-story-behind-the-welfare-queen-stereotype.

46. Sreenivisan, "The True Story Behind the 'Welfare Queen' Stereotype."

47. Josh Levin, *The Queen: The Forgotten Life Behind an American Myth* (Little, Brown and Company, 2019), 80.

48. Levin, *The Queen*, 198.

49. Levin, *The Queen*, 205.

50. Levin, *The Queen*, 196.

51. Levin, *The Queen*, 205.

52. Levin, *The Queen*, 207.

53. Levin, *The Queen*, 199–200.

54. Levin, *The Queen*, 196.

55. Levin, *The Queen*, 216–217.

56. Levin, *The Queen*, 60.

57. Levin, *The Queen*, 83.

58. Levin, *The Queen*, 2.

59. Levin, *The Queen*, 128.

60. Levin, *The Queen*, 246.

61. Levin, *The Queen*, 227.

62. Levin, *The Queen*, 106.

63. "Quick Facts: Government Benefits Fraud," United States Sentencing Commission, 2023, https://www.ussc.gov/research/quick-facts/government -benefits-fraud.

64. Peter Edelman, "The Worst Thing Bill Clinton Has Done," *The Atlantic*, March 1997, https://www.theatlantic.com/magazine/archive/1997 /03/the-worst-thing-bill-clinton-has-done/376797/.

65. Robin Toner, "New Senate Push on Welfare Revives Debate in Both Parties," the *New York Times*, September 9, 1995, https://www.nytimes

.com/1995/09/09/us/new-senate-push-on-welfare-revives-tensions-in
-both-parties.html

66. Office of the Assistant Secretary for Planning and Evaluation, "The
Personal Responsibility and Work Opportunity Reconciliation Act of
1996," U.S. Department of Health and Human Services, August 31, 1996,
https://aspe.hhs.gov/reports/personal-responsibility-work-opportunity
-reconciliation-act-1996.

67. Victoria M. Massie, "Lillie Harden Was Bill Clinton's Welfare Reform
Success Story. Welfare Reform Failed Her," *Vox*, August 23, 2016, https://
www.vox.com/2016/8/22/12583376/welfare-reform-history-clinton-lillie
-harden.

68. "Welfare Reform Bill Signing," C-SPAN transcript, 12:27:27, August 22,
1996, https://www.c-span.org/program/white-house-event/welfare-reform
-bill-signing/97777.

69. Gene Demby, "The Mothers Who Fought to Radically Reimagine Welfare," NPR, June 9, 2019, https://www.npr.org/sections/codeswitch/2019
/06/09/730684320/the-mothers-who-fought-to-radically-reimagine
-welfare.

70. Nathan J. Robinson, "It Didn't Pay Off," *Jacobin*, October 1, 2016, https://
jacobin.com/2016/10/clinton-welfare-reform-prwora-tanf-lillie-harden.

71. Gene Falk, "Temporary Assistance for Needy Families: The Decline in
Assistance Receipt Among Eligible Individuals," Congress.gov, April 10,
2023, https://www.congress.gov/crs-product/R47503.

72. Dylan Matthews, "'If the Goal Was to Get Rid of Poverty, We Failed':
The Legacy of the 1996 Welfare Reform," *Vox*, June 20, 2016, https://
www.vox.com/2016/6/20/11789988/clintons-welfare-reform.

73. Isabela Salas-Betsch, "The Economic Status of Single Mothers," Center
for American Progress, August 7, 2024, https://www.americanprogress
.org/article/the-economic-status-of-single-mothers.

74. Josh Getlin, "Law and Disorder: Tart, Tough-Talking Judge Judith
Sheindlin Presides Over the Grim Pageant of Dysfunction Known as
Manhattan's Family Court," *Los Angeles Times*, February 14, 1993,

https://www.latimes.com/archives/la-xpm-1993-02-14-vw-307-story
.html.

75. Josh Getlin, "The Improbable True Story of Judge Judy and the Reporter Who Made Her a Star," *Los Angeles Times*, June 8, 2021, https://www.latimes.com/entertainment-arts/tv/story/2021-06-08/judge-judy-final-episode-cbs-imdb-tv-amazon.

76. @vocable_brandon, "Judge Judy," TikTok, October 24, 2021, https://www.tiktok.com/@vocable_brandon/video/7428302079615094022?_r=1&_t=ZT-8vmU1mUzRhW.

77. News 24/7, "Judge Judy Gives Greedy Welfare Queen PERFECT Punishment After How She Spent Stolen Benefits," YouTube, March 20, 2018, https://www.youtube.com/watch?v=ss49IZP2JbU&t=45s.

78. Sarah Jaffe, "Judge Judy's Lifetime Achievement Is Teaching Us to Laugh at the Less Fortunate," *Slate*, June 26, 2019, https://slate.com/culture/2019/06/judge-judys-new-york-times-profile-downplays-her-troubling-history.html.

79. Nicole Einbinder, "'Judge Judy' Was Plagued by Sexual Harassment Claims, Drinking on the Job, and Racism, Former Employees Say," *Business Insider*, November 2, 2021, https://www.businessinsider.com/judge-judy-show-sexual-harassment-drinking-racism-accusations-2021-11.

80. "Judy Sheindlin," *Forbes*, May 28, 2024, https://www.forbes.com/profile/judy-sheindlin/.

81. @matshk1, "Terrible mother wants to party instead of taking care of kids. PART 2/3," TikTok, July 30, 2024, https://www.tiktok.com/@matshk1/video/7397474092166712607.

82. @zeezee4005, "Lazy mother refuses to pay child support and criticizes judge's job," TikTok, March 7, 2024, https://www.tiktok.com/@zeezee4005/video/7343776971836443935.

83. Afro Dye Tea, "Precious: Precious Fights Her Mom Full Scene," YouTube, May 3, 2021, https://www.youtube.com/watch?v=R77EdyEAvms.

84. Courtland Milloy, "'Precious' Is Bewildering," *Gainesville Sun*, November 25, 2009, https://www.gainesville.com/story/news/local/2009/11/26/precious-is-bewildering/31731727007/.

85. Carrie Rickey, "For Blacks, *Precious* Isn't So Precious," *Gainesville Sun*, March 10, 2010, https://www.gainesville.com/story/news/2010/03/11 /for-blacks-precious-isnt-so-precious/31747166007/.

86. Charlene Regester, "Monstrous Mother, Incestuous Father, and Terrorized Teen: Reading *Precious* as a Horror Film," *Journal of Film and Video* 67, no. 1 (April 1, 2015): 30–45, https://muse.jhu.edu/article/572154.

87. Roberts, "Introduction: A Benevolent Terror," in *Torn Apart: How the Child Welfare System Destroys Black Families—and How Abolition Can Build a Safer World* (Basic Books, 2022), 26, EPUB.

88. Dorothy Roberts interview conducted by author, April 2, 2024.

Chapter 8: Casey Anthony Is in the Book
On True Crime and Motherhood

1. Chuck Klosterman, "Hitler Is in the Book," in *I Wear the Black Hat* (Scribner, 2013), 183.

2. Klosterman, "Hitler Is in the Book."

3. Lynsey Eidell and Maggie Kreienberg, "Casey Anthony's Case: A Timeline of Her Murder Trial and Life After Acquittal," *People*, March 5, 2025, https://people.com/casey-anthony-case-complete-timeline-8422805.

4. Eidell and Kreienberg, "Casey Anthony's Case."

5. David Lohr, "Casey Anthony Trial: Suspect Called a 'Fun Party Girl' During Second Day of Testimony," *HuffPost*, May 25, 2011, https://www .huffpost.com/entry/casey-anthony-trial-fun-party-girl_n_867189.

6. Chris Rovzar, "Nancy Grace Explains What the Heck 'Tot Mom' Means," *New York*, July 12, 2011, https://nymag.com/intelligencer/2011 /07/nancy_grace_explains_what_the.html.

7. Aarti Shahani, "Casey Anthony Trial Shows the Limits of Forensic Science in Proving How a Child Died," ProPublica, July 5, 2011, https:// www.propublica.org/article/casey-anthony-trial-shows-the-limits-of -forensic-science-in-proving-how-a-c.

8. "Disturbing Theories About the Duct Tape Found with Caylee Anthony's Remains," Oxygen, May 21, 2018, https://www.oxygen.com/the-case

-of-caylee-anthony/disturbing-theories-duct-tape-caylee-anthony
-remains.

9. Associated Press, "Sex-Abuse Claim May Force Casey Anthony to Take the Stand," Jacksonville.com, May 27, 2011, https://www.jacksonville
.com/story/news/crime/2011/05/27/sex-abuse-claim-may-force-casey
-anthony-take-stand/15902351007/.

10. u/DeliciousGorilla, "Can anyone explain how a jury found Casey Anthony innocent?," r/TrueCrimeDiscussion, Reddit, 2024, https://www
.reddit.com/r/TrueCrimeDiscussion/comments/1evdga2/can_anyone
_explain_how_a_jury_found_casey_anthony/.

11. Graeme Massie, "South Park Skewers QAnon with Hillary and Oprah Drinking Kids' Blood and Microchip Vaccines: 'What You Believe Is Really Stupid,'" *The Independent*, March 11, 2021, https://www
.independent.co.uk/news/world/americas/south-park-qanon-trump
-vaccines-b1815570.html.

12. Marianna Spring, "Wayfair: The False Conspiracy About a Furniture Firm and Child Trafficking," BBC, July 15, 2020, https://www.bbc.com
/news/world-53416247.

13. Ej Dickson, "A Target Sex-Trafficking Hoax Is Going Viral on TikTok," *Rolling Stone*, April 7, 2021 https://www.rollingstone.com/culture
/culture-features/target-sex-trafficking-tiktok-hoax-1151665/.

14. Ej Dickson, "The Birth of QAmom," *Rolling Stone,* September 2, 2020, https://www.rollingstone.com/culture/culture-features/qanon-mom
-conspiracy-theory-parents-sex-trafficking-qamom-1048921/.

15. Sarah Naseer and Christopher St. Aubin, "True Crime Podcasts Are Popular in the U.S., Particularly Among Women and Those with Less Formal Education," Pew Research Center, June 20, 2023, https://www
.pewresearch.org/short-reads/2023/06/20/true-crime-podcasts-are
-popular-in-the-us-particularly-among-women-and-those-with-less
-formal-education/.

16. Amanda Vicary interview conducted by author, March 13, 2024.

17. Amanda M. Vicary and Chris R. Fraley, "Captured by True Crime: Why Are Women Drawn to Tales of Rape, Murder, and Serial Killers?," *So-*

cial Psychological and Personality Science 1, no. 81 (2010), https://www
.amandavicary.com/VicaryTrueCrime.pdf.

18. Vicary interview.

19. Jacob Smith, "What Are the Odds of Being a Serial Killer's Victim?,"
Casino.org, Oct. 6, 2022, https://www.casino.org/blog/what-are-the
-odds-of-being-a-serial-killers-victim/.

20. Erica L. Smith, "Female Murder Victims and Victim-Offender Relationship, 2021," Bureau of Justice Statistics, December 2022,
https://bjs.ojp.gov/female-murder-victims-and-victim-offender
-relationship-2021.

21. David Orenstein, "Analysis: 32 Years of U.S. Filicide Arrests," Brown
University, February 25, 2014, https://news.brown.edu/articles/2014/02
/filicide.

22. Philip J. Resnick, "Filicide in the United States," *Indian Journal of Psychiatry* 58, suppl. 2 (December 2016): 203–209, https://doi.org/10.4103
/0019-5545.196845.

23. Michelle Oberman, "Mothers Who Kill: Cross-Cultural Patterns in
and Perspectives on Contemporary Maternal Filicide," *International
Journal of Law and Psychiatry* 26, no. 5 (2003): 495–496, https://doi.org
/10.1016/S0160-2527(03)00083-9.Oberman, "Mothers Who Kill."

24. Sara G. West, "An Overview of Filicide," *Psychiatry (Edgmont)* 4, no. 2
(December 2007): 48–57, https://www.ncbi.nlm.nih.gov/pmc/articles/PMC
2922347/.

25. Marisol Bello and Meghan Hoyer, "Parents Who Do the Unthinkable—
Kill Their Children," *USA Today*, September 10, 2014, https://www
.usatoday.com/story/news/nation/2014/09/10/parents-kill-children-fbi
-data/15280259/.

26. Michelle Oberman interview conducted by author, March 21, 2024.

27. Oberman interview.

28. Oberman interview.

29. West, "An Overview of Filicide."

30. West, "An Overview of Filicide."

31. West, "An Overview of Filicide."

32. West, "An Overview of Filicide."
33. Kat Teurfs et al., "What Did Lori Vallow Daybell Do? A Full Time-line of the 'Doomsday Mom' Case," CBS News, April 23, 2025, https://www.cbsnews.com/news/lori-vallow-chad-daybell-what-did-they-do-doomsday-mom-murders-case-timeline/.
34. KC Baker, "Decades After Andrea Yates Killed Her 5 Children, Her Lawyer Places Flowers on Their Grave," *People*, March 8, 2025, https://people.com/andrea-yates-lawyer-flowers-children-grave-exclusive-11691942.
35. Emma Tucker, "2 Boys Drowned and a Deception That Gripped the Nation: Why the Susan Smith Case Is Still Intensely Felt 30 Years Later," CNN, November 21, 2024, https://www.cnn.com/2024/11/21/us/susan-smith-south-carolina-case-parole/index.html.
36. Lauren Matthias interview conducted by author, March 21, 2024.
37. John Matthias and Lauren Matthias, hosts, *Hidden: A True Crime Podcast*, "Beyond the Veil: The Many Extremes of Lori Vallow Daybell, Part 1," September 9, 2020, https://hiddentruecrime.podbean.com/e/beyond-the-veil-the-many-extremes-of-lori-vallow-daybell-part-i/.
38. Matthias and Matthias, "Beyond the Veil."
39. Michelle Williams, "Memories Haunt Kin of Dahmer's Victims," *Los Angeles Times*, August 2, 1992, https://www.latimes.com/archives/la-xpm-1992-08-02-mn-5678-story.html.
40. Vicary interview.
41. Matthias interview.
42. Richard Fetzer, "Chad Daybell's Family Says Shallow Graves of Tylee Ryan and JJ Vallow Were Not Dug by Their Dad," CBS News, July 20, 2022, https://www.cbsnews.com/news/chad-daybell-graves-tylee-ryan-jj-vallow-not-dug-dad/.
43. Resnick, "Filicide in the United States."
44. Resnick, "Filicide in the United States."
45. "Lindsay Clancy: Timeline of Events in the Case of Massachusetts Mom Accused of Killing Her 3 Children," *Inside Edition*, February 28, 2023,

https://www.insideedition.com/lindsay-clancy-timeline-of-events-in
-the-case-of-massachusetts-mom-accused-of-killing-her-3.

46. "Lindsay Clancy: Timeline of Events."

47. Matthew Nadler, "Offering Support in the Face of Terrible Tragedy," *Duxbury Clipper*, February 1, 2023, https://www.duxburyclipper.com /articles/offering-support-in-the-face-of-terrible-tragedy/.

48. Jessica Winter, "What We Still Don't Understand About Postpartum Psychosis," *New Yorker*, March 14, 2023, https://www.newyorker.com /science/annals-of-medicine/what-we-still-dont-understand-about -postpartum-psychosis.

49. Lindsay Dodgson, "Moms on TikTok Are Sharing Stories of Post-partum Psychosis After Lindsay Clancy Was Accused of Murdering Her 3 Kids," *Business Insider*, March 7, 2023, https://www.businessinsider .com/lindsay-clancy-tiktok-moms-share-stories-of-postpartum -psychosis-2023-3.

50. Matthias interview.

51. David R. Smith, "Trial of Lindsay Clancy, Mom Accused of Killing Kids, Rescheduled Again: A 60-Second Read," *Patriot Ledger*, May 30, 2025, https://www.patriotledger.com/story/news/courts/2025/05/30/lindsay -clancy-duxbury-ma-murder-kids-insanity-antidepressant-children -new-yorker-reporter-notes/83916592007/.

52. Marc Fortier, "'She Killed the Kids': Prosecutors Outline Chilling Time-line in Duxbury Tragedy," NBC 10 Boston, February 7, 2023, https:// www.nbcboston.com/news/local/she-killed-the-kids-prosecutors -outline-chilling-timeline-in-duxbury-tragedy/2966770/.

53. Luis Feldman, "'Can You Treat a Sociopath?': Lindsay Clancy Searched Online, Prosecutor Says," MassLive.com, October 26, 2023, https:// www.masslive.com/news/2023/10/can-you-treat-a-sociopath-lindsay -clancy-searched-online-prosecutor-says.html.

54. David R. Smith, "'Someone Who Got Sick': Judge Orders Lindsay Clan-cy's Husband Interview Notes Turned Over," *Patriot Ledger*, Febru-ary 17, 2025, https://www.patriotledger.com/story/news/courts/2025/02

/17/lindsay-clancy-duxbury-murder-trial-new-yorker-husband-patrick
-clancy-interview-notes-judge-order/78455095007/.

55. "Casey Anthony Entered a Hot Body Contest Four Days After Her Daughter's Disappearance and We're Still Not Over It," *In Touch*, May 18, 2018, https://www.intouchweekly.com/posts/casey-anthony-2008-hot-body-contest-photos-160307/.

56. Faith Karimi, "Casey Anthony Shares Her Version of Events in a New Docuseries. What You Need to Know," CNN, December 7, 2022, https://www.cnn.com/2022/12/07/us/casey-anthony-documentary-cec/index.html.

Chapter 9: The Perfect Storm
The Making of MAHA Moms, Anti-Vaxxers, and Housewife Insurrectionists

1. "Hearing to Consider the Nomination of Robert F. Kennedy, Jr., of California, to Be Secretary of Health and Human Services," United States Senate Committee on Finance, January 29, 2025, https://www.finance.senate.gov/hearings/hearingto-consider-the-nomination-of-robert-f-kennedy-jr-of-california-to-be-secretary-of-health-and-human-services.

2. Abby Turner and Andrew Kaczynski, "Robert F. Kennedy Jr. Repeatedly Suggested That Chemicals in Water Are Impacting Sexuality of Children," CNN, July 13, 2023, https://www.cnn.com/2023/07/13/politics/robert-kennedy-jr-chemicals-water-children-frogs.

3. C-SPAN, "Robert F. Kennedy Jr. Senate Confirmation Hearing to Be Secretary of Health & Human Services," YouTube, January 29, 2025, https://www.youtube.com/watch?v=NeeC7nGm6cI.

4. C-SPAN, "Robert F. Kennedy Jr. Senate Confirmation Hearing."

5. Robert F. Kennedy Jr. (@robertfkennedyjr), "Make America Healthy Again #MAHA," Instagram, August 25, 2024, https://www.instagram.com/p/C_GDAIhPgc6/?hl=en.

6. Diana Falzone, "What Does RFK Jr.'s 'Make America Healthy Again' Movement Aim to Do?," NewsNation, April 15, 2025, https://www.newsnationnow.com/health/rfk-jr-maha-make-america-healthy-again/.

7. Anna Merlan, "Meet the Conspiracy-Peddling Gossip Blogger Who's Cast Herself as a Trump-RFK Player," *Mother Jones*, October 15, 2024, https://www.motherjones.com/politics/2024/10/jessica-reed-kraus-houseinhabit/.

8. Kase Wickman, "Cheryl Hines, Megyn Kelly, and Vani Hari Form RFK Jr.'s MAHA Cheer Squad at First Confirmation Hearing," *Vanity Fair*, January 29, 2025, https://www.vanityfair.com/style/story/cheryl-hines-megyn-kelly-vani-hari-rfk-jr-maha-confirmation-hearing.

9. Wickman, "Cheryl Hines, Megyn Kelly, and Vani Hari."

10. Wickman, "Cheryl Hines, Megyn Kelly, and Vani Hari;" Ej Dickson, "Jewel Joined the Inauguration Festivities, Too," *The Cut*, January 21, 2025, https://www.thecut.com/article/jewel-performed-rfk-jr-maha-ball-trump-inauguration.html.

11. Jacqueline Capriotti interview conducted by author, May 14, 2025.

12. Olivia Reingold, "Can These Moms Get RFK Jr. Confirmed?," *Free Press*, January 30, 2025, https://www.thefp.com/p/maha-moms-rfk-jr-hhs-senate-hearing-trump-vaccines.

13. Ceara Foley interview conducted by author, March 30, 2025.

14. Alaina Demopoulos, "Rise of the Maha Moms: The Momfluencers Embracing RFK's Push for a 'Healthier' America," *The Guardian*, January 13, 2025, https://www.theguardian.com/lifeandstyle/2025/jan/13/rfk-jr-moms-health-trump.

15. Adam Gabbatt, "Robert F. Kennedy Jr. Brushes Off Sexual Assault Allegation: 'I Am Who I Am,'" *The Guardian*, July 2, 2024, https://www.theguardian.com/us-news/article/2024/jul/02/robert-f-kennedy-jr-sexual-assault-allegation-response.

16. Charmaine Patterson, "RFK Jr. Wanted to 'Possess' and 'Impregnate' Journalist Olivia Nuzzi, Her Ex Reportedly Alleges in Court Filing," *People*, October 15, 2024, https://people.com/rfk-jr-wanted-to-possess-and-impregnate-journalist-olivia-nuzzi-her-ex-alleges-in-court-filing-8728707.

17. Rachel Treisman, "RFK Jr. Admits to Dumping a Dead Bear in Central Park, Solving a Decade-Old Mystery," NPR, August 5, 2024, https://

www.npr.org/2024/08/05/nx-s1-5063939/rfk-jr-central-park-bear-bicycle.

18. Ej Dickson, "The Birth of QAmom," *Rolling Stone*, September 2, 2020, https://www.rollingstone.com/culture/culture-features/qanon-mom-conspiracy-theory-parents-sex-trafficking-qamom-1048921/.

19. Will Sommer interview conducted by author, April 30, 2024.

20. Dickson, "The Birth of QAmom."

21. David Gilbert, "A Far Right Moms Group Is Targeting Students. These Women Are Fighting Back," *Vice*, May 22, 2023, https://www.vice.com/en/article/moms-for-liberty-book-banning-lgbtq/.

22. "Moms for Liberty Uses False and Inflammatory Language to Vilify LGBTQ People," GLAAD, December 5, 2023, https://glaad.org/moms-for-liberty-groomer-rhetoric-anti-lgbtq/.

23. Associated Press, "Woman Pleads Guilty to Calling in Hoax Bomb Threat at Boston Children's Hospital," NBC News, September 28, 2023, https://www.nbcnews.com/nbc-out/out-news/woman-pleads-guilty-calling-hoax-bomb-threat-boston-childrens-hospital-rcna117956.

24. Amy Nakamura, "OnPolitics: Congress Subpoenas Mother-Daughter Duo Behind Jan. 6 Rally," *USA Today*, October 25, 2021, https://www.usatoday.com/story/news/politics/2021/10/25/mother-daughter-duo-behind-jan-6-rally-testify-before-house/8541734002/.

25. Erin Mansfield, Donovan Slack, and Savannah Behrmann, "This Mother-Daughter Duo Planned the Jan. 6 Rally. Now the House Committee Wants to Hear From Them, Too," *USA Today*, October 24, 2021, https://www.usatoday.com/story/news/2021/10/24/january-6-rally-organizers-called-before-congressional-committee/8536515002/?gnt-cfr=1&gca-cat=p

26. Alfred Branch, "CT Mother and Daughter Charged in Jan. 6 U.S. Capitol Riot: Feds," Patch.com, September 14, 2021, https://patch.com/connecticut/across-ct/ct-mother-daughter-charged-jan-6-u-s-capitol-riot-feds.

27. Wilson Wong, "Feds Arrest Woman Accused of Using Bullhorn to Direct Rioters During Capitol Siege," NBC News, February 5, 2021, https://

www.nbcnews.com/news/us-news/feds-arrest-woman-accused-using
-bullhorn-direct-rioters-during-capitol-n1256861.

28. Ryan J. Reilly, "Women Put 'Friendly Face' on Jan. 6 Attack, Extremism
Research Argues in New Study," NBC News, April 26, 2022, https://
www.nbcnews.com/politics/national-security/women-put-friendly
-face-jan-6-attack-extremism-research-argues-new-stu-rcna25831.

29. Steven Ross Johnson and Elliott Davis Jr., "How Key Demographic
Groups Voted in the 2024 Election," *U.S. News and World Report*, November 6, 2024, https://www.usnews.com/news/national-news/articles
/2024-11-06/how-5-key-demographic-groups-helped-trump-win-the
-2024-election.

30. Ej Dickson, "How QAnon and Pizzagate Conspiracy Theorists Got a
'Trolls' Doll Pulled from Stores," *Rolling Stone*, August 7, 2020, https://
www.rollingstone.com/culture/culture-features/trolls-hasbro-doll-pizza
gate-qanon-1041202/.

31. Pooja Salhotra and Jayme Lozano Carver, "A Second Texas Child Has
Died from Measles; RFK Jr. Visits," *Texas Tribune*, April 6, 2025, https://
www.texastribune.org/2025/04/06/measles-texas-outbreak-death
-unvaccinated/.

32. Ted Conover, "Please I Will Give Anything for You to Come Back,"
Outside, February 20, 2024, https://www.outsideonline.com/outdoor
-adventure/exploration-survival/colorado-off-grid-deaths/.

33. Ej Dickson and Brittany Spanos, "People Blamed an Influencer's
Murder-Suicide on the Eclipse. What Really Happened?," *Rolling Stone*,
June 14, 2024, https://www.rollingstone.com/culture/culture-features
/danielle-johnson-astrologer-murder-suicide-story-1235039610/.

34. Eviane Leidig, *The Women of the Far Right: Social Media Influencers
and Online Radicalization* (Columbia University Press, 2023), 119–120.

35. Erin Blakemore, "'Ku Klux Kiddies': The KKK's Little-Known Youth
Movement," History.com, January 8, 2019, https://www.history.com
/articles/kkk-youth-recruitment-1920s.

36. Emily Cataneo, "A Brief History of the Women's KKK," JSTOR Daily, October 14, 2020, https://daily.jstor.org/a-brief-history-of-the-womens-kkk/.

37. Seyward Darby, *Sisters in Hate: American Women on the Front Lines of White Nationalism* (Little, Brown and Company, 2020), 140–141.

38. Darby, *Sisters in Hate*, 105–108.

39. Darby, *Sisters in Hate*, 125.

40. Sara Petersen, "Trump's Mommies," *In Pursuit of Clean Countertops* (Substack), July 26, 2024, https://sarapetersen.substack.com/p/trumps -mommies.

41. Laura Geggel, "'Vast Majority' of Online Anti-Vaxxers Are Women," Live Science, December 29, 2017, https://www.livescience.com/61305-most -online-anti-vaxxers-are-women.html.

42. Stephanie Alice Baker and Michael James Walsh, "'A Mother's Intu-ition: It's Real and We Have to Believe in It': How the Maternal Is Used to Promote Vaccine Refusal on Instagram," *Information, Communica-tion & Society* 26, no. 8 (January 23, 2023): 1675–1692, https://doi.org /10.1080/1369118X.2021.2021269.

43. Aja Romano, "Karen: The Anti-Vaxxer Soccer Mom with Speak-to-the -Manager Hair, Explained," *Vox*, February 5, 2020, https://www.vox .com/2020/2/5/21079162/karen-name-insult-meme-manager.

44. Alfred Lubrano, "Anti-Vaccine Parents Are Often White, College-Educated, Whole Foods Moms," *Philadelphia Inquirer*, April 10, 2019, https://www.inquirer.com/news/middle-class-working-class-vaccine -anti-vaxxers-measles-cdc-20190410.html.

45. Courtney Thornton and Jennifer A. Reich, "Black Mothers and Vaccine Refusal: Gendered Racism, Healthcare, and the State," *Gender & Soci-ety* 36, no. 4 (June 6, 2022): 525–552, https://doi.org/10.1177/08912432 221102150.

46. Kat Stafford, "Why Do So Many Black Women Die in Pregnancy? One Reason: Doctors Don't Take Them Seriously," Associated Press, May 23, 2023, https://projects.apnews.com/features/2023/from-birth-to-death/ black-women-maternal-mortality-rate.html.

47. Ej Dickson, "Death of Sha-Asia Washington, Pregnant 26-Year-Old Black Woman, Highlights Devastating Trend," *Rolling Stone*, July 9, 2020, https://www.rollingstone.com/culture/culture-features/shaasia

-washington-death-woodhull-hospital-black-maternal-mortality-rate
-1026069/.

48. "Women and Pain: Disparities in Experience and Treatment," Harvard Health Publishing, October 9, 2017, https://www.health.harvard
.edu/blog/women-and-pain-disparities-in-experience-and-treatment
-2017100912562.

49. Vital Signs, "Many Women Report Mistreatment During Pregnancy and Delivery," CDC.gov, September 29, 2023, https://www.cdc.gov/vital
signs/respectful-maternity-care/index.html.

50. Johanna Richlin, "Vaccine-Skeptical Mothers Say Bad Health Care Experiences Made Them Distrust the Medical System," *Maine Morning Star*, March 12, 2024, https://mainemorningstar.com/2024/03/12
/vaccine-skeptical-mothers-say-bad-health-care-experiences-made
-them-distrust-the-medical-system/.

51. Ceara Foley interview conducted by author, March 30, 2025.

52. Foley interview.

53. Foley interview.

54. Liz Weil, "I Can Hear Thoughts," *The Cut*, April 23, 2025, https://www
.thecut.com/article/telepathy-tapes-families-autism-ky-dickens.html.

55. Foley interview.

56. parkslopeboy, "Indecisive I Don't Know Gif," Tenor, https://tenor.com
/view/indecisive-i-dont-know-not-sure-larry-david-gif-5682454.

57. Foley interview.

58. Ali Swenson, "Moms for Liberty Chapter Apologizes for Quoting Hitler in Its Newsletter," Associated Press, June 22, 2023, https://apnews
.com/article/moms-for-liberty-adolf-hitler-newsletter-quote-bcce698e
901b9e782970030ccd710512.

59. Red Ice.TV, "Journalist Concerned Right-Wingers Aren't Consuming Seed Oils," Rumble, 2024, https://rumble.com/v3gv9x8-journalist
-concerned-right-wingers-arent-consuming-seed-oils.html.

60. Candace Owens (@RealCandaceO), "OMG!! It gets worse. The journalist who wrote a hit piece on me also believes we need to 'stop getting caught up in our knee-jerk reaction to adults having sex with

children' and we need to instead support the creation of child robots that pedophiles can have sex with," X, February 27, 2025, https://x.com /RealCandaceO/status/1895257112537944511.

Chapter 10: Lighter, Easier, and More Joyful
The Eternal Appeal of Trad Wives and Momfluencers

1. Hannah Neeleman (@ballerinafarm), "The hens are laying again!," Instagram, May 11, 2023, https://www.instagram.com/p/CsGzfRDrcNu /?hl=en.

2. Julia Moskin, "Tycoon or Tradwife? The Woman Behind Ballerina Farm Makes Her Own Path," *New York Times*, December 3, 2024, https://www .nytimes.com/2024/12/03/dining/ballerina-farm-hannah-neeleman .html.

3. Hannah Neeleman (@ballerinafarm and @ballerinafarmstore), "For Mothers Day, flowers please! This year we're offering 3 different bundles of flower varieties. Each one stunning, just what momma needs. Ballerinafarmflowers.com," Instagram, April 18, 2024, https://www .instagram.com/reel/C549AayLqKl/.

4. Hannah Neeleman (@ballerinafarm), "Ballerina Farm Grilled Mozzarella Sandwiches," Instagram, October 21, 2022, https://www.instagram .com/reel/Cj9qZ1JDC2N/.

5. Hannah Neeleman (@ballerinafarm), Instagram, accessed April 27, 2025, https://www.instagram.com/ballerinafarm/.

6. Hannah Neeleman (@ballerinafarm), "Just a little family, wanting to farm and make a life in the country. We had a dream, to sell our farm products direct to consumers. In Utah, in the West, and the whole country. It started with just a few boxes a week. Then it grew, and @fedex has been there every step of the way. FedEx knows that today's consumers want speed, convenience, and visibility. This means residential deliveries any day of the week with FedEx Home Delivery as well as enabling consumer choice on when and where to receive orders. And our FedEx driv-

ers do just that. It's been a great 4 years. Can't wait for the next four years. #fedexsmallbusiness #sponsored," Instagram, April 23, 2022, https://www.instagram.com/ballerinafarm/p/CcrlEIIOAi8/?img_index=1.

7. "Enamel Sourdough Bowl," BallerinaFarm.com, https://ballerinafarm.com/products/enamel-sourdough-bowl.

8. Syeda Khaula Saad, "PSA: It's Time to Talk About the Husband Behind Ballerina Farm's Trad Wife Content," Betches, July 30, 2024, https://betches.com/ballerina-farm-husband-daniel-neeleman/.

9. Ballerina Farm, "Loved making this rose blossom meringue roulade with fresh pomegranates at school," YouTube, March 26, 2025, https://www.youtube.com/watch?v=oIYZJ_oJKDI.

10. Brian Marks, "Ballerina Farm's Hannah Neeleman Cooks with Her Kids on $30K Aga Stove Before Church After Viral Tradwife Story Put Marriage Under Microscope," *Daily Mail*, August 13, 2024, https://www.dailymail.co.uk/tvshowbiz/article-13737813/Ballerina-Farms-Hannah-Neeleman-cooks-kids-30K-Aga-stove-church-viral-tradwife-story-marriage-microscope.html.

11. Moskin, "Tycoon or Tradwife?"

12. Ayesha Rascoe, "'Trad Wives' Are Trending. What Does That Say About Feminism Today?," NPR, January 28, 2024, https://www.npr.org/2024/01/28/1227453741/trad-wives-are-trending-what-does-that-say-about-feminism-today.

13. Hannah Neeleman (@ballerinafarm), "We love a good hamburger," Instagram, May 31, 2025, https://www.instagram.com/reel/DKPjhILtvbr/?igsh=MXRoMnZnNW1maTVuYQ==.

14. Megan Agnew, "My Day with the Trad Wife Queen and What It Taught Me," *Sunday Times*, July 29, 2024, https://www.thetimes.com/world/us-world/article/my-day-with-the-trad-wife-queen-and-what-i-really-thought-of-her-qmbmmhkp8.

15. Hannah Neeleman (@ballerinafarm), "What I've been thinking lately . . . ," Instagram, July 31, 2024, https://www.instagram.com/p/C-GeBacSJx2/?hl=en.

16. Agnew, "My Day with the Trad Wife Queen."

17. Kedibone (@_kgalilelo), "oh my I'm eating up with Ballerina farm Times article . . . It was only a matter of time," X, September 13, 2024, https://x.com/_kgalilelo/status/1834535035598155830.

18. FriedChicken (@NabilaShiraz), "#BallerinaFarm," X, July 26, 2024, https://x.com/NabilaShiraz/status/1816892591188644176/photo/1.

19. Taylor Lorenz, *Extremely Online: The Untold Story of Fame, Influence, and Power on the Internet* (Simon & Schuster, 2023), 23.

20. Lorenz, *Extremely Online*, 20.

21. Chavie Lieber, "She Was the Queen of the 'Mommy Bloggers.' Then Her Life Fell Apart," *Vox*, May 2, 2019, https://www.vox.com/the-high light/2019/4/25/18512620/dooce-heather-armstrong-depression -valedictorian-of-being-dead.

22. Heather Armstrong interview conducted by author, October 23, 2018.

23. Lorenz, *Extremely Online*, 20.

24. Lorenz, *Extremely Online*, 20.

25. Sam Cabral, "Heather Armstrong: 'Queen of Mommy Blogging' Dead at 47," BBC, May 10, 2023, https://www.bbc.com/news/world-us-canada -65553608.

26. Joanna Pepin interview conducted by author, September 1, 2023.

27. Amanda Perelli, "The Creator Economy Is a $250 Billion Industry and It's Here to Stay," *Business Insider*, November 18, 2023, https://www .businessinsider.com/creator-economy-250-billion-market-and-here -to-stay-2023-11.

28. Sara Petersen interview conducted by author, August 20, 2023.

29. Katie Hicks, "Black Influencers Are Still Facing Pay Inequity," Marketing Brew, February 21, 2023, https://www.marketingbrew.com/stories /2023/02/21/black-influencers-are-still-facing-pay-inequity.

30. Donnya Negera interview conducted by author, December 28, 2023.

31. Shanicia Boswell interview conducted by author, September 18, 2024.

32. Sara Petersen interview conducted by author, August 24, 2023.

33. MK Fleming interview conducted by author, December 18, 2023.

34. u/imahater02, "CallingCPSoninfluencer," r/snarkingonthesnarkers, Reddit, 2022, https://www.reddit.com/r/snarkingonthesnarkers/comments/yj50cb/calling_cps_on_influencer/.

35. The Dad Challenge Podcast, "Dougherty Dozen Goes Shopping for Z's Birthday 2 Minutes Before Her Birthday," YouTube, April 14, 2025, https://www.youtube.com/watch?v=MJwVDw1WvZw.

36. Ej Dickson, "On the Internet, Everyone's a Bad Mom," *The Cut*, December 21, 2024, https://www.thecut.com/article/nurse-hannah-tiktok-controversy-mom-shaming.html.

37. Mattea Bubalo, "Who Is Ruby Franke, the Parenting Influencer Jailed for Child Abuse?," BBC, February 21, 2024, https://www.bbc.com/news/world-us-canada-66719859.

38. Zach Crenshaw, "'A Failure of the System': Kids Told DCS and Police About Prior 'YouTube Mom' Abuse," ABC 15 Arizona, May 14, 2021, https://www.abc15.com/news/region-central-southern-az/maricopa/a-failure-of-the-system-kids-told-dcs-and-police-about-prior-youtube-mom-abuse.

39. Chayenne, "A Simple Favor: Stephanie Vlog | Anna Kendrick," YouTube, August 6, 2018, https://www.youtube.com/watch?v=co-vgHXxbDg.

40. Sonja Haller, "Anna Kendrick of 'A Simple Favor' Thinks Mommy Bloggers Are 'Creepy,'" *USA Today*, September 12, 2018, https://www.usatoday.com/story/life/allthemoms/2018/09/12/anna-kendrick-simple-favor-thinks-mommy-bloggers-creepy/1281230002/.

41. Petersen interview.

42. Sarah Adams interview conducted by author, December 19, 2023.

43. Mom.uncharted, TikTok, accessed September 11, 2025, https://www.tiktok.com/@mom.uncharted?lang=en.

44. Adams interview.

45. Adams interview.

46. Hannah Neeleman (@ballerinafarm), "Our spring sojourn to rural France was of fairy tale-quality. Stomping through lush green pastures silhouetted against ancient castles, we peeked briefly into the ag-

ricultural engine that has propelled France's ambitions for hundreds of years," Instagram, April 18, 2023, https://www.instagram.com/p/CrGX-wDLOBU/?hl=en&img_index=1.

47. Olivia Little, "STUDY: Tradwife Influencers Are Quietly Spreading Far-Right Conspiracy Theories," Media Matters, May 1, 2024, https://www.mediamatters.org/tiktok/study-tradwife-influencers-are-quietly-spreading-far-right-conspiracy-theories.

48. Nara Smith (@naraazizasmith), "#easyrecipe #homecooking #fyp #snack #cheetos #marriage," TikTok, August 28, 2024, https://www.tiktok.com/@naraazizasmith/video/7408308154531990826?lang=en.

49. Azrin Tan, "The Weird, Wild, and Unrealistic Glamour of Nara Smith's Kitchen," *Vogue* Singapore, August 22, 2024, https://vogue.sg/nara-smith-kitchen-style/.

50. Olyn Smith, "Shattering the Myths: Why Getting Married Young Was My Best Decision Yet," *Evie*, February 8, 2025, https://www.eviemagazine.com/post/why-marrying-young-wasn-t-a-mistake-for-me-and-why-it-might-not-be-for-you-either.

51. *Evie*, Instagram monthly total followers, Social Blade, https://socialblade.com/instagram/user/eviemagazine.

52. Anna Silman, "Now Comes the Womanosphere: The Anti-Feminist Media Telling Women to Be Thin, Fertile, and—Republican," *The Guardian*, April 24, 2025, https://www.theguardian.com/us-news/2025/apr/24/womanosphere-conservative-women.

53. Carmen Schober, "The Trad Wife Aesthetic Is Popular Because Women Are Tired of Ugliness," *Evie*, January 25, 2025, https://www.eviemagazine.com/post/the-trad-wife-aesthetic-is-popular-because-women-are-tired-of-ugliness.

54. Carter Sherman, "The Rise of Pronatalism: Why Musk, Vance, and the Right Want Women to Have More Babies," *The Guardian*, March 11, 2025, https://www.theguardian.com/us-news/2025/mar/11/what-is-pronatalism-right-wing-republican.

55. Fleming interview.

56. "HB 1627–2023–24: Protecting the interests of minor children featured on for-profit family vlogs," Washington State Legislature, September 22, 2024, https://app.leg.wa.gov/billsummary?BillNumber=1627&Year=2023 &Initiative=false.

57. Faith Karimi, "The First Social Media Babies Are Adults Now. Some Are Pushing for Laws to Protect Kids from Their Parents' Oversharing," CNN, May 29, 2024, https://www.cnn.com/2024/05/29/us/social -media-children-influencers-cec.

58. Ayesha Rascoe, "The Sunday Story: Permission to Share," *Up First* (transcript), NPR, July 9, 2023, https://www.npr.org/transcripts/1186221489.

59. Kathryn Jezer-Morton, "What Worries Me About Making a Family into a Brand," *Mothers Under the Influence* (Substack), December 10, 2021, https://mothersundertheinfluence.substack.com/p/what-worries -me-about-making-a-family.

60. Jack Alban, "'This Is Weird': Popular Mom Creator Maia Knight Faces Backlash from Fans After She Stopped Showing Her Kids' Faces Online," Daily Dot, December 26, 2022, https://www.dailydot.com/unclick /mom-tiktoker-maia-knight/.

61. Kalya Kuefler, "This Influencer Started a Haircare Brand—and Its Products Are Blowing Up on TikTok," Yahoo! Style, August 6, 2023, https://ca.style.yahoo.com/amber-fillerup-clark-dae-interview-1600 00735.html.

62. Spill Sesh (@spillsesh_yt), "#maiaknight," TikTok, September 23, 2023, https://www.tiktok.com/@spillsesh_yt/video/7180465287899254059.

63. Maia Knight (@maiaknight), TikTok, April 26, 2025, https://www.tik tok.com/@maiaknight/video/7497604420625042718.

64. Maia Knight (@maiaknight), TikTok, March 25, 2025, https://www.tik tok.com/@maiaknight/video/7485809537136725294.

65. Maia Knight (@maiaknight), TikTok, December 18, 2023, https://www .tiktok.com/@maiaknight/video/7314053637045521707.

66. Heather Armstrong interview conducted by author, October 23, 2018.

Chapter 11: The Rise of the Huns
In Defense of MLM Mommies

1. Toby Axelrod Dickson, Facebook, https://www.facebook.com/toby.axel roddickson/posts/pfbid0U3GGkRFcAKurPXaQZUGBPcqdMnhjE8ic qw4qBwATZErwErCyaX3ncdtqKGgmb1Gl.

2. Toby Axelrod Dickson (@pixielanetobydickson), Instagram, January 27, 2023, https://www.instagram.com/p/Cn7445HDFO5/.

3. Toby Axelrod Dickson (@pixielanetobydickson), "Buttery soft gowns and headband/hat sets by Pixielane make the perfect gift for the newborns in your life, #babyshower #babygirl #babyboy," Instagram, October 18, 2021, https://www.instagram.com/p/CVL0p2FARPD/.

4. "Solid Leggings," LulaRoe, https://lularoe.com/products/solid-leggings.

5. Alden Wicker, "Multilevel-Marketing Companies Like LuLaRoe Are Forcing People into Debt and Psychological Crisis," Quartz, August 6, 2017, https://qz.com/1039331/mlms-like-avon-and-lularoe-are-sending -people-into-debt-and-psychological-crisis.

6. "Multi-Level Marketing Business and Pyramid Schemes," Federal Trade Commission Consumer Advice, July 2022, https://consumer .ftc.gov/articles/multi-level-marketing-businesses-pyramid-schemes #pyramid.

7. Amanda May, "Rodan + Fields Revises MLM Model, Causing Job Cuts," Cosmetics Business, July 16, 2024, https://cosmeticsbusiness.com /rodan-and-fields-revises-mlm-business-model.

8. "FTC Takes Action Against doTERRA Distributors for False COVID-19 Health Claims," Federal Trade Commission, March 3, 2023, https:// www.ftc.gov/news-events/news/press-releases/2023/03/ftc-takes -action-against-doterra-distributors-false-covid-19-health-claims.

9. Amy McCarthy, "The Multilevel Truth Behind Small Town America's Latest Tea Obsession," Eater, March 3, 2022, https://www.eater .com/22958985/loaded-teas-herbalife-mlm-silver-lining-lessons-dupes -nutrition-clubs.

10. William Keep interview conducted by author, April 18, 2023.

11. "Multi-Level Marketing Businesses and Pyramid Schemes," Federal Trade Commission Consumer Advice.

12. Bridget Read, *Little Bosses Everywhere: How the Pyramid Scheme Shaped America* (Crown, 2025), 6–8.

13. Jon M. Taylor, *The Case (for and) Against Multi-Level Marketing* (Consumer Awareness Institute, 2012): 7–1, https://www.ftc.gov/sites/default/files/documents/public_comments/trade-regulation-rule-disclosure-requirements-and-prohibitions-concerning-business-opportunities-ftc.r511993-00008%C2%A0/00008-57281.pdf.

14. Taylor, *The Case (for and) Against Multi-Level Marketing*.

15. Taylor, *The Case (for and) Against Multi-Level Marketing*.

16. r/antiMLM, Reddit, https://www.reddit.com/r/antiMLM/.

17. u/lazycat881, "Hun pays downline $$ from her own pocket," r/antiMLM, Reddit, October 18, 2024, https://www.reddit.com/r/antiMLM/comments/1g6fmsd/hun_pays_downline_from_her_own_pocket/.

18. u/1imaginewag0ns, "So my mom started working with Herbalife about 2 years ago, she's gotten so attached to it that she neglected me. She claims to have tons of money, but we had to move out of our house cause she couldnt afford it. I feel bad for the people who look up to my 'mom,'" r/antiMLM, Reddit, https://www.reddit.com/r/antiMLM/comments/c3mo31/so_my_mom_started_working_with_herbalife_about_2/.

19. u/Kaitlynnbeaver, "They'll do literally anything but go to the doctor," r/antiMLM, Reddit, 2024, https://www.reddit.com/r/antiMLM/comments/1940hak/theyll_do_literally_anything_but_go_to_the_doctor/.

20. LuLaRoe, "We Are LuLaRoe," YouTube, January 16, 2022, https://www.youtube.com/watch?v=y6SHebWhri0&t=32s.

21. u/Timely_Objective_585, "Living the DREAM life," r/antiMLM, Reddit, October 17, 2024, https://www.reddit.com/r/antiMLM/comments/1g6ed15/living_the_dream_life/.

22. Read, "Introduction: Not a Pyramid Scheme," in *Little Bosses Everywhere*, 13.

23. Rick Perlstein, "The Eye on the Pyramids (Part 3: MLMs and the Conservative Republican Infrastructure)," *The Nation*, July 18, 2013, https://

www.thenation.com/article/archive/eye-pyramids-part-3-mlms-and -conservative-republican-infrastructure/.

24. Carlie Porterfield, "Betsy DeVos Reportedly Made $225 Million— or More—During Her Time in Trump's Cabinet," *Forbes*, March 22, 2021, https://www.forbes.com/sites/carlieporterfield/2021/03/22/betsy -devos-reportedly-made-225-million---or-more---during-her-time-in -trumps-cabinet/.

25. Will Anderson, "Beware the 'Christian' Pitch to Join Multilevel Marketing," January 28, 2022, https://www.thegospelcoalition.org/article /multilevel-marketing-christians/.

26. Orla McGrath, "Expert Explains Why Mormon Women Embrace Multi-Level Marketing," *Colorado Arts and Sciences Magazine*, University of Colorado Boulder, April 24, 2023, https://www.colorado .edu/asmagazine/2023/04/24/expert-explains-why-mormon-women -embrace-multi-level-marketing.

27. Read, *Little Bosses Everywhere*, 6, 11.

28. Jo Piazza interview conducted by author, May 16, 2024.

29. "About Us," PixieLane, https://pixielane.com/pages/about-us.

30. Emily Lynn Paulson interview conducted by author, May 16, 2024.

31. Emily Lynn Paulson, *Hey, Hun: Sales, Sisterhood, Supremacy, and the Other Lies Behind Multilevel Marketing* (Row House, 2023): 39.

32. Paulson, *Hey, Hun*, 17.

33. Paulson interview, 1:45.

34. Paulson, *Hey, Hun*, 75.

35. Paulson, *Hey, Hun*, 36.

36. Paulson, *Hey, Hun*, 39.

37. Paulson interview.

38. Paulson interview.

39. Paulson, *Hey, Hun*, 49–50.

40. Paulson interview.

41. Meg Conley, "Motherhood in America Is a Multilevel Marketing Scheme," Medium, December 7, 2020, https://gen.medium.com/mother hood-in-america-is-a-multilevel-marketing-scheme-f4ec1f536b04.

42. Paulson, *Hey Hun*, 20.

43. Paulson, *Hey Hun, 9.*

44. Paulson interview.

45. Paulson interview.

46. Emily Stewart, "MLMs Might Not Be Able to Get Away with Their Shady Promises Much Longer," *Vox*, October 22, 2021, https://www.vox.com /the-goods/22732586/ftc-mlm-rohit-chopra-business-opportunity-rule.

47. Rachel Tillman, "TikTok Bans Multilevel Marketing in Updated Community Guidelines," NY1, December 17, 2020, https://ny1.com/nyc /all-boroughs/news/2020/12/17/tiktok-bans-multi-level-marketing -pyramid-ponzi-schemes.

48. Shannon Sollitt, "Employees at doTERRA Didn't Know Layoffs Were Coming. Here Are the Signs," *Salt Lake Tribune*, May 27, 2024, https:// www.sltrib.com/news/education/2024/05/27/employees-doterra -didnt-know/.

49. Paulson interview.

50. Paulson interview.

51. Toby Dickson interview conducted by author, May 16, 2024.

52. Dickson interview.

53. Dickson interview.

Conclusion: Ramsay Bolton Was Right
If You Think This Has a Happy Ending, You Haven't Been Paying Attention

1. Piratevisionsam, "If you think this has a happy ending, you haven't been paying attention . . . ," YouTube, June 3, 2013, https://www.youtube .com/watch?v=FT4_Fefew78.

2. Emily Lynn Paulson interview conducted by author, May 16, 2024.

3. Peter Kerr, "Michel Foucault, French Historian," *New York Times*, June 26, 1984, https://www.nytimes.com/1984/06/26/obituaries/michel -foucault-french-historian.html.

4. *Michael Pollan or Michel Foucault?* (blog), last updated January 29, 2011, https://michaelpollanormichelfoucault.blogspot.com/.

About the Author

Ej Dickson is a senior writer at *New York* magazine's *The Cut*. She previously worked as a senior culture writer for *Rolling Stone*. She has contributed to *The New York Times*, *The Washington Post*, *GQ*, *Elle*, and many other publications. She lives in Brooklyn with her husband, their two children, and their three-legged dog, Ringo.

About the Typeface

Minion was designed by Robert Slimbach for Adobe in 1990. Inspired by old-style Renaissance typefaces, it was chosen for this project to represent the timeless, noble grind of motherhood; Minion is reliable, adaptable, and provides a strong visual foundation for the narrative it supports.